A MEMOIR OF JANE AUSTEN

A Memoir of Jane Austen

by her nephew
JAMES AUSTEN-LEIGH

with

The Watsons

&

Lady Susan

by
JANE AUSTEN

Introduction by
J. H. STAPE

Wordsworth Reference

In loving memory of
MICHAEL TRAYLER
the founder of Wordsworth Editions

I

Readers who are interested in other titles from
Wordsworth Editions are invited to visit our website at
www.wordsworth-editions.com

For our latest list and a full mail-order service, contact
Bibliophile Books, 5 Thomas Road, London E14 7BN
TEL: +44 (0)20 7515 9222 FAX: +44 (0)20 7538 4115
E-MAIL: orders@bibliophilebooks.com

First published in 2007 by Wordsworth Editions Limited
8B East Street, Ware, Hertfordshire SG12 9HJ

ISBN 978 1 84022 560 0

Typeset in Great Britain by Antony Gray
Printed and bound by Clays Ltd, St Ives plc

Contents

Introduction

Based upon recollections of a well-known person, a 'memoir', a term borrowed from the French, tends to be more casually structured than biography. Less subject to the demands of chronology and tending, on the whole, to avoid slants, angles and the grinding of axes, the memoir is freer and sometimes less self-conscious. Its main concern lies with recording an intimate glimpse of a family member, a friend or acquaintance, interesting, for whatever reason, to the wide public. Although not a full-scale biography, the present work is somewhat modestly titled, for *A Memoir of Jane Austen*, 'By her Nephew, the Rev. J. E. Austen Leigh, Vicar of Bray', as its publisher Bentley advertised it, was, on its publication on 16 December 1869 (the volume bears an 1870 imprint date), the fullest public discussion of the writer's activities, family connections and personal habits.

Two factors motivated Austen-Leigh's seeing his recollections of his 'dear Aunt Jane' into print: the rise in interest in Jane Austen's writings since about the 1830s, and the ageing and passing of those family members who had known her. Augmented by the first publication of some of his aunt's few surviving letters, his memoir more closely resembles a full-scale, if short and generalised, biography compared with what had, until then, appeared before the public.

The 'Biographical Notice of the Author' (1818), appended to the posthumously published *Northanger Abbey and Persuasion* by Jane Austen's brother Henry, consists of a mere handful of pages of affectionate admiration – and frustratingly few facts. Even its expanded and revised version of 1833, published as a *Memoir*, remains general, 'a tribute due to her memory' loudly bewailing the fact that the materials for a more precise account 'cannot be obtained'. James Austen-Leigh's sister Caroline Austen (1805–80) published another privileged and brief account, *My Aunt Jane Austen: A Memoir* (1867). Motivated by her desire to leave for posterity 'some record' of her aunt's 'life and character', Caroline Austen mingled personal recollections of visits to the Chawton House with considerable affection and remarks on her aunt's personal habits – her perpetual reading, her love of music, her 'sweetness of manner'. She presents a detailed and useful description of her aunt's decline and death on which her brother relied for the set-piece ending of his own work. Loving in its observations, it is small scale in its ambitions, adopts a plain style and, like Henry Austen's two writings about his beloved sister, is little concerned with details of fact and date.

Caroline Austen's account none the less marked a departure in the public dissemination of the nature of her personality and the facts of Austen's life. The death of Jane Austen's surviving brother, Admiral Sir Francis Austen, at the age of ninety-one in 1865, seems to have stimulated awareness that family memories should be preserved before they inevitably faded. The task fell to James Edward Austen-Leigh (1798–1874), the only son of Jane Austen's brother James. Austen-Leigh had spent his earliest years and young manhood in the rectory that had been his aunt's home, received her encouragement on a novel that he had begun and, representing his father who was too ill to be present, had attended her funeral service at Winchester Cathedral.

Educated at Winchester and at Exeter College, Oxford, he was ordained in 1823, and, following in his father's and grandfather's footsteps, became a country clergyman. A man of seventy when, by his own confession, he somewhat reluctantly agreed to put down his own and his family's recollections, he must, at a time of short life spans, have been aware of the pressures of mortality. He was certainly conscious of the fragility of memory – he speaks of 'the difficulty of recovering little facts and feelings which had been merged half a century deep in oblivion' – and its tendency to exaggerate, both for ill and for good. He could have been no less keenly aware of a duty – that workhorse term of the mid- and late-Victorian era – that had befallen him: to pass on to the future a vision of his aunt that was, as he saw it, true to her personality and appropriate to her achievement.

Whatever the more recent criticism of his work for its reticence and its emphases, the Austen family, on the whole, chose well. Discretion, judgement, judiciousness, necessary to the successful cure of souls, were important qualifications for exposing to public light what was then known of Jane Austen's life. Like any family boasting a famous relative, the Austens were torn by contrary impulses: a desire to protect intimate family history from mere curiosity contradicted the simultaneous desire to set the record straight. Proud of the growing recognition of Jane Austen's literary achievement, they were, none the less, deeply influenced by the temper of their time, one little inclined to reveal intimacies and to air private emotions in public. The line between careful protection and outright censorship was an extremely fine one, and the *Memoir* is thus shot through with a sense of mid-Victorian proprieties.

An authorised account of Jane Austen's life would need to reflect something of the delicate shading and discrimination characteristic of her writing (although Austen-Leigh's singularly lacks a sense of wit). And it goes without saying that the writing itself would need to be decorous to do justice to perceptions of extreme subtlety matched by a prose that is no less so. Careful appraisal would be placed alongside what the family saw as Jane Austen's essential good humour, her delicacy of insight and her remarkable 'gentleness' of character. Capturing the personality of his aunt in a way that would satisfy both his family and public interest would prove a challenging task that Austen-Leigh seems to have risen to for his own age although he has less satisfied the curiosity of ours. Constrained not only by the lack of details that his Uncle Henry had vigorously bemoaned, Austen-Leigh faced the responsibility of conveying the family's attitude. To reveal but not to disclose too much of a life that he saw mainly as an inner one, lived out in the country and little marked by drama or what the public would consider extraordinary, might indeed have taxed a professional writer more imaginatively inclined.

There was, moreover, the question of evidence, particularly vexed in this case. The destruction of much of Jane Austen's correspondence by her devoted and protective sister Cassandra (1773–1845) was evidently intended to hamper, if not stop dead, any prospective chronicler of her sister's life. Cassandra's attitude as regards the revelation of personal details about her sister and family is controlling: large tracts of Jane Austen's life were to remain forever off limits, the victims of stern propriety. Austen-Leigh would in the main have to restrict himself to family memories rather than to documents, some letters and Austen's then-unpublished juvenilia apart.

Every would-be biographer confronts gaps of knowledge and conflicting versions of the 'same' event, and faces the temptation to speculate where the documented facts begin to thin out. The case of Jane Austen is an extreme version of this general state of affairs. A mere hundred or so letters survived Cassandra's conflagration, and James Austen-Leigh did not have complete access even to these, some surviving that he did not know of. How well and how accurately, in any case, do they represent her? Even the handful he presents strike him as uninteresting: 'the reader must be warned not to expect too much from them'. Praising their clarity of style and the light touch of humour that runs through them, he none the less discourages: 'they treat only of the details of domestic life'. (The modern reader discerns here the limitations of a male viewpoint, and one might regret the diffidence of Austen-Leigh's sister Caroline in her recollections, for a gentlewoman would surely have felt more sympathetically towards precisely such 'details'.)

On the other hand, Austen-Leigh possessed several advantages that would stand him in good stead in fulfilling a task that he had somewhat reluctantly undertaken. Delicate and nuanced discriminations about human character were the clergyman's stock-in-trade, and, given the challenges Austen-Leigh faced in recounting his aunt's life in a way that would do justice to it, he must have frequently relied, consciously or not, upon his professional training. In addition to his personal observations of his aunt from his childhood and young manhood, and those recounted to him by his sister and other close relatives, he could call upon his many years of experience in the pulpit and, figuratively in any case, in the confessional. The local clergyman was privy to a community's and an individual's secret life, called upon to understand and to sympathise with the varied impulses and moods of those under his care, to mend fences, to articulate values and to persuade of a vision that vaunted itself as holding the master key to human experience.

Despite 'being unaccustomed to write for publication', as he confesses in his Postscript to the *Memoir*, Austen-Leigh was, in fact, a writer of sorts, not only attempting his hand at verse and fiction in his earlier years, but also, and much more relevantly, producing his weekly sermon, a literary form that imposes several virtues upon its practitioners, not the least being concision and clarity. Steeped in the cadences of the King James Bible and the Book of Common Prayer, he enjoyed a training in language that included Greek and Latin and that was deep and highly disciplined. The *Memoir* possesses an undeniable stylistic distinction, its prose style sacrificing the elegant, the ornate and the pedantic for a rigorous clarity and accessibility typical of the sermon. Even in discussing so humble topic as hand-spinning, Austen-Leigh's patrician cadences are well worth savouring for an old-fashioned grace and balance:

> The term 'spinster' still testifies to its having been the ordinary employment of the English young woman. It was the labour assigned to the ejected nuns by the rough earl who said, 'Go spin, ye jades, go spin.' It was the employment at which Roman matrons and Grecian princesses presided amongst their handmaids . . . But, at last, this time-honoured domestic manufacture is quite extinct among us – crushed by the power of steam, overborne by a countless host of spinning jennies, and I can only just remember some of its last struggles for existence in the Steventon cottages.

The basis of his life's work, a country clergyman's learning had to be worn lightly, just as interesting an audience and holding its attention was mastered during the course of his duties. Skilled in presenting ideas and arguments in a language sufficiently simple and unadorned to communicate effectively with a congregation, Austen-Leigh could likewise draw upon long experience in interpretation, argument and discretion. Trained in biblical exegesis and engaged in mediating the intricacies of Christian doctrine to his flock, he possessed skills that could, almost effortlessly, be transferred to the writing of biography.

Running contrary to the dictum of the novelist and biographer Ford Madox Ford that 'there is no great man that is not belittled and rendered common by his biographer', Austen-Leigh's *Memoir* presents his subject almost too gingerly, with an elegant discrimination that smoothes out any potential rough spots in Austen's life and in that of her immediate relatives. This is not to say that it labours under a tendency towards the hagiographic, but to admit that it narrowly skirts doing so. The novelist Fay Weldon in commenting upon Austen-Leigh's *Memoir* accuses the writer of doing Jane Austen a disservice in his insistence upon her 'genteelness', which, according to Weldon, thereby tended to relegate her to the list of 'delicate' lady writers rather than to the first rank of English novelists, where she so clearly belongs. Still other critics see in the *Memoir* the beginning of 'the dear Aunt Jane' cult. *The Times* review of Austen-Leigh's work nicely summarises the view of her that would long prevail, until a recent preoccupation with fissures and silences has demanded a more nuanced and complex view of her life: 'she seems, as far as we can see, to have passed her whole life without one thought of the outer world' (17 January 1870). As an impression garnered from Austen-Leigh, this is, on the whole, a just one. But, to be fair to him, it is one informed by the view of the woman as 'the angel in the house', innocent of a knowledge of life's rougher sides, and very much of its time. This view has been corrected, and even refuted, by scholarly work on Austen's life during the past half century. Not only has the occasional bite of her wit been reappraised but even a 'regulated hatred' in her for her characters has been discovered, as readings of her work emphasise our own darker preoccupations. (For instance, an interpretation of *Mansfield Park* can turn upon the brutalities of the slave trade.)

Yet, however much biographers may shape an attitude towards a writer, the works in the end must speak for themselves. Thus, for all the influence of Austen-Leigh's portrait on later biographies of Jane Austen, her writing has won a much wider audience than that she enjoyed not only in her own lifetime but also during the mid-Victorian era when the importance of her work was becoming increasingly evident. No less a figure than the essayist and educator Thomas Macaulay expressed an interest in writing her biography. Austen-Leigh's account, whatever its deficiencies, came at a historically significant moment when the Victorians began to look back quizzically on the Regency period, so different in its deepest impulses from theirs. Thanks to Austen-Leigh's descriptive skills, one of the real and enduring interests of this *Memoir* is its detailed presentation of an earlier, more genteel era when etiquette served not only as an index of breeding but also of moral fibre, and when the country gentry, secure of its place in the scheme of things before the onslaught of the Industrial Revolution, expended its energies in gardening, balls, visits to fashionable spas and country and seaside rambles.

However wanting Austen-Leigh's *Memoir* might appear from a post-Freudian or a feminist perspective, it continues to offer several, not negligible, pleasures. Its sense of narrative development, its judicious emphases and very modesty of intention can, in the main, be considered strengths. Its occasional snobbishness, general conventionality and reticence testify as much to mid-Victorian tastes and values as they do to the author's personality. Austen-Leigh's respectful biography – strikingly at odds with the protocols of our expansive 'tell-it-all' time – perhaps disappoints most in conveying little about the life of the artist. Begging off the task of literary criticism (the business, after all, of the critic), Austen-Leigh none the less comments briefly on Austen's writing, discerning more maturity and depth in her later work. In his stress on the novelist's photographic realism, however, he renders less than justice to either the subtleties or the careful narrative structuring of a writer whom Virginia Woolf called 'the most perfect artist among women'.

This edition reprints Austen-Leigh's second, slightly revised, edition of the *Memoir*, issued in 1871, to which is appended Austen's *Lady Susan*, an epistolary novella written in 1793–4, and *The Watsons*, a fragmentary novel, written in 1803–5. The modern reader can thus share the experience of this volume's original readers whose sense of discovery and pleasure was deepened by works then as wholly unknown as the biographical facts revealed by Jane Austen's conscientious and affectionate nephew.

J. H. STAPE
Research Fellow in St Mary's College,
Strawberry Hill, London

A MEMOIR OF JANE AUSTEN

He knew of no one but himself who was inclined to the work. This is no uncommon motive. A man sees something to be done, knows of no one who will do it but himself, and so is driven to the enterprise.

HELPS' *Life of Columbus*, ch. i.

Preface

The Memoir of my Aunt, Jane Austen, has been received with more favour than I had ventured to expect. The notices taken of it in the periodical press, as well as letters addressed to me by many with whom I am not personally acquainted, show that an unabated interest is still taken in every particular that can be told about her. I am thus encouraged not only to offer a second edition of the Memoir, but also to enlarge it with some additional matter which I might have scrupled to intrude on the public if they had not thus seemed to call for it. In the present edition, the narrative is somewhat enlarged, and a few more letters are added; with a short specimen of her childish stories. The cancelled chapter of *Persuasion* is given, in compliance with wishes both publicly and privately expressed. A fragment of a story entitled 'The Watsons' is printed; and extracts are given from a novel which she had begun a few months before her death; but the chief addition is a short tale never before published, called 'Lady Susan'. I regret that the little which I have been able to add could not appear in my first edition; as much of it was either unknown to me, or not at my command, when I first published; and I hope that I may claim some indulgent allowance for the difficulty of recovering little facts and feelings which had been merged half a century deep in oblivion.

November 17, 1870.

I

*Introductory Remarks – Birth of Jane Austen – Her Family
Connections – Their Influence on her Writings*

More than half a century has passed away since I, the youngest of
the mourners,[*] attended the funeral of my dear aunt Jane in
Winchester Cathedral; and now, in my old age, I am asked whether
my memory will serve to rescue from oblivion any events of her life
or any traits of her character to satisfy the enquiries of a generation
of readers who have been born since she died. Of events her life was
singularly barren: few changes and no great crisis ever broke the
smooth current of its course. Even her fame may be said to have
been posthumous: it did not attain to any vigorous life till she had
ceased to exist. Her talents did not introduce her to the notice of
other writers, or connect her with the literary world, or in any
degree pierce through the obscurity of her domestic retirement. I
have therefore scarcely any materials for a detailed life of my aunt;
but I have a distinct recollection of her person and character; and
perhaps many may take an interest in a delineation, if any such can
be drawn, of that prolific mind whence sprung the Dashwoods and
Bennets, the Bertrams and Woodhouses, the Thorpes and Mus-
groves, who have been admitted as familiar guests to the firesides of
so many families, and are known there as individually and intimately
as if they were living neighbours. Many may care to know whether
the moral rectitude, the correct taste, and the warm affections with
which she invested her ideal characters, were really existing in the
native source whence those ideas flowed, and were actually
exhibited by her in the various relations of life. I can indeed bear
witness that there was scarcely a charm in her most delightful
characters that was not a true reflection of her own sweet temper
and loving heart. I was young when we lost her; but the impressions
made on the young are deep, and though in the course of fifty years

---

[*] I went to represent my father, who was too unwell to attend himself, and
thus I was the only one of my generation present.

I have forgotten much, I have not forgotten that 'Aunt Jane' was the delight of all her nephews and nieces. We did not think of her as being clever, still less as being famous; but we valued her as one always kind, sympathising, and amusing. To all this I am a living witness, but whether I can sketch out such a faint outline of this excellence as shall be perceptible to others may be reasonably doubted. Aided, however, by a few survivors* who knew her, I will not refuse to make the attempt. I am the more inclined to undertake the task from a conviction that, however little I may have to tell, no one else is left who could tell so much of her.

Jane Austen was born on December 16, 1775, at the Parsonage House of Steventon in Hampshire. Her father, the Revd George Austen, was of a family long established in the neighbourhood of Tenterden and Sevenoaks in Kent. I believe that early in the seven-teenth century they were clothiers. Hasted, in his history of Kent, says: 'The clothing business was exercised by persons who possessed most of the landed property in the Weald, insomuch that almost all the ancient families of these parts, now of large estates and genteel rank in life, and some of them ennobled by titles, are sprung from ancestors who have used this great staple manufacture, now almost unknown here.' In his list of these families Hasted places the Austens, and he adds that these clothiers 'were usually called the Gray Coats of Kent; and were a body so numerous and united that at county elections whoever had their vote and interest was almost certain of being elected'. The family still retains a badge of this origin; for their livery is of that peculiar mixture of light blue and white called Kentish grey, which forms the facings of the Kentish militia.

Mr George Austen had lost both his parents before he was nine years old. He inherited no property from them; but was happy in

---

* My chief assistants have been my sisters, Mrs B. Lefroy and Miss Austen, whose recollections of our aunt are, on some points, more vivid than my own. I have not only been indebted to their memory for facts, but have sometimes used their words. Indeed some passages towards the end of the work were entirely written by the latter.

  I have also to thank some of my cousins, and especially the daughters of Admiral Charles Austen, for the use of letters and papers which had passed into their hands, without which this Memoir, scanty as it is, could not have been written.

having a kind uncle, Mr Francis Austen, a successful lawyer at Tunbridge, the ancestor of the Austens of Kippington, who, though he had children of his own, yet made liberal provision for his orphan nephew. The boy received a good education at Tunbridge School, whence he obtained a scholarship, and subsequently a fellowship, at St John's College, Oxford. In 1764 he came into possession of the two adjoining Rectories of Deane and Steventon in Hampshire; the former purchased for him by his generous uncle Francis, the latter given by his cousin Mr Knight. This was no very gross case of plurality, according to the ideas of that time, for the two villages were little more than a mile apart, and their united populations scarcely amounted to three hundred. In the same year he married Cassandra, youngest daughter of the Revd Thomas Leigh, of the family of Leighs of Warwickshire, who, having been a fellow of All Souls, held the College living of Harpsden, near Henley-upon-Thames. Mr Thomas Leigh was a younger brother of Dr Theophilus Leigh, a personage well known at Oxford in his day, and his day was not a short one, for he lived to be ninety, and held the Mastership of Balliol College for above half a century. He was a man more famous for his sayings than his doings, overflowing with puns and witticisms and sharp retorts; but his most serious joke was his practical one of living much longer than had been expected or intended. He was a fellow of Corpus, and the story is that the Balliol men, unable to agree in electing one of their own number to the Mastership, chose him, partly under the idea that he was in weak health and likely soon to cause another vacancy. It was afterwards said that his long incumbency had been a judgment on the Society for having elected an *Out-College Man*.* I imagine that the front of Balliol towards Broad Street which has recently been pulled down must have been built, or at least restored, while he was Master, for the Leigh arms were placed under the cornice at the corner nearest to Trinity gates. The beautiful building lately erected has destroyed this record, and thus 'monuments themselves memorials need'.

His fame for witty and agreeable conversation extended beyond the bounds of the University. Mrs Thrale, in a letter to Dr Johnson,

* There seems to have been some doubt as to the validity of this election; for Hearne says that it was referred to the Visitor, who confirmed it. (Hearne's *Diaries*, v.2.)

writes thus: 'Are you acquainted with Dr Leigh,* the Master of Balliol College, and are you not delighted with his gaiety of manners and youthful vivacity, now that he is eighty-six years of age? I never heard a more perfect or excellent pun than his, when some one told him how, in a late dispute among the Privy Councillors, the Lord Chancellor struck the table with such violence that he split it. "No, no, no," replied the Master; "I can hardly persuade myself that he *split* the *table*, though I believe he *divided* the *Board*." '

Some of his sayings of course survive in family tradition. He was once calling on a gentleman notorious for never opening a book, who took him into a room overlooking the Bath Road, which was then a great thoroughfare for travellers of every class, saying rather pompously, 'This, Doctor, I call my study.' The Doctor, glancing his eye round the room, in which no books were to be seen, replied, 'And very well named too, sir, for you know Pope tells us, "The proper *study* of mankind is *Man*." ' When my father went to Oxford he was honoured with an invitation to dine with this dignified cousin. Being a raw undergraduate, unaccustomed to the habits of the University, he was about to take off his gown, as if it were a great coat, when the old man, then considerably turned eighty, said, with a grim smile, 'Young man, you need not strip: we are not going to fight.' This humour remained in him so strongly to the last that he might almost have supplied Pope with another instance of 'the ruling passion strong in death', for only three days before he expired, being told that an old acquaintance was lately married, having recovered from a long illness by eating eggs, and that the wits said that he had been egged on to matrimony, he immediately trumped the joke, saying, 'Then may the yoke sit easy on him.' I do not know from what common ancestor the Master of Balliol and his great-niece Jane Austen, with some others of the family, may have derived the keen sense of humour which they certainly possessed.

Mr and Mrs George Austen resided first at Deane, but removed in 1771 to Steventon, which was their residence for about thirty years. They commenced their married life with the charge of a little child, a son of the celebrated Warren Hastings, who had been committed to the care of Mr Austen before his marriage, probably

---

* Mrs Thrale writes Dr *Lee*, but there can be no doubt of the identity of person.

through the influence of his sister, Mrs Hancock, whose husband at that time held some office under Hastings in India. Mr Gleig, in his *Life of Hastings*, says that his son George, the offspring of his first marriage, was sent to England in 1761 for his education, but that he had never been able to ascertain to whom this precious charge was entrusted, nor what became of him. I am able to state, from family tradition, that he died young, of what was then called putrid sore throat; and that Mrs Austen had become so much attached to him that she always declared that his death had been as great a grief to her as if he had been a child of her own.

About this time, the grandfather of Mary Russell Mitford, Dr Russell, was Rector of the adjoining parish of Ashe; so that the parents of two popular female writers must have been intimately acquainted with each other.

As my subject carries me back about a hundred years, it will afford occasions for observing many changes gradually effected in the manners and habits of society, which I may think it worth while to mention. They may be little things, but time gives a certain importance even to trifles, as it imparts a peculiar flavour to wine. The most ordinary articles of domestic life are looked on with some interest, if they are brought to light after being long buried; and we feel a natural curiosity to know what was done and said by our forefathers, even though it may be nothing wiser or better than what we are daily doing or saying ourselves. Some of this generation may be little aware how many conveniences, now considered to be necessaries and matters of course, were unknown to their grand-fathers and grandmothers. The lane between Deane and Steventon has long been as smooth as the best turnpike road; but when the family removed from the one residence to the other in 1771, it was a mere cart track, so cut up by deep ruts as to be impassable for a light carriage. Mrs Austen, who was not then in strong health, performed the short journey on a feather-bed, placed upon some soft articles of furniture in the waggon which held their household goods. In those days it was not unusual to set men to work with shovel and pickaxe to fill up ruts and holes in roads seldom used by carriages, on such special occasions as a funeral or a wedding. Ignorance and coarseness of language also were still lingering even upon higher levels of society than might have been expected to retain such mists. About this time, a neighbouring squire, a man of many acres, referred the following difficulty to Mr Austen's decision: 'You know all about these sort of things. Do tell us. Is Paris in France, or France in Paris? for my wife has been disputing with me about it.' The same gentleman, narrating some conversation which he had heard between the rector and his wife, represented the latter as beginning her reply to her husband with a round oath; and when his daughter called him to task, reminding him that Mrs Austen never swore, he replied, 'Now, Betty, why do you pull me up for nothing? that's neither here nor there; you know very well that's only *my way of telling the story*.' Attention has lately been called by a celebrated writer to the inferiority of the clergy to the laity of England two centuries ago. The charge no doubt is true, if the rural clergy are to be compared with that higher section of country gentlemen who went into parliament, and mixed in London society, and took the lead in their several counties; but it might be found less true if they were to be compared, as in all fairness they ought to be, with that lower section with whom they usually associated. The smaller landed proprietors, who seldom went farther from home than their county town, from the squire with his thousand acres to the yeoman who cultivated his hereditary property of one or two hundred, then formed a numerous class – each the aristocrat of his own parish; and there was probably a greater difference in manners and refinement between this class and that immediately above them than could now be found between any two persons who rank as gentlemen. For in the progress of civilisation, though all orders may make some progress, yet it is most perceptible in the lower. It is a process of 'levelling up'; the rear rank 'dressing up', as it were, close to the front rank. When Hamlet mentions, as something which he had 'for *three years taken* note of', that 'the toe of the peasant comes so near the heel of the courtier', it was probably intended by Shakspeare as a satire on his own times; but it expressed a principle which is working at all times in which society makes any progress. I believe that a century ago the improvement in most country parishes began with the clergy; and that in those days a rector who chanced to be a gentleman and a scholar found himself superior to his chief parishioners in information and manners, and became a sort of centre of refinement and politeness.

Mr Austen was a remarkably good-looking man, both in his youth and his old age. During his year of office at Oxford he had been called the 'handsome Proctor'; and at Bath, when more than seventy years old, he attracted observation by his fine features and abundance of snow-white hair. Being a good scholar he was able to prepare two of his sons for the University, and to direct the studies of his other children, whether sons or daughters, as well as to increase his income by taking pupils.

In Mrs Austen also was to be found the germ of much of the ability which was concentrated in Jane, but of which others of her children had a share. She united strong common sense with a lively imagination, and often expressed herself, both in writing and in conversation, with epigrammatic force and point. She lived, like many of her family, to an advanced age. During the last years of her life she endured continual pain, not only patiently but with characteristic cheerfulness. She once said to me, 'Ah, my dear, you find me just where you left me – on the sofa. I sometimes think that God Almighty must have forgotten me; but I dare say He will come for me in His own good time.' She died and was buried at Chawton, January 1827, aged eighty-eight.

*   *   *

Her own family were so much, and the rest of the world so little, to Jane Austen, that some brief mention of her brothers and sister is necessary in order to give any idea of the objects which principally occupied her thoughts and filled her heart, especially as some of them, from their characters or professions in life, may be supposed to have had more or less influence on her writings: though I feel some reluctance in bringing before public notice persons and circumstances essentially private.

Her eldest brother James, my own father, had, when a very young man, at St John's College, Oxford, been the originator and chief supporter of a periodical paper called the *Loiterer*, written somewhat on the plan of the *Spectator* and its successors, but nearly confined to subjects connected with the University. In after life he used to speak very slightingly of this early work, which he had the better right to do, as, whatever may have been the degree of their merits, the best papers had certainly been written by himself. He was well read in English literature, had a correct taste, and wrote readily and happily, both in prose and verse. He was more than ten years older than Jane, and had, I believe, a large share in directing her reading and forming her taste.

Her second brother, Edward, had been a good deal separated from the rest of the family, as he was early adopted by his cousin, Mr Knight, of Godmersham Park in Kent and Chawton House in Hampshire; and finally came into possession both of the property and the name. But though a good deal separated in childhood, they were much together in after life, and Jane gave a large share of her affections to him and his children. Mr Knight was not only a very amiable man, kind and indulgent to all connected with him, but possessed also a spirit of fun and liveliness, which made him especially delightful to all young people.

Her third brother, Henry, had great conversational powers, and inherited from his father an eager and sanguine disposition. He was a very entertaining companion, but had perhaps less steadiness of purpose, certainly less success in life, than his brothers. He became a clergyman when middle-aged; and an allusion to his sermons will be found in one of Jane's letters. At one time he resided in London, and was useful in transacting his sister's business with her publishers.

Her two youngest brothers, Francis and Charles, were sailors during that glorious period of the British navy which comprises the close of the last and the beginning of the present century, when it was impossible for an officer to be almost always afloat, as these brothers were, without seeing service which, in these days, would be considered distinguished. Accordingly, they were continually engaged in actions of more or less importance, and sometimes gained promotion by their success. Both rose to the rank of Admiral, and carried out their flags to distant stations.

Francis lived to attain the very summit of his profession, having died, in his ninety third year, G.C.B. and Senior Admiral of the Fleet, in 1865. He possessed great firmness of character, with a strong sense of duty, whether due from himself to others, or from others to himself. He was consequently a strict disciplinarian; but, as he was a very religious man, it was remarked of him (for in those days, at least, it was remarkable) that he maintained this discipline without ever uttering an oath or permitting one in his presence. On one occasion, when ashore in a seaside town, he was spoken of as 'the officer who kneeled at church'; a custom which now happily would not be thought peculiar.

Charles was generally serving in frigates or sloops; blockading harbours, driving the ships of the enemy ashore, boarding gunboats, and frequently making small prizes. At one time he was absent from England on such services for seven years together. In later life he commanded the *Bellerophon*, at the bombardment of St Jean d'Acre in 1840. In 1850 he went out in the *Hastings*, in command of the East India and China station, but on the breaking out of the Burmese war he transferred his flag to a steam sloop, for the purpose of getting up the shallow waters of the Irrawaddy, on board of which he died of cholera in 1852, in the seventy-fourth year of his age. His sweet temper and affectionate disposition, in which he resembled his sister Jane, had secured to him an unusual portion of attachment, not only from his own family, but from all the officers and common sailors who served under him. One who was with him at his death has left this record of him: 'Our good Admiral won the hearts of all by his gentleness and kindness while he was struggling with disease, and endeavouring to do his duty as Commander-in-chief of the British naval forces in these waters. His death was a great grief to the whole fleet. I know that I cried bitterly when I found he was dead.' The Order in Council of the Governor-General of India, Lord Dalhousie, expresses 'admiration of the staunch high spirit which, notwithstanding his age and previous sufferings, had led the Admiral to take his part in the trying service which has closed his career'.

These two brothers have been dwelt on longer than the others because their honourable career accounts for Jane Austen's partiality for the Navy, as well as for the readiness and accuracy with which she wrote about it. She was always very careful not to meddle with matters which she did not thoroughly understand. She never touched upon politics, law, or medicine, subjects which some novel writers have ventured on rather too boldly, and have treated, perhaps, with more brilliancy than accuracy. But with ships and sailors she felt herself at home, or at least could always trust to a brotherly critic to keep her right. I believe that no flaw has ever been found in her seamanship either in *Mansfield Park* or in *Persuasion*.

But dearest of all to the heart of Jane was her sister Cassandra, about three years her senior. Their sisterly affection for each other could scarcely be exceeded. Perhaps it began on Jane's side with the feeling of deference natural to a loving child towards a kind elder sister. Something of this feeling always remained; and even in the maturity of her powers, and in the enjoyment of increasing success, she would still speak of Cassandra as of one wiser and better than herself. In childhood, when the elder was sent to the school of a Mrs Latournelle, in the Forbury at Reading, the younger went with her, not because she was thought old enough to profit much by the instruction there imparted, but because she would have been miserable without her sister; her mother observing that 'if Cassandra were going to have her head cut off, Jane would insist on sharing her fate'. This attachment was never interrupted or weakened. They lived in the same home, and shared the same bedroom, till separated by death. They were not exactly alike. Cassandra's was the colder and calmer disposition; she was always prudent and well judging, but with less outward demonstration of feeling and less sunniness of temper than Jane possessed. It was remarked in her family that 'Cassandra had the *merit* of having her temper always under command, but that Jane had the *happiness* of a temper that never required to be commanded'. When *Sense and Sensibility* came out, some persons, who knew the family slightly, surmised that the two elder Miss Dashwoods were intended by the author for her sister and herself; but this could not be the case. Cassandra's character might indeed represent the '*sense*' of Elinor, but Jane's had little in common with the '*sensibility*' of Marianne. The young woman who, before the age of twenty, could so clearly discern the failings of Marianne Dashwood, could hardly have been subject to them herself.

This was the small circle, continually enlarged, however, by the increasing families of four of her brothers, within which Jane Austen found her wholesome pleasures, duties, and interests, and beyond which she went very little into society during the last ten years of her life. There was so much that was agreeable and attractive in this family party that its members may be excused if they were inclined to live somewhat too exclusively within it. They might see in each other much to love and esteem, and something to admire. The family talk had abundance of spirit and vivacity, and was never troubled by disagreements even in little matters, for it was not their habit to dispute or argue with each other: above all, there was strong family affection and firm union, never to be broken but by death. It cannot be doubted that all this had its influence on the author in the construction of her stories, in which a family party usually supplies the narrow stage, while the interest is made to revolve round a few actors.

It will be seen also that though her circle of society was small, yet she found in her neighbourhood persons of good taste and cultivated minds. Her acquaintance, in fact, constituted the very class from which she took her imaginary characters, ranging from the member of parliament, or large landed proprietor, to the young curate or younger midshipman of equally good family; and I think that the influence of these early associations may be traced in her writings, especially in two particulars. First, that she is entirely free from the vulgarity, which is so offensive in some novels, of dwelling on the outward appendages of wealth or rank, as if they were things to which the writer was unaccustomed; and, secondly, that she deals as little with very low as with very high stations in life. She does not go lower than the Miss Steeles, Mrs Elton, and John Thorpe, people of bad taste and underbred manners, such as are actually found sometimes mingling with better society. She has nothing resembling the Brangtons, or Mr Dubster and his friend Tom Hicks, with whom Madame D'Arblay loved to season her stories, and to produce striking contrasts to her well-bred characters.

Steventon Parsonage

2

*Description of Steventon – Life at Steventon – Changes of
Habits and Customs in the last Century*

As the first twenty-five years, more than half of the brief life of Jane
Austen, were spent in the parsonage of Steventon, some description
of that place ought to be given. Steventon is a small rural village
upon the chalk hills of north Hants, situated in a winding valley
about seven miles from Basingstoke. The South-Western railway
crosses it by a short embankment, and, as it curves round, presents a
good view of it on the left hand to those who are travelling down the
line, about three miles before entering the tunnel under Popham
Beacon. It may be known to some sportsmen, as lying in one of the
best portions of the Vine Hunt. It is certainly not a picturesque
country; it presents no grand or extensive views; but the features are
small rather than plain. The surface continually swells and sinks, but
the hills are not bold, nor the valleys deep; and though it is
sufficiently well clothed with woods and hedgerows, yet the poverty
of the soil in most places prevents the timber from attaining a large
size. Still it has its beauties. The lanes wind along in a natural curve,

continually fringed with irregular borders of native turf, and lead to pleasant nooks and corners. One who knew and loved it well very happily expressed its quiet charms, when he wrote:

> True taste is not fastidious, nor rejects,
> Because they may not come within the rule
> Of composition pure and picturesque,
> Unnumbered simple scenes which fill the leaves
> Of Nature's sketch book.

Of this somewhat tame country, Steventon, from the fall of the ground, and the abundance of its timber, is certainly one of the prettiest spots; yet one cannot be surprised that, when Jane's mother, a little before her marriage, was shown the scenery of her future home, she should have thought it unattractive, compared with the broad river, the rich valley, and the noble hills which she had been accustomed to behold at her native home near Henley-upon-Thames.

The house itself stood in a shallow valley, surrounded by sloping meadows, well sprinkled with elm trees, at the end of a small village of cottages, each well provided with a garden, scattered about prettily on either side of the road. It was sufficiently commodious to hold pupils in addition to a growing family, and was in those times considered to be above the average of parsonages; but the rooms were finished with less elegance than would now be found in the most ordinary dwellings. No cornice marked the junction of wall and ceiling; while the beams which supported the upper floors projected into the rooms below in all their naked simplicity, covered only by a coat of paint or whitewash: accordingly it has since been considered unworthy of being the Rectory house of a family living, and about forty-five years ago it was pulled down for the purpose of erecting a new house in a far better situation on the opposite side of the valley.

North of the house, the road from Deane to Popham Lane ran at a sufficient distance from the front to allow a carriage drive, through turf and trees. On the south side the ground rose gently, and was occupied by one of those old-fashioned gardens in which vegetables and flowers are combined, flanked and protected on the east by one of the thatched mud walls common in that country, and over-shadowed by fine elms. Along the upper or southern side of this garden, ran a terrace of the finest turf, which must have been in the writer's thoughts when she described Catharine Morland's childish delight in 'rolling down the green slope at the back of the house'.

But the chief beauty of Steventon consisted in its hedgerows. A hedgerow, in that country, does not mean a thin formal line of quickset, but an irregular border of copse-wood and timber, often wide enough to contain within it a winding footpath, or a rough cart track. Under its shelter the earliest primroses, anemones, and wild hyacinths were to be found; sometimes, the first bird's-nest; and, now and then, the unwelcome adder. Two such hedgerows radiated, as it were, from the parsonage garden. One, a continuation of the turf terrace, proceeded westward, forming the southern boundary of the home meadows; and was formed into a rustic shrubbery, with occasional seats, entitled 'The Wood Walk'. The other ran straight up the hill, under the name of 'The Church Walk', because it led to the parish church, as well as to a fine old manor-house, of Henry VIII's time, occupied by a family named Digweed, who have for more than a century rented it, together with the chief farm in the parish. The church itself – I speak of it as it then was, before the improvements made by the present rector –

> A little spireless fane,
> Just seen above the woody lane,

might have appeared mean and uninteresting to an ordinary observer; but the adept in church architecture would have known that it must have stood there some seven centuries, and would have found beauty in the very narrow early English windows, as well as in the general proportions of its little chancel, while its solitary position, far from the hum of the village, and within sight of no habitation, except a glimpse of the grey manor-house through its circling screen of sycamores, has in it something solemn and appropriate to the last resting-place of the silent dead. Sweet violets, both purple and white, grow in abundance beneath its south wall. One may imagine for how many centuries the ancestors of those little flowers have occupied that undisturbed, sunny nook, and may think how few living families can boast of as ancient a tenure of their land. Large elms protrude their rough branches; old hawthorns shed their annual blossoms over the graves; and the hollow yew-tree must be at least coeval with the church.

But whatever may be the beauties or defects of the surrounding scenery, this was the residence of Jane Austen for twenty-five years. This was the cradle of her genius. These were the first objects which inspired her young heart with a sense of the beauties of nature. In strolls along those wood-walks, thick-coming fancies rose in her mind, and gradually assumed the forms in which they came forth to the world. In that simple church she brought them all into subjection to the piety which ruled her in life, and supported her in death.

The home at Steventon must have been, for many years, a pleasant and prosperous one. The family was unbroken by death, and seldom visited by sorrow. Their situation had some peculiar advantages beyond those of ordinary rectories. Steventon was a family living. Mr Knight, the patron, was also proprietor of nearly the whole parish. He never resided there, and consequently the rector and his children came to be regarded in the neighbourhood as a kind of representatives of the family. They shared with the principal tenant the command of an excellent manor, and enjoyed, in this reflected way, some of the consideration usually awarded to landed proprietors. They were not rich, but, aided by Mr Austen's powers of teaching, they had enough to afford a good education to their sons and daughters, to mix in the best society of the neighbourhood, and to exercise a liberal hospitality to their own relations and friends. A carriage and a pair of horses were kept. This might imply a higher style of living in our days than it did in theirs. There were then no assessed taxes. The carriage, once bought, entailed little further expense; and the horses probably, like Mr Bennet's, were often employed on farm work. Moreover, it should be remembered that a pair of horses in those days were almost necessary, if ladies were to move about at all; for neither the condition of the roads nor the style of carriage-building admitted of any comfortable vehicle being drawn by a single horse. When one looks at the few specimens still remaining of coach-building in the last century, it strikes one that the chief object of the builders must have been to combine the greatest possible weight with the least possible amount of accommodation.

The family lived in close intimacy with two cousins, Edward and Jane Cooper, the children of Mrs Austen's eldest sister, and Dr Cooper, the vicar of Sonning, near Reading. The Coopers lived for some years at Bath, which seems to have been much frequented in those days by clergymen retiring from work. I believe that Cassandra and Jane sometimes visited them there, and that Jane thus acquired the intimate knowledge of the topography and customs of Bath, which enabled her to write *Northanger Abbey* long before she resided there herself. After the death of their own parents, the two young Coopers paid long visits at Steventon. Edward Cooper did not live undistinguished. When an undergraduate at Oxford, he gained the prize for Latin hexameters on 'Hortus Anglicus' in 1791; and in later life he was known by a work on prophecy, called 'The Crisis', and other religious publications, especially for several volumes of Sermons, much preached in many pulpits in my youth. Jane Cooper was married from her uncle's house at Steventon, to Captain, afterwards Sir Thomas Williams, under whom Charles Austen served in several ships. She was a dear friend of her namesake, but was fated to become a cause of great sorrow to her, for a few years after the marriage she was suddenly killed by an accident to her carriage.

There was another cousin closely associated with them at Steventon, who must have introduced greater variety into the family circle. This was the daughter of Mr Austen's only sister, Mrs Hancock. This cousin had been educated in Paris, and married to a Count de Feuillade, of whom I know little more than that he perished by the guillotine during the French Revolution. Perhaps his chief offence was his rank; but it was said that the charge of 'incivism,' under which he suffered, rested on the fact of his having laid down some arable land into pasture – a sure sign of his intention to embarrass the Republican Government by producing a famine! His wife escaped through danger and difficulties to England, was received for some time into her uncle's family, and finally married her cousin Henry Austen. During the short peace of Amiens, she and her second husband went to France, in the hope of recovering some of the Count's property, and there narrowly escaped being included amongst the *détenus*. Orders had been given by Buonaparte's government to detain all English travellers, but at the posthouses Mrs Henry Austen gave the necessary orders herself, and her French was so perfect that she passed everywhere for a native, and her husband escaped under this protection.

She was a clever woman, and highly accomplished, after the French rather than the English mode; and in those days, when intercourse with the Continent was long interrupted by war, such an element in the society of a country parsonage must have been a rare acquisition. The sisters may have been more indebted to this cousin than to Mrs La Tournelle's teaching for the considerable knowledge of French which they possessed. She also took the principal parts in the private theatricals in which the family several times indulged, having their summer theatre in the barn, and their winter one within the narrow limits of the dining-room, where the number of the audience must have been very limited. On these occasions, the prologues and epilogues were written by Jane's eldest brother, and some of them are very vigorous and amusing. Jane was only twelve years old at the time of the earliest of these representations, and not more than fifteen when the last took place. She was, however, an early observer, and it may be reasonably supposed that some of the incidents and feelings which are so vividly painted in the Mansfield Park theatricals are due to her recollections of these entertainments.

Some time before they left Steventon, one great affliction came upon the family. Cassandra was engaged to be married to a young clergyman. He had not sufficient private fortune to permit an immediate union; but the engagement was not likely to be a hopeless or a protracted one, for he had a prospect of early preferment from a nobleman with whom he was connected both by birth and by personal friendship. He accompanied this friend to the West Indies, as chaplain to his regiment, and there died of yellow fever, to the great concern of his friend and patron, who afterwards declared that, if he had known of the engagement, he would not have permitted him to go out to such a climate. This little domestic tragedy caused great and lasting grief to the principal sufferer, and could not but cast a gloom over the whole party. The sympathy of Jane was probably, from her age, and her peculiar attachment to her sister, the deepest of all.

Of Jane herself I know of no such definite tale of love to relate. Her reviewer in the *Quarterly* of January 1821 observes, concerning the attachment of Fanny Price to Edmund Bertram: 'The silence in which this passion is cherished, the slender hopes and enjoyments by which it is fed, the restlessness and jealousy with which it fills a mind naturally active, contented, and unsuspicious, the manner in which it tinges every event, and every reflection, are painted with a vividness and a detail of which we can scarcely conceive anyone but a female, and we should almost add, a female writing from recollection, capable.' This conjecture, however probable, was wide of the mark. The picture was drawn from the intuitive perceptions of genius, not from personal experience. In no circumstance of her life was there any similarity between herself and her heroine in *Mansfield Park*. She did not indeed pass through life without being the object of warm affection. In her youth she had declined the addresses of a gentleman who had the recommendations of good character, and connections, and position in life, of everything, in fact, except the subtle power of touching her heart. There is, however, one passage of romance in her history with which I am imperfectly acquainted, and to which I am unable to assign name, or date, or place, though I have it on sufficient authority. Many years after her death, some circumstances induced her sister Cassandra to break through her habitual reticence, and to speak of it. She said that, while staying at some seaside place, they became acquainted with a gentleman, whose charm of person, mind, and manners was such that Cassandra thought him worthy to possess and likely to win her sister's love. When they parted, he expressed his intention of soon seeing them again; and Cassandra felt no doubt as to his motives. But they never again met. Within a short time they heard of his sudden death. I believe that, if Jane ever loved, it was this unnamed gentleman; but the acquaintance had been short, and I am unable to say whether her feelings were of such a nature as to affect her happiness.

Any description that I might attempt of the family life at Steventon, which closed soon after I was born, could be little better than a fancy-piece. There is no doubt that if we could look into the households of the clergy and the small gentry of that period, we should see some things which would seem strange to us, and should miss many more to which we are accustomed. Every hundred years, and especially a century like the last, marked by an extraordinary advance in wealth, luxury, and refinement of taste, as well as in the mechanical arts which embellish our houses, must produce a great change in their aspect. These changes are always at work; they are going on now, but so silently that we take no note of them. Men soon forget the small objects which they leave behind them as they drift down the stream of life. As Pope says –

> Nor does life's stream for observation stay;
> It hurries all too fast to mark their way.

Important inventions, such as the applications of steam, gas, and electricity, may find their places in history; but not so the alterations, great as they may be, which have taken place in the appearance of our dining- and drawing-rooms. Who can now record the degrees by which the custom prevalent in my youth of asking each other to take wine together at dinner became obsolete? Who will be able to fix, twenty years hence, the date when our dinners began to be carved and handed round by servants, instead of smoking before our eyes and noses on the table? To record such little matters would indeed be 'to chronicle small beer'. But, in a slight memoir like this, I may be allowed to note some of those changes in social habits which give a colour to history, but which the historian has the greatest difficulty in recovering.

At that time the dinner-table presented a far less splendid appearance than it does now. It was appropriated to solid food, rather than to flowers, fruits, and decorations. Nor was there much glitter of plate upon it; for the early dinner hour rendered candlesticks unnecessary, and silver forks had not come into general use: while the broad rounded end of the knives indicated the substitute generally used instead of them.[*]

The dinners too were more homely, though not less plentiful and savoury; and the bill of fare in one house would not be so like that in another as it is now, for family receipts were held in high estimation. A grandmother of culinary talent could bequeath to her descendant fame for some particular dish, and might influence the family dinner for many generations.

---

[*] The celebrated Beau Brummel, who was so intimate with George IV as to be able to quarrel with him, was born in 1771. It is reported that when he was questioned about his parents, he replied that it was long since he had heard of them, but that he imagined the worthy couple must have cut their own throats by that time, because when he last saw them they were eating peas with their knives. Yet Brummel's father had probably lived in good society; and was certainly able to put his son into a fashionable regiment, and to leave him £30,000.[†] Raikes believes that he had been Secretary to Lord North. Thackeray's idea that he had been a footman cannot stand against the authority of Raikes, who was intimate with the son.

[†] Raikes's *Memoirs*, vol. ii, p. 207.

Dos est magna parentium
Virtus.

One house would pride itself on its ham, another on its game-pie, and a third on its superior furmity, or tansey-pudding. Beer and home-made wines, especially mead, were more largely consumed. Vegetables were less plentiful and less various. Potatoes were used, but not so abundantly as now; and there was an idea that they were to be eaten only with roast meat. They were novelties to a tenant's wife who was entertained at Steventon Parsonage, certainly less than a hundred years ago; and when Mrs Austen advised her to plant them in her own garden, she replied, 'No, no; they are very well for you gentry, but they must be terribly *costly to rear*.'

But a still greater difference would be found in the furniture of the rooms, which would appear to us lamentably scanty. There was a general deficiency of carpeting in sitting-rooms, bedrooms, and passages. A pianoforte, or rather a spinnet or harpsichord, was by no means a necessary appendage. It was to be found only where there was a decided taste for music, not so common then as now, or in such great houses as would probably contain a billiard-table. There would often be but one sofa in the house, and that a stiff, angular, uncomfortable article. There were no deep easy-chairs, nor other appliances for lounging; for to lie down, or even to lean back, was a luxury permitted only to old persons or invalids. It was said of a nobleman, a personal friend of George III and a model gentleman of his day, that he would have made the tour of Europe without ever touching the back of his travelling carriage. But perhaps we should be most struck with the total absence of those elegant little articles which now embellish and encumber our drawing-room tables. We should miss the sliding bookcases and picture-stands, the letter-weighing machines and envelope cases, the periodicals and illustrated newspapers – above all, the countless swarm of photograph books which now threaten to swallow up all space. A small writing-desk, with a smaller work-box, or netting-case, was all that each young lady contributed to occupy the table; for the large family work-basket, though often produced in the parlour, lived in the closet.

There must have been more dancing throughout the country in those days than there is now: and it seems to have sprung up more spontaneously, as if it were a natural production, with less fastidiousness as to the quality of music, lights, and floor. Many country towns had a monthly ball throughout the winter, in some of which the same apartment served for dancing and tea-room. Dinner parties more frequently ended with an extempore dance on the carpet, to the music of a harpsichord in the house, or a fiddle from the village. This was always supposed to be for the entertainment of the young people, but many, who had little pretension to youth, were very ready to join in it. There can be no doubt that Jane herself enjoyed dancing, for she attributes this taste to her favourite heroines; in most of her works, a ball or a private dance is mentioned, and made of importance.

Many things connected with the ball-rooms of those days have now passed into oblivion. The barbarous law which confined the lady to one partner throughout the evening must indeed have been abolished before Jane went to balls. It must be observed, however, that this custom was in one respect advantageous to the gentleman, inasmuch as it rendered his duties more practicable. He was bound to call upon his partner the next morning, and it must have been convenient to have only one lady for whom he was obliged

> To gallop all the country over,
> The last night's partner to behold,
> And humbly hope she caught no cold.

But the stately minuet still reigned supreme; and every regular ball commenced with it. It was a slow and solemn movement, expressive of grace and dignity, rather than of merriment. It abounded in formal bows and courtesies, with measured paces, forwards, backwards and sideways, and many complicated gyrations. It was executed by one lady and gentleman, amidst the admiration, or the criticism, of surrounding spectators. In its earlier and most palmy days, as when Sir Charles and Lady Grandison delighted the company by dancing it at their own wedding, the gentleman wore a dress sword, and the lady was armed with a fan of nearly equal dimensions. Addison observes that 'women are armed with fans, as men with swords, and sometimes do more execution with them'. The graceful carriage of each weapon was considered a test of high breeding. The clownish man was in danger of being tripped up by his sword getting between his legs: the fan held clumsily looked more of a burden than an ornament; while in the hands of an adept it could be made to speak a language of its own.* It was not everyone who felt qualified to make this public exhibition, and I have been told that those ladies who intended to dance minuets, used to distinguish themselves from others by wearing a particular kind of lappet on their head-dress. I have heard also of another curious proof of the respect in which this dance was held. Gloves immaculately clean were considered requisite for its due performance, while gloves a little soiled were thought good enough for a country dance; and accordingly some prudent ladies provided themselves with two pairs for their several purposes. The minuet expired with the last century: but long after it had ceased to be danced publicly it was taught to boys and girls, in order to give them a graceful carriage.

Hornpipes, cotillons, and reels, were occasionally danced; but the chief occupation of the evening was the interminable country dance, in which all could join. This dance presented a great show of enjoyment, but it was not without its peculiar troubles. The ladies and gentlemen were ranged apart from each other in opposite rows, so that the facilities for flirtation, or interesting intercourse, were not so great as might have been desired by both parties. Much heart-burning and discontent sometimes arose as to *who* should stand above *whom*, and especially as to who was entitled to the high privilege of calling and leading off the first dance: and no little indignation was felt at the lower end of the room when any of the leading couples retired prematurely from their duties, and did not condescend to dance up and down the whole set. We may rejoice that these causes of irritation no longer exist; and that if such feelings as jealousy, rivalry, and discontent ever touch celestial bosoms in the modern ball-room they must arise from different and more recondite sources.

I am tempted to add a little about the difference of personal habits.

---

* See *Spectator*, No. 102, on the Fan Exercise. Old gentlemen who had survived the fashion of wearing swords were known to regret the disuse of that custom, because it put an end to one way of distinguishing those who had, from those who had not, been used to good society. To wear the sword easily was an art which, like swimming and skating, required to be learned in youth. Children could practise it early with their toy swords adapted to their size.

It may be asserted as a general truth, that less was left to the charge and discretion of servants, and more was done, or superintended, by the masters and mistresses. With regard to the mistresses, it is, I believe, generally understood, that at the time to which I refer, a hundred years ago, they took a personal part in the higher branches of cookery, as well as in the concoction of home-made wines, and distilling of herbs for domestic medicines, which are nearly allied to the same art. Ladies did not disdain to spin the thread of which the household linen was woven. Some ladies liked to wash with their own hands their choice china after breakfast or tea. In one of my earliest child's books, a little girl, the daughter of a gentleman, is taught by her mother to make her own bed before leaving her chamber. It was not so much that they had not servants to do all these things for them, as that they took an interest in such occupations. And it must be borne in mind how many sources of interest enjoyed by this generation were then closed, or very scantily opened to ladies. A very small minority of them cared much for literature or science. Music was not a very common, and drawing was a still rarer, accomplishment; needlework, in some form or other, was their chief sedentary employment.

But I doubt whether the rising generation are equally aware how much gentlemen also did for themselves in those times, and whether some things that I can mention will not be a surprise to them. Two homely proverbs were held in higher estimation in my early days than they are now – 'The master's eye makes the horse fat'; and, 'If you would be well served, serve yourself'. Some gentlemen took pleasure in being their own gardeners, performing all the scientific, and some of the manual, work themselves. Well-dressed young men of my acquaintance, who had their coat from a London tailor, would always brush their evening suit themselves, rather than entrust it to the carelessness of a rough servant, and to the risks of dirt and grease in the kitchen; for in those days servants' halls were not common in the houses of the clergy and the smaller country gentry. It was quite natural that Catherine Morland should have contrasted the magnificence of the offices at Northanger Abbey with the few shapeless pantries in her father's parsonage. A young man who expected to have his things packed or unpacked for him by a servant, when he travelled, would have been thought exceptionally fine, or exceptionally lazy. When my uncle undertook to teach me to shoot, his first lesson was how to clean my own gun. It was thought meritorious on the evening of a hunting day, to turn out after dinner, lanthorn in hand, and visit the stable, to ascertain that the horse had been well cared for. This was of the more importance, because, previous to the introduction of clipping, about the year 1820, it was a difficult and tedious work to make a long-coated hunter dry and comfortable, and was often very imperfectly done. Of course, such things were not practised by those who had gamekeepers, and stud-grooms, and plenty of well-trained servants; but they were practised by many who were unequivocally gentle-men, and whose grandsons, occupying the same position in life, may perhaps be astonished at being told that 'such things were'.

I have drawn pictures for which my own experience, or what I heard from others in my youth, have supplied the materials. Of course, they cannot be universally applicable. Such details varied in various circles, and were changed very gradually; nor can I pretend to tell how much of what I have said is descriptive of the family life at Steventon in Jane Austen's youth. I am sure that the ladies there had nothing to do with the mysteries of the stew-pot or the preserving-pan; but it is probable that their way of life differed a little from ours, and would have appeared to us more homely. It may be that useful articles, which would not now be produced in drawing-rooms, were hemmed, and marked, and darned in the old-fashioned parlour. But all this concerned only the outer life; there was as much cultivation and refinement of mind as now, with probably more studied courtesy and ceremony of manner to visitors; whilst certainly in that family literary pursuits were not neglected.

I remember to have heard of only two little things different from modern customs. One was, that on hunting mornings the young men usually took their hasty breakfast in the kitchen. The early hour at which hounds then met may account for this; and probably the custom began, if it did not end, when they were boys; for they hunted at an early age, in a scrambling sort of way, upon any pony or donkey that they could procure, or, in default of such luxuries, on foot. I have been told that Sir Francis Austen, when seven years old, bought on his own account, it must be supposed with his father's permission, a pony for a guinea and a half; and after riding him with great success for two seasons, sold him for a guinea more. One may wonder how the child could have so much money, and how the animal could have been obtained for so little. The same authority informs me that his first cloth suit was made from a scarlet habit, which, according to the fashion of the times, had been his mother's usual morning dress. If all this is true, the future admiral of the British Fleet must have cut a conspicuous figure in the hunting-field. The other peculiarity was that, when the roads were dirty, the sisters took long walks in pattens. This defence against wet and dirt is now seldom seen. The few that remain are banished from good society, and employed only in menial work; but a hundred and fifty years ago they were celebrated in poetry, and considered so clever a contrivance that Gay, in his *Trivia*, ascribes the invention to a god stimulated by his passion for a mortal damsel, and derives the name 'Patten' from 'Patty'.

> The patten now supports each frugal dame,
> Which from the blue-eyed Patty takes the name.

But mortal damsels have long ago discarded the clumsy implement. First it dropped its iron ring and became a clog; afterwards it was fined down into the pliant galoshe – lighter to wear and more effectual to protect – a no less manifest instance of gradual improvement than Cowper indicates when he traces through eighty lines of poetry his 'accomplished sofa' back to the original three-legged stool.

As an illustration of the purposes which a patten was intended to serve, I add the following epigram, written by Jane Austen's uncle, Mr Leigh Perrot, on reading in a newspaper the marriage of Captain Foote to Miss Patten:

> Through the rough paths of life, with a patten your guard,
>   May you safely and pleasantly jog;
> May the knot never slip, nor the ring press too hard,
>   Nor the *Foot* find the *Patten* a clog.

At the time when Jane Austen lived at Steventon, a work was carried on in the neighbouring cottages which ought to be recorded, because it has long ceased to exist.

Up to the beginning of the present century, poor women found profitable employment in spinning flax or wool. This was a better occupation for them than straw plaiting, inasmuch as it was carried on at the family hearth, and did not admit of gadding and gossiping about the village. The implement used was a long narrow machine of wood, raised on legs, furnished at one end with a large wheel, and at the other with a spindle on which the flax or wool was loosely wrapped, connected together by a loop of string. One hand turned the wheel, while the other formed the thread. The outstretched arms, the advanced foot, the sway of the whole figure backwards and forwards, produced picturesque attitudes, and displayed whatever of grace or beauty the work-woman might possess.[*] Some ladies were fond of spinning, but they worked in a quieter manner, sitting at a neat little machine of varnished wood, like Tunbridge ware, generally turned by the foot, with a basin of water at hand to supply the moisture required for forming the thread, which the cottager took by a more direct and natural process from her own mouth. I remember two such elegant little wheels in our own family.

It may be observed that this hand-spinning is the most primitive of female accomplishments, and can be traced back to the earliest times. Ballad poetry and fairy tales are full of allusions to it. The term 'spinster' still testifies to its having been the ordinary employment of the English young woman. It was the labour assigned to the ejected nuns by the rough earl who said, 'Go spin, ye jades, go spin.' It was the employment at which Roman matrons and Grecian princesses presided amongst their handmaids. Heathen mythology celebrated it in the three Fates spinning and measuring out the thread of human life. Holy Scripture honours it in those 'wise-hearted women' who 'did spin with their hands, and brought that which they had spun' for the construction of the Tabernacle in the wilderness: and an old English proverb carries it still farther back to the time 'when Adam delved and Eve span'. But, at last, this time-honoured domestic manufacture is quite extinct amongst us – crushed by the power of steam, overborne by a countless host of spinning jennies, and I can only just remember some of its last struggles for existence in the Steventon cottages.

---

[*] Mrs Gaskell, in her tale of *Sylvia's Lovers*, declares that this hand-spinning rivalled harp-playing in its gracefulness.

Steventon Manor House

3

*Early Compositions – Friends at Ashe – A very old Letter – Lines
on the Death of Mrs Lefroy – Observations on Jane Austen's
Letter-writing – Letters*

I know little of Jane Austen's childhood. Her mother followed a custom, not unusual in those days, though it seems strange to us, of putting out her babies to be nursed in a cottage in the village. The infant was daily visited by one or both of its parents, and frequently brought to them at the parsonage, but the cottage was its home, and must have remained so till it was old enough to run about and talk; for I know that one of them, in after life, used to speak of his foster mother as 'Movie', the name by which he had called her in his infancy. It may be that the contrast between the parsonage house and the best class of cottages was not quite so extreme then as it would be now, that the one was somewhat less luxurious, and the other less squalid. It would certainly seem from the results that it was a wholesome and invigorating system, for the children were all strong and healthy. Jane was probably treated like the rest in this respect. In childhood every available opportunity of instruction was made use of. According to the ideas of the time, she was well educated, though not highly accomplished, and she certainly enjoyed that important element of mental training, associating at home with persons of cultivated intellect. It cannot be doubted that her early years were bright and happy, living, as she did, with indulgent parents, in a cheerful home, not without agreeable variety of society. To these sources of enjoyment must be added the first stirrings of talent within her, and the absorbing interest of original composition. It is impossible to say at how early an age she began to write. There are copy books extant containing tales some of which must have been composed while she was a young girl, as they had amounted to a considerable number by the time she was sixteen. Her earliest stories are of a slight and flimsy texture, and are generally intended to be nonsensical, but the nonsense has much spirit in it. They are usually preceded by a dedication of mock solemnity to some one of her family. It would seem that the grandiloquent dedications prevalent in those days had not escaped her youthful penetration. Perhaps the most characteristic feature in these early productions is that, however puerile the matter, they are always composed in pure simple English, quite free from the over-ornamented style which might be expected from so young a writer. One of her juvenile effusions is given, as a specimen of the kind of transitory amusement which June was continually supplying to the family party.

The Mystery: An unfinished Comedy

DEDICATION

To the Revd George Austen

Sir – I humbly solicit your patronage to the following Comedy, which, though an unfinished one, is, I flatter myself, as complete a *Mystery* as any of its kind.

I am, Sir, your most humble Servant,

THE AUTHOR.

The Mystery: A Comedy

DRAMATIS PERSONAE

Men	*Women*
Col. Elliott	Fanny Elliot
Old Humbug	Mrs Humbug
Young Humbug	*and*
Sir Edward Spangle	Daphne
and	
Corydon	

ACT I

SCENE I – A garden

Enter CORYDON.

CORYDON: But hush: I am interrupted.   [*Exit Corydon.*

Enter OLD HUMBUG *and his* SON, *talking.*

OLD HUMBUG: It is for that reason that I wish you to follow my advice. Are you convinced of its propriety?

YOUNG HUMBUG: I am, sir, and will certainly act in the manner you have pointed out to me.

OLD HUMBUG: Then let us return to the house.   [*Exeunt.*

SCENE II – A parlour in HUMBUG's house.
MRS HUMBUG *and* FANNY *discovered at work.*

MRS HUMBUG: You understand me, my love?

FANNY: Perfectly, ma'am: pray continue your narration.

MRS HUMBUG: Alas! it is nearly concluded; for I have nothing more to say on the subject.

FANNY: Ah! here is Daphne.

Enter DAPHNE.

DAPHNE: My dear Mrs Humbug, how d'ye do? Oh! Fanny, it is all over.

FANNY: Is it indeed!

MRS HUMBUG: I'm very sorry to hear it.

FANNY: Then 'twas to no purpose that I –

DAPHNE: None upon earth.

MRS HUMBUG: And what is to become of —— ?

DAPHNE: Oh! 'tis all settled. (*Whispers to* MRS HUMBUG.)

FANNY: And how is it determined?

DAPHNE: I'll tell you. (*Whispers to* FANNY.)

MRS HUMBUG: And is he to – ?

DAPHNE: I'll tell you all I know of the matter. (*Whispers to* MRS HUMBUG *and* FANNY.)

FANNY: Well, now I know everything about it, I'll go away.

MRS HUMBUG *and* DAPHNE: And so will I.   [*Exeunt.*

SCENE III – The curtain rises,
and discovers SIR EDWARD SPANGLE reclined in
an elegant attitude on a sofa fast asleep.

Enter COL. ELLIOTT.

COL. E.: My daughter is not here, I see. There lies Sir Edward. Shall I tell him the secret? No, he'll certainly blab it. But he's asleep, and won't hear me; – so I'll e'en venture. (*Goes up to* SIR EDWARD, *whispers to him, and exit.*)

END OF THE FIRST ACT

FINIS.

*   *   *

Her own mature opinion of the desirableness of such an early habit of composition is given in the following words of a niece:

As I grew older, my aunt would talk to me more seriously of my reading and my amusements. I had taken early to writing verses and stories, and I am sorry to think how I troubled her with reading them. She was very kind about it, and always had some praise to bestow, but at last she warned me against spending too much time upon them. She said – how well I recollect it! – that she knew writing stories was a great amusement, and *she* thought a harmless one, though many people, she was aware, thought otherwise; but that at my age it would be bad for me to be much taken up with my own compositions. Later still – it was after she had gone to Winchester – she sent me a message to this effect, that if I would take her advice I should cease writing till I was sixteen; that she had herself often wished she had read more, and written less in the corresponding years of her own life.

As this niece was only twelve years old at the time of her aunt's death, these words seem to imply that the juvenile tales to which I have referred had, some of them at least, been written in her childhood.

But between these childish effusions, and the composition of her living works, there intervened another stage of her progress, during which she produced some stories, not without merit, but which she never considered worthy of publication. During this preparatory period her mind seems to have been working in a very different direction from that into which it ultimately settled. Instead of presenting faithful copies of nature, these tales were generally burlesques, ridiculing the improbable events and exaggerated sentiments which she had met with in sundry silly romances. Something of this fancy is to be found in *Northanger Abbey*, but she soon left it far behind in her subsequent course. It would seem as if she were first taking note of all the faults to be avoided, and curiously considering how she ought *not* to write before she attempted to put forth her strength in the right direction. The family have, rightly, I think, declined to let these early works be published. Mr Shortreed observed very pithily of Walter Scott's early rambles on the borders, 'He was makin' himsell a' the time; but he didna ken, may be, what he was about till years had passed. At first he thought of little, I dare say, but the queerness and the fun.' And so, in a humbler way, Jane Austen was 'makin' hersell', little thinking of future fame, but caring only for 'the queerness and the fun'; and it would be as unfair to expose this preliminary process to the world, as it would be to display all that goes on behind the curtain of the theatre before it is drawn up.

It was, however, at Steventon that the real foundations of her fame were laid. There some of her most successful writing was composed at such an early age as to make it surprising that so young a woman could have acquired the insight into character, and the nice observation of manners which they display. *Pride and Prejudice*, which some consider the most brilliant of her novels, was the first finished, if not the first begun. She began it in October 1796, before she was twenty-one years old, and completed it in about ten months, in August 1797. The title then intended for it was 'First Impressions'. *Sense and Sensibility* was begun, in its present form, immediately after the completion of the former, in November 1797, but something similar in story and character had been written earlier under the title of 'Elinor and Marianne'; and if, as is probable, a good deal of this earlier production was retained, it must form the earliest specimen of her writing that has been given to the world. *Northanger Abbey*, though not prepared for the press till 1803, was certainly first composed in 1798.

Amongst the most valuable neighbours of the Austens were Mr and Mrs Lefroy and their family. He was rector of the adjoining parish of Ashe; she was sister to Sir Egerton Brydges, to whom we are indebted for the earliest notice of Jane Austen that exists. In his autobiography, speaking of his visits at Ashe, he writes thus: 'The nearest neighbours of the Lefroys were the Austens of Steventon. I remember Jane Austen, the novelist, as a little child. She was very intimate with Mrs Lefroy, and much encouraged by her. Her mother was a Miss Leigh, whose paternal grandmother was sister to the first Duke of Chandos. Mr Austen was of a Kentish family, of which several branches have been settled in the Weald of Kent, and some are still remaining there. When I knew Jane Austen, I never suspected that she was an authoress; but my eyes told me that she was fair and handsome, slight and elegant, but with cheeks a little too full.' One may wish that Sir Egerton had dwelt rather longer on the subject of these memoirs, instead of being drawn away by his extreme love for genealogies to her great-grandmother and ancestors. That great grandmother however lives in the family records as Mary Brydges, a daughter of Lord Chandos, married in Westminster Abbey to Theophilus Leigh of Addlestrop in 1698. When a girl she had received a curious letter of advice and reproof, written by her mother from Constantinople. Mary, or 'Poll', was remaining in England with her grandmother, Lady Bernard, who seems to have been wealthy and inclined to be too indulgent to her granddaughter. This letter is given. Any such authentic document, two hundred years old, dealing with domestic details, must possess some interest. This is remarkable, not only as a specimen of the homely language in which ladies of rank then expressed themselves, but from the sound sense which it contains. Forms of expression vary, but good sense and right principles are the same in the nineteenth that they were in the seventeenth century.

MY DEARES POLL – Yr letters by Cousin Robbert Serle arrived here not before the 27th of Aprill, yett were they hartily wellcome to us, bringing ye joyful news which a great while we had longed for of my most dear Mother & all other relations & friends good health which I beseech God continue to you all, & as I observe in yrs to yr Sister Betty ye extraordinary kindness of (as I may truly say) the best Mothr & Gnd Mothr in the world in pinching herself to make you fine, so I cannot but admire her great good Housewifry in affording you so very plentifull an allowance, & yett to increase her Stock at the rate I find she hath done; & think I can never sufficiently mind you how very much it is yr duty on all occasions to pay her yr gratitude in all humble submission & obedience to all her commands soe long as you live. I must tell you 'tis to her bounty & care in ye greatest measure you are like to owe yr well living in this world, & as you cannot but be very sensible you are an extra-ordinary charge to her so it behoves you to take particular heed tht in ye whole course of yr life, you render her a proportionable comfort, especially since 'tis ye best way you can ever hope to make her such amends as God requires of yr hands. but Poll! it grieves me a little & yt I am forced to take notice of & reprove you for some vaine expressions in yr lettrs to yr Sister – you say concerning yr allowance 'you aime to bring yr bread & cheese even' in this I do not discommend you, for a foule shame indeed it would be should you out run the Constable having soe liberall a provision made you for yr maintenance – but ye reason you give for yr resolution I cannot at all approve for you say 'to spend more you can't' thats because you have it not to spend, otherwise it seems you would. So yt 'tis yr Grandmothrs discretion & not yours tht keeps you from extravagancy, which plainly appears in ye close of yr sentence, saying yt you think it simple covetousness to save out of yrs but 'tis my opinion if you lay all on yr back 'tis ten tymes a greater sin & shame thn to save some what out of soe large an allowance in yr purse to help you at a dead lift. Child, we all know our beginning, but who knows his end? Ye best use tht can be made of fair weathr is to provide against foule & 'tis great discretion & of noe small commendations for a young woman betymes to shew herself housewifly & frugal. Yr Mother neither Maide nor wife ever yett bestowed forty pounds a yeare on herself & yett if you never fall undr a worse reputation in ye world thn she (I thank God for it) hath hitherto done, you need not repine at it, & you cannot be ignorant of ye difference tht was between my fortune & what you are to expect. You ought likewise to consider tht you have seven brothers & sisters & you are all one man's children & therefore it is very unreasonable that one should expect to be preferred in finery soe much above all ye rest for 'tis impossible you should soe much mistake yr ffather's condition as to fancy he is able to allow every one of you forty pounds a yeare a piece, for such an allowance with the charge of their diett over and above will amount to at least five hundred pounds a yeare, a sum yr poor ffather can ill spare, besides doe but bethink yrself what a ridiculous sight it will be when yr grandmothr & you come to us to have noe less thn seven waiting gentlewomen in one house, for what reason can you give why every one of yr Sistrs should not have every one of ym a Maide as well as you, & though you may spare to pay yr maide's wages out of yr allowance yett you take no care of ye unnecessary charge you put yr ffathr to in yr increase of his family, whereas if it were not a piece of pride to have ye name of keeping yr maide she yt waits on yr good Grandmother might easily doe as formerly you know she hath done, all ye business you have for a maide unless as you grow oldr you grow a veryer Foole which God forbid!

Poll, you live in a place where you see great plenty & splendour but let not ye allurements of earthly pleasures tempt you to forget or neglect ye duty of a good Christian in dressing yr bettr part which is yr soule, as will best please God. I am not against yr going decent & neate as becomes yr ffathers daughter but to clothe yrself rich & be running into every gaudy fashion can never become yr circumstances & instead of doing you creditt & getting you a good prefernt it is ye readiest way you can take to slight all sober men from ever thinking of matching thmselves with women that live above thyr fortune, & if this be a wise way of spending money judge you! & besides, doe but reflect what an od sight it will be to a stranger that comes to our house to see yr Grandmothr yr Mothr & all yr Sisters in a plane dress & you only trickd up like a bartlemew-babby – you know what sort of people those are tht can't faire well but they must cry rost meate now what effect could you imagine yr writing in such a high straine to yr Sisters could have but either to provoke thm to envy you or murmur against us. I must tell you neithr of yr Sisters have ever had twenty pounds a yeare allowance from us yett, & yett theyr dress hath not disparaged neithr thm nor us & without incurring ye censure of simple covetousness they will have some what to shew out of their saving that will doe thm creditt & I expect yt you tht are theyr elder Sister shd rather sett thm examples of ye like nature thn tempt thm from treading in ye steps of their good Grandmothr & poor Mothr. This is not half what might be saide on this occasion but believing thee to be a very good natured dutyfull child I shd have thought it a great deal too much but yt having in my coming hither past through many most desperate dangers I cannot forbear thinking & preparing myself for all events, & therefore not knowing how it may please God to dispose of us I conclude it my duty to God & thee my dr child to lay this matter as home to thee as I could, assuring you my daily prayers are not nor shall not be wanting that God may give you grace always to remember to make a right use of this truly affectionate counsell of yr poor Mothr. & though I speak very plaine down-right english to you yett I would not have you doubt but that I love you as hartily as any child I have & if you serve God and take good courses I promise you my kindness to you shall be according to yr own hart's desire, for you may be certain I can aime at nothing in what I have now writ but yr real good which to promote shall be ye study & care day & night

Of my dear Poll thy truly affectionate Mothr.

ELIZA CHANDOS.
Pera of Galata, May ye 6th 1686.

P.S. – Thy ffathr & I send thee our blessing, & all thy brothrs & sistrs theyr service. Our harty & affectionate service to my brothr & sistr Childe & all my dear cozens. When you see my Lady Worster & cozen Howlands pray present thm my most humble service.

This letter shows that the wealth acquired by trade was already manifesting itself in contrast with the straitened circumstances of some of the nobility. Mary Brydges's 'poor ffather', in whose household economy was necessary, was the King of England's ambassador at Constantinople; the grandmother, who lived in 'great plenty and splendour', was the widow of a Turkey merchant. But then, as now, it would seem, rank had the power of attracting and absorbing wealth.

At Ashe also Jane became acquainted with a member of the Lefroy family, who was still living when I began these memoirs, a few months ago; the Right Hon. Thomas Lefroy, late Chief Justice of Ireland. One must look back more than seventy years to reach the time when these two bright young persons were, for a short time, intimately acquainted with each other, and then separated on their several courses, never to meet again; both destined to attain some distinction in their different ways, one to survive the other for more than half a century, yet in his extreme old age to remember and speak, as he sometimes did, of his former companion, as one to be much admired, and not easily forgotten by those who had ever known her.

Mrs Lefroy herself was a remarkable person. Her rare endowments of goodness, talents, graceful person, and engaging manners, were sufficient to secure her a prominent place in any society into which she was thrown; while her enthusiastic eagerness of disposition rendered her especially attractive to a clever and lively girl. She was killed by a fall from her horse on Jane's birthday, December 16, 1804. The following lines to her memory were written by Jane four years afterwards, when she was thirty-three years old. They are given, not for their merits as poetry, but to show how deep and lasting was the impression made by the elder friend on the mind of the younger:

To the Memory of Mrs Lefroy

1

The day returns again, my natal day;
   What mix'd emotions in my mind arise!
Beloved Friend; four years have passed away
   Since thou wert snatched for ever from our eyes.

2

The day commemorative of my birth,
   Bestowing life, and light, and hope to me,
Brings back the hour which was thy last on earth.
   O! bitter pang of torturing memory!

3

Angelic woman! past my power to praise
   In language meet thy talents, temper, mind,

Thy solid worth, thy captivating grace,
 Thou friend and ornament of human kind.

4

But come, fond Fancy, thou indulgent power;
 Hope is desponding, chill, severe, to thee:
Bless thou this little portion of an hour;
 Let me behold her as she used to be.

5

I see her here with all her smiles benign,
 Her looks of eager love, her accents sweet,
That voice and countenance almost divine,
 Expression, harmony, alike complete.

6

Listen! It is not sound alone, 'tis sense,
 'Tis genius, taste, and tenderness of soul:
'Tis genuine warmth of heart without pretence,
 And purity of mind that crowns the whole.

7

She speaks! 'Tis eloquence, that grace of tongue,
 So rare, so lovely, never misapplied
By her, to palliate vice, or deck a wrong:
 She speaks and argues but on virtue's side.

8

Hers is the energy of soul sincere;
 Her Christian spirit, ignorant to feign,
Seeks but to comfort, heal, enlighten, cheer,
 Confer a pleasure or prevent a pain.

9

Can aught enhance such goodness? yes, to me
 Her partial favour from my earliest years
Consummates all: ah! give me but to see
 Her smile of love! The vision disappears.

10

'Tis past and gone. We meet no more below.
 Short is the cheat of Fancy o'er the tomb.

Oh! might I hope to equal bliss to go,
　　To meet thee, angel, in thy future home.

11

Fain would I feel an union with thy fate:
　　Fain would I seek to draw an omen fair
From this connection in our earthly date.
　　Indulge the harmless weakness. Reason, spare.

The loss of their first home is generally a great grief to young persons of strong feeling and lively imagination; and Jane was exceedingly unhappy when she was told that her father, now seventy years of age, had determined to resign his duties to his eldest son, who was to be his successor in the Rectory of Steventon, and to remove with his wife and daughters to Bath. Jane had been absent from home when this resolution was taken; and, as her father was always rapid both in forming his resolutions and in acting on them, she had little time to reconcile herself to the change.

*　　*　　*

A wish has sometimes been expressed that some of Jane Austen's letters should be published. Some entire letters, and many extracts, will be given in this memoir; but the reader must be warned not to expect too much from them. With regard to accuracy of language indeed every word of them might be printed without correction. The style is always clear, and generally animated, while a vein of humour continually gleams through the whole; but the materials may be thought inferior to the execution, for they treat only of the details of domestic life. There is in them no notion of politics or public events; scarcely any discussions on literature, or other subjects of general interest. They may be said to resemble the nest which some little bird builds of the materials nearest at hand, of the twigs and mosses supplied by the tree in which it is placed; curiously constructed out of the simplest matters.

Her letters have very seldom the date of the year, or the signature of her christian name at full length; but it has been easy to ascertain their dates, either from the post-mark, or from their contents.

*　　*　　*

The two following letters are the earliest that I have seen. They were both written in November 1800; before the family removed from Steventon. Some of the same circumstances are referred to in both.

The first is to her sister Cassandra, who was then staying with their brother Edward at Godmersham Park, Kent:

Steventon, Saturday evening, Nov. 8th.

MY DEAR CASSANDRA – I thank you for so speedy a return to my two last, and particularly thank you for your anecdote of Charlotte Graham and her cousin, Harriet Bailey, which has very much amused both my mother and myself. If you can learn anything farther of that interesting affair, I hope you will mention it. I have two messages; let me get rid of them, and then my paper will be my own. Mary fully intended writing to you by Mr Chute's frank, and only happened entirely to forget it, but will write soon; and my father wishes Edward to send him a memorandum of the price of the hops. The tables are come, and give general contentment. I had not expected that they would so perfectly suit the fancy of us all three, or that we should so well agree in the disposition of them; but nothing except their own surface can have been smoother. The two ends put together form one constant table for everything, and the centre piece stands exceedingly well under the glass, and holds a great deal most commodiously, without looking awkwardly. They are both covered with green baize, and send their best love. The Pembroke has got its destination by the sideboard, and my mother has great delight in keeping her money and papers locked up. The little table which used to stand there has most conveniently taken itself off into the best bedroom; and we are now in want only of the chiffonniere, which is neither finished nor come. So much for that subject; I now come to another, of a very different nature, as other subjects are very apt to be. Earle Harwood has been again giving uneasiness to his family and talk to the neighbourhood; in the present instance, however, he is only unfortunate, and not in fault.

About ten days ago, in cocking a pistol in the guard-room at Marcau, he accidentally shot himself through the thigh. Two young Scotch surgeons in the island were polite enough to propose taking off the thigh at once, but to that he would not consent; and accordingly in his wounded state was put on board a cutter and conveyed to Haslar Hospital, at Gosport, where the bullet was extracted, and where he now is, I hope, in a fair way of doing well. The surgeon of the hospital wrote to the family on the occasion, and John Harwood went down to him immediately, attended by James,[*] whose object in going was to be the means of bringing back the earliest intelligence to Mr and Mrs Harwood, whose anxious sufferings, particularly those of the latter, have of course been dreadful. They went down on Tuesday, and James came back the next day, bringing such favourable accounts as greatly to lessen the distress of the family at Deane, though it will probably be a long while before Mrs Harwood can be quite at ease. *One* most material comfort, however, they have; the assurance of its being really an accidental wound, which is not only positively declared by Earle himself, but is likewise testified by the particular direction of the bullet. Such a wound could not have been received in a duel. At present he is going on very well, but the surgeon will not declare him to be in no danger.[†] Mr Heathcote met with a genteel little accident the other day in hunting. He got off to lead his horse over a hedge, or a house, or something, and his horse in his haste trod upon his leg, or rather ancle, I believe, and it is not certain whether the small bone is not broke. Martha has accepted Mary's invitation for Lord Portsmouth's ball. He has not yet sent out his own invitations, but *that* does not signify; Martha comes, and a ball there is to be. I think it will be too early in her mother's absence for me to return with her.

Sunday Evening – We have had a dreadful storm of wind in the fore part of this day, which has done a great deal of mischief among our trees. I was sitting alone in the dining-room when an odd kind of crash startled me – in a moment afterwards it was repeated. I then went to the window, which I reached just in time to see the last of our two highly valued elms descend into the Sweep ! ! ! ! The other, which had fallen, I suppose, in the first crash, and which was the nearest to the pond, taking a more easterly direction, sunk among our screen of chestnuts and firs, knocking down one spruce-fir, beating off the head of another, and stripping the two corner chestnuts of several branches in its fall. This is not all. One large

---

* James, the writer's eldest brother.
† The limb was saved.

elm out of the two on the left-hand side as you enter what I call the elm walk, was likewise blown down; the maple bearing the weathercock was broke in two, and what I regret more than all the rest is, that all the three elms which grew in Hall's meadow, and gave such ornament to it, are gone; two were blown down, and the other so much injured that it cannot stand. I am happy to add, however, that no greater evil than the loss of trees has been the consequence of the storm in this place, or in our immediate neighbourhood. We grieve, therefore, in some comfort.

I am yours ever,

J. A.

The next letter, written four days later than the former, was addressed to Miss Lloyd, an intimate friend, whose sister (my mother) was married to Jane's eldest brother:

Steventon, Wednesday evening, Nov. 12th.

MY DEAR MARTHA – I did not receive your note yesterday till after Charlotte had left Deane, or I would have sent my answer by her, instead of being the means, as I now must be, of lessening the elegance of your new dress for the Hurstbourne ball by the value of 3*d*. You are very good in wishing to see me at Ibthorp so soon, and I am equally good in wishing to come to you. I believe our merit in that respect is much upon a par, our self-denial mutually strong. Having paid this tribute of praise to the virtue of both, I shall here have done with panegyric, and proceed to plain matter of fact. In about a fortnight's time I hope to be with you. I have two reasons for not being able to come before. I wish so to arrange my visit as to spend some days with you after your mother's return. In the 1st place, that I may have the pleasure of seeing her, and in the 2nd, that I may have a better chance of bringing you back with me. Your promise in my favour was not quite absolute, but if your will is not perverse, you and I will do all in our power to overcome your scruples of conscience. I hope we shall meet next week to talk all this over, till we have tired ourselves with the very idea of my visit before my visit begins. Our invitations for the 19th are arrived, and very curiously are they worded.* Mary mentioned to

* The invitation, the ball dress, and some other things in this and the preceding letter refer to a ball annually given at Hurstbourne Park, on

you yesterday poor Earle's unfortunate accident, I dare say. He does not seem to be going on very well. The two or three last posts have brought less and less favourable accounts of him. John Harwood has gone to Gosport again to-day. We have two families of friends now who are in a most anxious state; for though by a note from Catherine this morning there seems now to be a revival of hope at Manydown, its continuance may be too reasonably doubted. Mr Heathcote,* however, who has broken the small bone of his leg, is so good as to be going on very well. It would be really too much to have three people to care for.

You distress me cruelly by your request about books. I cannot think of any to bring with me, nor have I any idea of our wanting them. I come to you to be talked to, not to read or hear reading; I can do that at home; and indeed I am now laying in a stock of intelligence to pour out on you as my share of the conversation. I am reading Henry's *History of England*, which I will repeat to you in any manner you may prefer, either in a loose, desultory, unconnected stream, or dividing my recital, as the historian divides it himself, into seven parts: – The Civil and Military: Religion: Constitution: Learning and Learned Men: Arts and Sciences: Commerce, Coins, and Shipping: and Manners. So that for every evening in the week there will be a different subject. The Friday's lot – Commerce, Coins, and Shipping – you will find the least entertaining; but the next evening's portion will make amends. With such a provision on my part, if you will do yours by repeating the French Grammar, and Mrs Stent† will now and then ejaculate some wonder about the cocks and hens, what can we want? Farewell for a short time. We all unite in best love, and I am your very affectionate

                                                            J. A.

_____

the anniversary of the Earl of Portsmouth's marriage with his first wife. He was the Lord Portsmouth whose eccentricities afterwards became notorious, and the invitations, as well as other arrangements about these balls, were of a peculiar character.

* The father of Sir William Heathcote, of Hursley, who was married to a daughter of Mr Bigg Wither, of Manydown, and lived in the neighbourhood.

† A very dull old lady, then residing with Mrs Lloyd.

The two next letters must have been written early in 1801, after the removal from Steventon had been decided on, but before it had taken place. They refer to the two brothers who were at sea, and give some idea of a kind of anxieties and uncertainties to which sisters are seldom subject in these days of peace, steamers, and electric telegraphs. At that time ships were often windbound or becalmed, or driven wide of their destination; and sometimes they had orders to alter their course for some secret service; not to mention the chance of conflict with a vessel of superior power – no improbable occurrence before the battle of Trafalgar. Information about relatives on board men-of-war was scarce and scanty, and often picked up by hearsay or chance means; and every scrap of intelligence was proportionably valuable:

My Dear Cassandra – I should not have thought it necessary to write to you so soon, but for the arrival of a letter from Charles to myself. It was written last Saturday from off the Start, and conveyed to Popham Lane by Captain Boyle, on his way to Midgham. He came from Lisbon in the *Endymion*. I will copy Charles's account of his conjectures about Frank: 'He has not seen my brother lately, nor does he expect to find him arrived, as he met Captain Inglis at Rhodes, going up to take command of the *Petrel*, as he was coming down; but supposes he will arrive in less than a fortnight from this time, in some ship which is expected to reach England about that time with dispatches from Sir Ralph Abercrombie.' The event must show what sort of a conjuror Captain Boyle is. The *Endymion* has not been plagued with any more prizes. Charles spent three pleasant days in Lisbon.

They were very well satisfied with their royal passenger,[*] whom they found jolly and affable, who talks of Lady Augusta as his wife, and seems much attached to her.

When this letter was written, the *Endymion* was becalmed, but Charles hoped to reach Portsmouth by Monday or Tuesday. He received my letter, communicating our plans, before he left England; was much surprised, of course, but is quite reconciled to them, and means to come to Steventon once more while Steventon is ours.

---

[*] The Duke of Sussex, son of George III, married, without royal consent, to the Lady Augusta Murray.

From a letter written later in the same year:

Charles has received £30 for his share of the privateer, and expects £10 more; but of what avail is it to take prizes if he lays out the produce in presents to his sisters? He has been buying gold chains and topaze crosses for us. He must be well scolded. The *Endymion* has already received orders for taking troops to Egypt, which I should not like at all if I did not trust to Charles being removed from her somehow or other before she sails. He knows nothing of his own destination, he says, but desires me to write directly, as the *Endymion* will probably sail in three or four days. He will receive my yesterday's letter, and I shall write again by this post to thank and reproach him. We shall be unbearably fine.

4

The family removed to Bath in the spring of 1801, where they
resided first at No. 4 Sydney Terrace, and afterwards in Green Park
Buildings. I do not know whether they were at all attracted to Bath
by the circumstance that Mrs Austen's only brother, Mr Leigh
Perrot, spent part of every year there. The name of Perrot, together
with a small estate at Northleigh in Oxfordshire, had been
bequeathed to him by a great uncle. I must devote a few sentences to
this very old and now extinct branch of the Perrot family; for one of
the last survivors, Jane Perrot, married to a Walker, was Jane
Austen's great grandmother, from whom she derived her Christian
name. The Perrots were settled in Pembrokeshire at least as early as
the thirteenth century. They were probably some of the settlers
whom the policy of our Plantagenet kings placed in that county,
which thence acquired the name of 'England beyond Wales', for the
double purpose of keeping open a communication with Ireland from
Milford Haven, and of overawing the Welsh. One of the family
seems to have carried out this latter purpose very vigorously; for it is
recorded of him that he slew *twenty-six men* of Kemaes, a district of
Wales, and *one wolf*. The manner in which the two kinds of game are
classed together, and the disproportion of numbers, are remarkable;
but probably at that time the wolves had been so closely killed down,
that *lupicide* was become a more rare and distinguished exploit than
homicide. The last of this family died about 1778, and their property
was divided between Leighs and Musgraves, the larger portion
going to the latter. Mr Leigh Perrot pulled down the mansion, and
sold the estate to the Duke of Marlborough, and the name of these
Perrots is now to be found only on some monuments in the church
of Northleigh.

Mr Leigh Perrot was also one of several cousins to whom a life
interest in the Stoneleigh property in Warwickshire was left, after

the extinction of the earlier Leigh peerage, but he compromised his claim to the succession in his lifetime. He married a niece of Sir Montague Cholmeley of Lincolnshire. He was a man of considerable natural power, with much of the wit of his uncle, the Master of Balliol, and wrote clever epigrams and riddles, some of which, though without his name, found their way into print; but he lived a very retired life, dividing his time between Bath and his place in Berkshire called Scarlets. Jane's letters from Bath make frequent mention of this uncle and aunt.

The unfinished story, now published under the title of 'The Watsons', must have been written during the author's residence in Bath. In the autumn of 1804 she spent some weeks at Lyme, and became acquainted with the Cobb, which she afterwards made memorable for the fall of Louisa Musgrove. In February 1805, her father died at Bath, and was buried at Walcot Church. The widow and daughters went into lodgings for a few months, and then removed to Southampton. The only records that I can find about her during those four years are the three following letters to her sister; one from Lyme, the others from Bath. They show that she went a good deal into society, in a quiet way, chiefly with ladies; and that her eyes were always open to minute traits of character in those with whom she associated:

Extract from a letter from Jane Austen to her Sister

Lyme, Friday, Sept. 14 (1804).

MY DEAR CASSANDRA – I take the first sheet of fine striped paper to thank you for your letter from Weymouth, and express my hopes of your being at Ibthorp before this time. I expect to hear that you reached it yesterday evening, being able to get as far as Blandford on Wednesday. Your account of Weymouth contains nothing which strikes me so forcibly as there being no ice in the town. For every other vexation I was in some measure prepared, and particularly for your disappointment in not seeing the Royal Family go on board on Tuesday, having already heard from Mr Crawford that he had seen you in the very act of being too late. But for there being no ice, what could prepare me! You found my letter at Andover, I hope, yesterday, and have now for many hours been satisfied that your kind anxiety on my behalf was as much thrown away as kind anxiety usually is. I continue quite well; in proof of which I have bathed again this morning. It was absolutely necessary that I should have the little fever and indisposition which I had: it has been all the fashion this week in Lyme. We are quite settled in our lodgings by this time, as you may suppose, and everything goes on in the usual order. The servants behave very well, and make no difficulties, though nothing certainly can exceed the inconvenience of the offices, except the general dirtiness of the house and furniture, and all its inhabitants. I endeavour, as far as I can, to supply your place, and be useful, and keep things in order. I detect dirt in the water decanters, as fast as I can, and keep everything as it was under your administration . . . The ball last night was pleasant, but not full for Thursday. My father staid contentedly till half-past nine (we went a little after eight), and then walked home with James and a lanthorn, though I believe the lanthorn was not lit, as the moon was up; but sometimes this lanthorn may be a great convenience to him. My mother and I staid about an hour later. Nobody asked me the two first dances; the two next I danced with Mr Crawford, and had I chosen to stay longer might have danced with Mr Granville, Mrs Granville's son, whom my dear friend Miss A. introduced to me, or with a new odd-looking man who had been eyeing me for some time, and at last, without any introduction, asked me if I meant to dance again. I think he must be Irish by his ease, and because I imagine him to belong to the honbl B.'s, who are son, and son's wife of an Irish viscount, bold queer-looking people, just fit to be quality at Lyme. I called yesterday morning (ought it not in strict propriety to be termed yester-morning?) on Miss A. and was introduced to her father and mother. Like other young ladies she is considerably genteeler than her parents. Mrs A. sat darning a pair of stockings the whole of my visit. But do not mention this at home, lest a warning should act as an example. We afterwards walked together for an hour on the Cobb; she is very converseable in a common way; I do not perceive wit or genius, but she has sense and some degree of taste, and her manners are very engaging. She seems to like people rather too easily.

Yours affectly,

J. A.

Letter from Jane Austen to her sister Cassandra at Ibthorp, alluding to the sudden death of Mrs Lloyd at that place:

25 Gay Street (Bath), Monday, April 8, 1805.

MY DEAR CASSANDRA – Here is a day for you. Did Bath or Ibthorp ever see such an 8th of April? It is March and April together; the glare of the one and the warmth of the other. We do nothing but walk about. As far as your means will admit, I hope you profit by such weather too. I dare say you are already the better for change of place. We were out again last night. Miss Irvine invited us, when I met her in the Crescent, to drink tea with them, but I rather declined it, having no idea that my mother would be disposed for another evening visit there so soon; but when I gave her the message, I found her very well inclined to go; and accordingly, on leaving Chapel, we walked to Lansdown. This morning we have been to see Miss Chamberlaine look hot on horseback. Seven years and four months ago we went to the same riding-house to see Miss Lefroy's performance![*] What a different set are we now moving in! But seven years, I suppose, are enough to change every pore of one's skin and every feeling of one's mind. We did not walk long in the Crescent yesterday. It was hot and not crowded enough; so we went into the field, and passed close by S. T. and Miss S.[†] again. I have not yet seen her face, but neither her dress nor air have anything of the dash or stylishness which the Browns talked of; quite the contrary; indeed, her dress is not even smart, and her appearance very quiet. Miss Irvine says she is never speaking a word. Poor wretch; I am afraid she is en *pénitence*. Here has been that excellent Mrs Coulthart calling, while my mother was out, and I was believed to be so. I always respected her, as a good-hearted friendly woman. And the Browns have been here; I find their affidavits on the table. The *Ambuscade* reached Gibraltar on the 9th of March, and found all well; so say the papers. We have had no letters from anybody, but we expect to hear from Edward tomorrow, and from you soon afterwards. How happy they are at Godmersham now! I shall be very glad of a letter from Ibthorp, that I may know how you all are, but particularly yourself. This is nice weather for Mrs J. Austen's going to Speen, and I hope she will have a pleasant visit there. I expect a prodigious account of the

---

[*] Here is evidence that Jane Austen was acquainted with Bath before it became her residence in 1801. See p. 34.

[†] A gentleman and lady lately engaged to be married.

christening dinner; perhaps it brought you at last into the company of Miss Dundas again.

Tuesday – I received your letter last night, and wish it may be soon followed by another to say that all is over; but I cannot help thinking that nature will struggle again, and produce a revival. Poor woman! May her end be peaceful and easy as the exit we have witnessed! And I dare say it will. If there is no revival, suffering must be all over; even the consciousness of existence, I suppose, was gone when you wrote. The nonsense I have been writing in this and in my last letter seems out of place at such a time, but I will not mind it; it will do you no harm, and nobody else will be attacked by it. I am heartily glad that you can speak so comfortably of your own health and looks, though I can scarcely comprehend the latter being really approved. Could travelling fifty miles produce such an immediate change? You were looking very poorly here, and everybody seemed sensible of it. Is there a charm in a hack postchaise? But if there were, Mrs Craven's carriage might have undone it all. I am much obliged to you for the time and trouble you have bestowed on Mary's cap, and am glad it pleases her; but it will prove a useless gift at present, I suppose. Will not she leave Ibthorp on her mother's death? As a companion you are all that Martha can be supposed to want, and in that light, under these circumstances, your visit will indeed have been well timed.

Thursday – I was not able to go on yesterday; all my wit and leisure were bestowed on letters to Charles and Henry. To the former I wrote in consequence of my mother's having seen in the papers that the *Urania* was waiting at Portsmouth for the convoy for Halifax. This is nice, as it is only three weeks ago that you wrote by the *Camilla*. I wrote to Henry because I had a letter from him in which he desired to hear from me very soon. His to me was most affectionate and kind, as well as entertaining; there is no merit to him in *that*; he cannot help being amusing. He offers to meet us on the sea coast, if the plan of which Edward gave him some hint takes place. Will not this be making the execution of such a plan more desirable and delightful than ever? He talks of the rambles we took together last summer with pleasing affection.

Yours ever,

J. A.

From the same to the same.

> *Gay St, Sunday evening, April 21 (1805).*

MY DEAR CASSANDRA – I am much obliged to you for writing to me again so soon; your letter yesterday was quite an unexpected pleasure. Poor Mrs Stent! it has been her lot to be always in the way; but we must be merciful, for perhaps in time we may come to be Mrs Stents ourselves, unequal to anything, and unwelcome to everybody . . . My morning engagement was with the Cookes, and our party consisted of George and Mary, a Mr L., Miss B., who had been with us at the concert, and the youngest Miss W. Not Julia; we have done with her; she is very ill; but Mary. Mary W.'s turn is actually come to be grown up, and have a fine complexion, and wear great square muslin shawls. I have not expressly enumerated myself among the party, but there I was, and my cousin George was very kind, and talked sense to me every now and then, in the intervals of his more animated fooleries with Miss B., who is very young, and rather handsome, and whose gracious manners, ready wit, and solid remarks, put me somewhat in mind of my old acquaintance L. L. There was a monstrous deal of stupid quizzing and common-place nonsense talked, but scarcely any wit; all that bordered on it or on sense came from my cousin George, whom altogether I like very well. Mr B. seems nothing more than a tall young man. My evening engagement and walk was with Miss A., who had called on me the day before, and gently upbraided me in her turn with a change of manners to her since she had been in Bath, or at least of late. Unlucky me! that my notice should be of such consequence, and my manners so bad! She was so well disposed, and so reasonable, that I soon forgave her, and made this engagement with her in proof of it. She is really an agreeable girl, so I think I may like her; and her great want of a companion at home, which may well make any tolerable acquaintance important to her, gives her another claim on my attention. I shall endeavour as much as possible to keep my intimacies in their proper place, and prevent their clashing. Among so many friends, it will be well if I do not get into a scrape; and now here is Miss Blashford come. I should have gone distracted if the Bullers had staid . . . When I tell you I have been visiting a countess this morning, you will immediately, with great justice, but no truth, guess it to be Lady Roden. No: it is Lady Leven, the mother of Lord Balgonie. On receiving a message from Lord and Lady Leven through the Mackays, declaring their intention of waiting on us, we thought it right to go to them. I hope we have not done too much, but the friends and admirers of Charles must be attended to. They seem very reasonable, good sort of people, very civil, and full of his praise.* We were shewn at first into an empty drawing-room, and presently in came his lordship, not knowing who we were, to apologise for the servant's mistake, and to say himself what was untrue, that Lady Leven was not within. He is a tall gentlemanlike looking man, with spectacles, and rather deaf. After sitting with him ten minutes we walked away; but Lady Leven coming out of the dining parlour as we passed the door, we were obliged to attend her back to it, and pay our visit over again. She is a stout woman, with a very handsome face. By this means we had the pleasure of hearing Charles's praises twice over. They think themselves excessively obliged to him, and estimate him so highly as to wish Lord Balgonie, when he is quite recovered, to go out to him. There is a pretty little Lady Marianne of the party, to be shaken hands with, and asked if she remembered Mr Austen . . .

I shall write to Charles by the next packet, unless you tell me in the meantime of your intending to do it.

Believe me, if you chuse,

Yr affte Sister.

Jane did not estimate too highly the 'Cousin George' mentioned in the foregoing letter; who might easily have been superior in sense and wit to the rest of the party. He was the Revd George Leigh Cooke, long known and respected at Oxford, where he held important offices, and had the privilege of helping to form the minds of men more eminent than himself. As Tutor in Corpus Christi College, he became instructor to some of the most distinguished undergraduates of that time: amongst others to Dr Arnold, the Revd John Keble, and Sir John Coleridge. The latter

* It seems that Charles Austen, then first lieutenant of the *Endymion*, had had an opportunity of showing attention and kindness to some of Lord Leven's family.

has mentioned him in terms of affectionate regard, both in his Memoir of Keble, and in a letter which appears in Dean Stanley's *Life of Arnold*. Mr Cooke was also an impressive preacher of earnest awakening sermons. I remember to have heard it observed by some of my undergraduate friends that, after all, there was more good to be got from George Cooke's plain sermons than from much of the more laboured oratory of the University pulpit. He was frequently Examiner in the schools, and occupied the chair of the Sedleian Professor of Natural Philosophy, from 1810 to 1853.

Before the end of 1805, the little family party removed to Southampton. They resided in a commodious old-fashioned house in a corner of Castle Square.

I have no letters of my aunt, nor any other record of her, during her four years' residence at Southampton; and though I now began to know, and, what was the same thing, to love her myself, yet my observations were only those of a young boy, and were not capable of penetrating her character, or estimating her powers. I have, however, a lively recollection of some local circumstances at Southampton, and as they refer chiefly to things which have been long ago swept away, I will record them. My grandmother's house had a pleasant garden, bounded on one side by the old city walls; the top of this wall was sufficiently wide to afford a pleasant walk, with an extensive view, easily accessible to ladies by steps. This must have been a part of the identical walls which witnessed the embarkation of Henry V before the battle of Agincourt, and the detection of the conspiracy of Cambridge, Scroop, and Grey, which Shakespeare has made so picturesque; when, according to the chorus in *Henry V*, the citizens saw

> The well-appointed King at Hampton Pier
> Embark his royalty.

Among the records of the town of Southampton, they have a minute and authentic account, drawn up at that time, of the encampment of Henry V near the town, before his embarkment for France. It is remarkable that the place where the army was encamped, then a low level plain, is now entirely covered by the sea, and is called Westport.* At that time Castle Square was occupied by

* See Wharton's note to Johnson and Steevens' Shakespeare.

a fantastic edifice, too large for the space in which it stood, though too small to accord well with its castellated style, erected by the second Marquis of Lansdowne, half-brother to the well-known statesman, who succeeded him in the title. The Marchioness had a light phaeton, drawn by six, and sometimes by eight little ponies, each pair decreasing in size, and becoming lighter in colour, through all the grades of dark brown, light brown, bay, and chestnut, as it was placed farther away from the carriage. The two leading pairs were managed by two boyish postilions, the two pairs nearest to the carriage were driven in hand. It was a delight to me to look down from the window and see this fairy equipage put together; for the premises of this castle were so contracted that the whole process went on in the little space that remained of the open square. Like other fairy works, however, it all proved evanescent. Not only carriage and ponies, but castle itself, soon vanished away, 'like the baseless fabric of a vision'. On the death of the Marquis in 1809, the castle was pulled down. Few probably remember its existence; and anyone who might visit the place now would wonder how it ever could have stood there.

In 1809 Mr Knight was able to offer his mother the choice of two houses on his property; one near his usual residence at Godmersham Park in Kent; the other near Chawton House, his occasional residence in Hampshire. The latter was chosen; and in that year the mother and daughters, together with Miss Lloyd, a near connection who lived with them, settled themselves at Chawton Cottage.

Chawton may be called the *second*, as well as the *last* home of Jane Austen; for during the temporary residences of the party at Bath and Southampton she was only a sojourner in a strange land; but here she found a real home amongst her own people. It so happened that during her residence at Chawton circumstances brought several of her brothers and their families within easy distance of the house. Chawton must also be considered the place most closely connected with her career as a writer; for there it was that, in the maturity of her mind, she either wrote or rearranged, and prepared for publication the books by which she has become known to the world. This was the home where, after a few years, while still in the prime of life, she began to droop and wither away, and which she left only in the last stage of her illness, yielding to the persuasion of friends hoping against hope.

This house stood in the village of Chawton, about a mile from Alton, on the right hand side, just where the road to Winchester branches off from that to Gosport. It was so close to the road that the front door opened upon it; while a very narrow enclosure, paled in on each side, protected the building from danger of collision with any runaway vehicle. I believe it had been originally built for an inn, for which purpose it was certainly well situated. Afterwards it had been occupied by Mr Knight's steward; but by some additions to the house, and some judicious planting and skreening, it was made a pleasant and commodious abode. Mr Knight was experienced and adroit at such arrangements, and this was a labour of love to him. A good-sized entrance and two sitting-rooms made the length of the house, all intended originally to look upon the road, but the large drawing-room window was blocked up and turned into a book-case, and another opened at the side which gave to view only turf and trees, as a high wooden fence and hornbeam hedge shut out the Winchester road, which skirted the whole length of the little domain. Trees were planted each side to form a shrubbery walk, carried round the enclosure, which gave a sufficient space for ladies' exercise. There was a pleasant irregular mixture of hedgerow, and gravel walk, and orchard, and long grass for mowing, arising from two or three little enclosures having been thrown together. The house itself was quite as good as the generality of parsonage-houses then were, and much in the same style; and was capable of receiving other members of the family as frequent visitors. It was sufficiently well furnished; everything inside and out was kept in good repair, and it was altogether a comfortable and ladylike establishment, though the means which supported it were not large.

I give this description because some interest is generally taken in the residence of a popular writer. Cowper's unattractive house in the street of Olney has been pointed out to visitors, and has even attained the honour of an engraving in Southey's edition of his works: but I cannot recommend any admirer of Jane Austen to undertake a pilgrimage to this spot. The building indeed still stands, but it has lost all that gave it its character. After the death of Mrs Cassandra Austen, in 1845, it was divided into tenements for labourers, and the grounds reverted to ordinary uses.

Chawton Church

5

Description of Jane Austen's person, character, and tastes

As my memoir has now reached the period when I saw a great deal
of my aunt, and was old enough to understand something of her
value, I will here attempt a description of her person, mind, and
habits. In person she was very attractive; her figure was rather tall
and slender, her step light and firm, and her whole appearance
expressive of health and animation. In complexion she was a clear
brunette with a rich colour; she had full round cheeks, with mouth
and nose small and well formed, bright hazel eyes, and brown hair
forming natural curls close round her face. If not so regularly
handsome as her sister, yet her countenance had a peculiar charm of
its own to the eyes of most beholders. At the time of which I am now
writing, she never was seen, either morning or evening, without a
cap; I believe that she and her sister were generally thought to have
taken to the garb of middle age earlier than their years or their
looks required; and that, though remarkably neat in their dress as

in all their ways, they were scarcely sufficiently regardful of the fashionable, or the becoming.

She was not highly accomplished according to the present standard. Her sister drew well, and it is from a drawing of hers that the likeness prefixed to this volume has been taken. Jane herself was fond of music, and had a sweet voice, both in singing and in conversation; in her youth she had received some instruction on the pianoforte; and at Chawton she practised daily, chiefly before breakfast. I believe she did so partly that she might not disturb the rest of the party who were less fond of music. In the evening she would sometimes sing, to her own accompaniment, some simple old songs, the words and airs of which, now never heard, still linger in my memory.

She read French with facility, and knew something of Italian. In those days German was no more thought of than Hindostanee, as part of a lady's education. In history she followed the old guides – Goldsmith, Hume, and Robertson. Critical enquiry into the usually received statements of the old historians was scarcely begun. The history of the early kings of Rome had not yet been dissolved into legend. Historic characters lay before the reader's eyes in broad light or shade, not much broken up by details. The virtues of King Henry VIII were yet undiscovered, nor had much light been thrown on the inconsistencies of Queen Elizabeth; the one was held to be an unmitigated tyrant, and an embodied Blue Beard; the other a perfect model of wisdom and policy. Jane, when a girl, had strong political opinions, especially about the affairs of the sixteenth and seventeenth centuries. She was a vehement defender of Charles I and his grandmother Mary; but I think it was rather from an impulse of feeling than from any enquiry into the evidence by which they must be condemned or acquitted. As she grew up, the politics of the day occupied very little of her attention, but she probably shared the feeling of moderate Toryism which prevailed in her family. She was well acquainted with the old periodicals from the *Spectator* downwards. Her knowledge of Richardson's works was such as no one is likely again to acquire, now that the multitude and the merits of our light literature have called off the attention of readers from that great master. Every circumstance narrated in *Sir Charles Grandison*, all that was ever said or done in the cedar parlour, was familiar to her; and the wedding days of Lady L. and Lady G. were as well remembered as if they had been living friends. Amongst her favourite writers, Johnson in prose, Crabbe in verse, and Cowper in both, stood high. It is well that the native good taste of herself and of those with whom she lived, saved her from the snare into which a sister novelist had fallen, of imitating the grandiloquent style of Johnson. She thoroughly enjoyed Crabbe; perhaps on account of a certain resemblance to herself in minute and highly finished detail; and would sometimes say, in jest, that, if she ever married at all, she could fancy being Mrs Crabbe; looking on the author quite as an abstract idea, and ignorant and regardless what manner of man he might be. Scott's poetry gave her great pleasure; she did not live to make much acquaintance with his novels. Only three of them were published before her death; but it will be seen by the following extract from one of her letters, that she was quite prepared to admit the merits of *Waverley*; and it is remarkable that, living, as she did, far apart from the gossip of the literary world, she should even then have spoken so confidently of his being the author of it:

Walter Scott has no business to write novels; especially good ones. It is not fair. He has fame and profit enough as a poet, and ought not to be taking the bread out of other people's mouths. I do not mean to like *Waverley*, if I can help it, but I fear I must. I am quite determined, however, not to be pleased with Mrs —'s, should I ever meet with it, which I hope I may not. I think I can be stout against anything written by her. I have made up my mind to like no novels really, but Miss Edgeworth's, E.'s, and my own.

It was not, however, what she *knew*, but what she *was*, that distinguished her from others. I cannot better describe the fascination which she exercised over children than by quoting the words of two of her nieces. One says:

As a very little girl I was always creeping up to aunt Jane, and following her whenever I could, in the house and out of it. I might not have remembered this but for the recollection of my mother's telling me privately, that I must not be troublesome to my aunt. Her first charm to children was great sweetness of manner. She seemed to love you, and you loved her in return. This, as well as I can now recollect, was what I felt in my early days, before I was old enough to be amused by her cleverness. But soon came the delight of her playful talk. She could make everything amusing to a child. Then, as I got older, when cousins came to share the entertainment, she would tell us the most delightful stories, chiefly of Fairyland, and her fairies had all characters of their own. The tale was invented, I am sure, at the moment, and was continued for two or three days, if occasion served.

Again:

When staying at Chawton, with two of her other nieces, we often had amusements in which my aunt was very helpful. She was the one to whom we always looked for help. She would furnish us with what we wanted from her wardrobe; and she would be the entertaining visitor in our make-believe house. She amused us in various ways. Once, I remember, in giving a conversation as between myself and my two cousins, supposing we were all grown up, the day after a ball.

Very similar is the testimony of another niece:

Aunt Jane was the general favourite with children; her ways with them being so playful, and her long circumstantial stories so delightful. These were continued from time to time, and were begged for on all possible and impossible occasions; woven, as she proceeded, out of nothing but her own happy talent for invention. Ah! if but one of them could be recovered! And again, as I grew older, when the original seventeen years between our ages seemed to shrink to seven, or to nothing, it comes back to me now how strangely I missed her. It had become so much a habit with me to put by things in my mind with a reference to her, and to say to myself, I shall keep this for aunt Jane.

A nephew of hers used to observe that his visits to Chawton, after the death of his aunt Jane, were always a disappointment to him. From old associations he could not help expecting to be particularly happy in that house; and never till he got there could he realise to himself how all its peculiar charm was gone. It was not only that the chief light in the house was quenched, but that the loss of it had cast a shade over the spirits of the survivors. Enough has been said to show her love for children, and her wonderful power of entertaining them; but her friends of all ages felt her enlivening influence. Her unusually quick sense of the ridiculous led her to play with all the commonplaces of everyday life, whether as regarded persons or things; but she never played with its serious duties or responsibilities, nor did she ever turn individuals into ridicule. With all her neighbours in the village she was on friendly, though not on intimate, terms. She took a kindly interest in all their proceedings, and liked to hear about them. They often served for her amusement; but it was her own nonsense that gave zest to the gossip. She was as far as possible from being censorious or satirical. She never abused them or *quizzed* them – *that* was the word of the day; an ugly word, now obsolete; and the ugly practice which it expressed is much less prevalent now than it was then. The laugh which she occasionally raised was by imagining for her neighbours, as she was equally ready to imagine for her friends or herself, impossible contingencies, or by relating in prose or verse some trifling anecdote coloured to her own fancy, or in writing a fictitious history of what they were supposed to have said or done, which could deceive nobody.

The following specimens may be given of the liveliness of mind which imparted an agreeable flavour both to her correspondence and her conversation:

On reading in the newspapers the marriage of
Mr Gell to Miss Gill, of Eastbourne

> At Eastbourne Mr Gell,
> From being perfectly well,
> Became dreadfully ill,
> For love of Miss Gill.
> So he said, with some sighs,
> I'm the slave of your *iis*;
> Oh, restore, if you please,
> By accepting my *ees*.

On the marriage of a middle-aged flirt with a Mr Wake, whom, it
was supposed, she would scarcely have accepted in her youth

> Maria, good-humoured, and handsome, and tall,
>   For a husband was at her last stake;
> And having in vain danced at many a ball,
>   Is now happy to *jump at a Wake*.

We were all at the play last night to see Miss O'Neil in Isabella. I do not think she was quite equal to my expectation. I fancy I want something more than can be. Acting seldom satisfies me. I took two pockethandkerchiefs, but had very little occasion for either. She is an elegant creature, however, and hugs Mr Young delightfully.

So, Miss B. is actually married, but I have never seen it in the papers; and one may as well be single if the wedding is not to be in print.

Once, too, she took it into her head to write the following mock panegyric on a young friend, who really was clever and handsome:

1

In measured verse I'll now rehearse
The charms of lovely Anna:
And, first, her mind is unconfined
Like any vast savannah.

2

Ontario's lake may fitly speak
Her fancy's ample bound:
Its circuit may, on strict survey
Five hundred miles be found.

3

Her wit descends on foes and friends
Like famed Niagara's Fall;
And travellers gaze in wild amaze,
And listen, one and all.

4

Her judgment sound, thick, black, profound,
Like transatlantic groves,
Dispenses aid, and friendly shade
To all that in it roves.

5

If thus her mind to be defined
America exhausts,
And all that's grand in that great land
In similes it costs –

6

Oh how can I her person try
    To image and portray?
How paint the face, the form how trace
    In which those virtues lay?

7

Another world must be unfurled,
    Another language known,
Ere tongue or sound can publish round
    Her charms of flesh and bone.

I believe that all this nonsense was nearly extempore, and that the fancy of drawing the images from America arose at the moment from the obvious rhyme which presented itself in the first stanza.

The following extracts are from letters addressed to a niece who was at that time amusing herself by attempting a novel, probably never finished, certainly never published, and of which I know nothing but what these extracts tell. They show the good-natured sympathy and encouragement which the aunt, then herself occupied in writing *Emma*, could give to the less matured powers of the niece. They bring out incidentally some of her opinions concerning compositions of that kind:

Extracts

Chawton, Aug. 10, 1814.

Your aunt C. does not like desultory novels, and is rather fearful that yours will be too much so; that there will be too frequent a change from one set of people to another, and that circumstances will be sometimes introduced, of apparent consequence, which will lead to nothing. It will not be so great an objection to me. I allow much more latitude than she does, and think nature and spirit cover many sins of a wandering story. And people in general do not care much about it, for your comfort . . .

Sept. 9.

You are now collecting your people delightfully, getting them exactly into such a spot as is the delight of my life. Three or four families in a country village is the very thing to work on; and I hope you will write a great deal more, and make full use of them while they are so very favourably arranged.

Sept. 28.

Devereux Forrester being ruined by his vanity is very good: but I wish you would not let him plunge into a 'vortex of dissipation'. I do not object to the thing, but I cannot bear the expression: it is such thorough novel slang; and so old that I dare say Adam met with it in the first novel that he opened.

Hans Place (Nov. 1814).

I have been very far from finding your book an evil, I assure you. I read it immediately, and with great pleasure. Indeed, I do think you get on very fast. I wish other people of my acquaintance could compose as rapidly. Julian's history was quite a surprise to me. You had not very long known it yourself, I suspect; but I have no objection to make to the circumstance; it is very well told, and his having been in love with the aunt gives Cecilia an additional interest with him. I like the idea; a very proper compliment to an aunt! I rather imagine, indeed, that nieces are seldom chosen but in compliment to some aunt or other. I dare say your husband was in love with me once, and would never have thought of you if he had not supposed me dead of a scarlet fever.

Jane Austen was successful in everything that she attempted with her fingers. None of us could throw spilikins in so perfect a circle, or take them off with so steady a hand. Her performances with cup and ball were marvellous. The one used at Chawton was an easy one, and she has been known to catch it on the point above an hundred times in succession, till her hand was weary. She sometimes found a resource in that simple game, when unable, from weakness in her eyes, to read or write long together. A specimen of her clear strong handwriting is here given. Happy would the compositors for the press be if they had always so legible a manuscript to work from. But the writing was not the only part of her letters which showed superior handiwork. In those days there was an art in folding and sealing. No adhesive envelopes made all easy. Some people's letters always looked loose and untidy; but her paper was sure to take the right folds, and her sealing-wax to drop into the right place. Her needlework both plain and ornamental was excellent, and might almost have put a sewing machine to shame. She was considered especially great in satin stitch. She spent much time in these occupations, and some of her merriest talk was over clothes which she and her companions were making, sometimes for themselves, and sometimes for the poor. There still remains a curious specimen of her needlework made for a sister-in-law, my mother. In a very small bag is deposited a little rolled up housewife, furnished with minikin needles and fine thread. In the housewife is a tiny pocket, and in the pocket is enclosed a slip of paper, on which, written as with a crow quill, are these lines:

> This little bag, I hope, will prove
>   To be not vainly made;
> For should you thread and needles want,
>   It will afford you aid.
>
> And, as we are about to part,
>   'Twill serve another end:
> For, when you look upon this bag,
>   You'll recollect your friend.

It is the kind of article that some benevolent fairy might be supposed to give as a reward to a diligent little girl. The whole is of flowered silk, and having been never used and carefully preserved, it is as fresh and bright as when it was first made seventy years ago; and shows that the same hand which painted so exquisitely with the pen could work as delicately with the needle.

I have collected some of the bright qualities which shone, as it were, on the surface of Jane Austen's character, and attracted most notice; but underneath them there lay the strong foundations of sound sense and judgment, rectitude of principle, and delicacy of feeling, qualifying her equally to advise, assist, or amuse. She was, in fact, as ready to comfort the unhappy, or to nurse the sick, as she was to laugh and jest with the light-hearted. Two of her nieces were grown up, and one of them was married, before she was taken away from them. As their minds became more matured, they were admitted into closer intimacy with her, and learned more of her graver thoughts; they know what a sympathising friend and judicious adviser they found her to be in many little difficulties and doubts of early womanhood.

I do not venture to speak of her religious principles: that is a subject on which she herself was more inclined to *think* and *act* than to *talk*, and I shall imitate her reserve; satisfied to have shown how much of Christian love and humility abounded in her heart, without presuming to lay bare the roots whence those graces grew. Some little insight, however, into these deeper recesses of the heart must be given, when we come to speak of her death.

6

Habits of Composition resumed after a long interval –
First publication – The interest taken by the
Author in the success of her Works

It may seem extraordinary that Jane Austen should have written so little during the years that elapsed between leaving Steventon and settling at Chawton; especially when this cessation from work is contrasted with her literary activity both before and after that period. It might rather have been expected that fresh scenes and new acquaintance would have called forth her powers; while the quiet life which the family led both at Bath and Southampton must have afforded abundant leisure for composition; but so it was that nothing which I know of, certainly nothing which the public have seen, was completed in either of those places. I can only state the fact, without assigning any cause for it; but as soon as she was fixed in her second home, she resumed the habits of composition which had been formed in her first, and continued them to the end of her life. The first year of her residence at Chawton seems to have been devoted to revising and preparing for the press *Sense and Sensibility*, and *Pride and Prejudice*; but between February 1811 and August 1816, she began and completed *Mansfield Park*, *Emma*, and *Persuasion*, so that the last five years of her life produced the same number of novels with those which had been written in her early youth. How she was able to effect all this is surprising, for she had no separate study to retire to, and most of the work must have been done in the general sitting-room, subject to all kinds of casual interruptions. She was careful that her occupation should not be suspected by servants, or visitors, or any persons beyond her own family party. She wrote upon small sheets of paper which could easily be put away, or covered with a piece of blotting paper. There was, between the front door and the offices, a swing door which creaked when it was opened; but she objected to having this little inconvenience remedied, because it gave her notice when anyone was coming. She was not, however, troubled with companions like her own Mrs Allen in *Northanger Abbey*, whose 'vacancy of mind and incapacity for thinking were such that, as she never talked a great deal, so she could never be entirely silent; and therefore, while she sat at work, if she lost her needle, or broke her thread, or saw a speck of dirt on her gown, she must observe it, whether there were anyone at leisure to answer her or not'. In that well-occupied female party there must have been many precious hours of silence during which the pen was busy at the little mahogany writing-desk,* while Fanny Price, or Emma Woodhouse, or Anne Elliott was growing into beauty and interest. I have no doubt that I, and my sisters and cousins, in our visits to Chawton, frequently disturbed this mystic process, without having any idea of the mischief that we were doing; certainly we never should have guessed it by any signs of impatience or irritability in the writer.

As so much had been previously prepared, when once she began to publish, her works came out in quick succession. *Sense and Sensibility* was published in 1811, *Pride and Prejudice* at the beginning of 1813, *Mansfield Park* in 1814, *Emma* early in 1816; *Northanger Abbey* and *Persuasion* did not appear till after her death, in 1818. It will be shown farther on why *Northanger Abbey*, though amongst the first written, was one of the last published. Her first three novels were published by Egerton, her last three by Murray. The profits of the four which had been printed before her death had not at that time amounted to seven hundred pounds.

I have no record of the publication of *Sense and Sensibility*, nor of the author's feelings at this her first appearance before the public; but the following extracts from three letters to her sister give a lively picture of the interest with which she watched the reception of *Pride and Prejudice*, and show the carefulness with which she corrected her compositions, and rejected much that had been written:

Chawton, Friday, January 29 (1813).
I hope you received my little parcel by J. Bond on Wednesday evening, my dear Cassandra, and that you will be ready to hear from me again on Sunday, for I feel that I must write to you to-day. I

---

* This mahogany desk, which has done good service to the public, is now in the possession of my sister, Miss Austen.

want to tell you that I have got my own darling child from London. On Wednesday I received one copy sent down by Falkener, with three lines from Henry to say that he had given another to Charles and sent a third by the coach to Godmersham . . . The advertisement is in our paper to-day for the first time: 18s. He shall ask £1 1s. for my two next, and £1 8s. for my stupidest of all. Miss B. dined with us on the very day of the book's coming, and in the evening we fairly set at it, and read half the first vol. to her, prefacing that, having intelligence from Henry that such a work would soon appear, we had desired him to send it whenever it came out, and I believe it passed with her unsuspected. She was amused, poor soul! *That* she could not help, you know, with two such people to lead the way, but she really does seem to admire Elizabeth. I must confess that I think her as delightful a creature as ever appeared in print, and how I shall be able to tolerate those who do not like *her* at least I do not know. There are a few typical errors; and a 'said he', or a 'said she', would sometimes make the dialogue more immediately clear; but 'I do not write for such dull elves' as have not a great deal of ingenuity themselves. The second volume is shorter than I could wish, but the difference is not so much in reality as in look, there being a larger proportion of narrative in that part. I have lop't and crop't so successfully, however, that I imagine it must be rather shorter than *Sense and Sensibility* altogether. Now I will try and write of something else.

Chawton, Thursday, February 4 (1813).

MY DEAR CASSANDRA – Your letter was truly welcome, and I am much obliged to you for all your praise; it came at a right time, for I had had some fits of disgust. Our second evening's reading to Miss B. had not pleased me so well, but I believe something must be attributed to my mother's too rapid way of getting on: though she perfectly understands the characters herself, she cannot speak as they ought. Upon the whole, however, I am quite vain enough and well satisfied enough. The work is rather too light, and bright, and sparkling; it wants shade; it wants to be stretched out here and there with a long chapter of sense, if it could be had; if not, of solemn specious nonsense, about something unconnected with the story; an essay on writing, a critique on Walter Scott, or the history of Buonaparté, or something that would form a contrast, and bring the reader with increased delight to the playfulness and epigrammatism of the general style ... The greatest blunder in the printing that I have met with is in page 220, v. 3, where two speeches are made into one. There might as well be no suppers at Longbourn; but I suppose it was the remains of Mrs Bennett's old Meryton habits.

The following letter seems to have been written soon after the last two: in February 1813:

This will be a quick return for yours, my dear Cassandra; I doubt its having much else to recommend it; but there is no saying; it may turn out to be a very long and delightful letter. I am exceedingly pleased that you can say what you do, after having gone through the whole work, and Fanny's praise is very gratifying. My hopes were tolerably strong of *her*, but nothing like a certainty. Her liking Darcy and Elizabeth is enough. She might hate all the others, if she would. I have her opinion under her own hand this morning, but your transcript of it, which I read first, was not, and is not, the less acceptable. To *me* it is of course all praise, but the more exact truth which she sends you is good enough ... Our party on Wednesday was not unagreeable, though we wanted a master of the house less anxious and fidgety, and more conversable. Upon Mrs —'s mentioning that she had sent the rejected addresses to Mrs H., I began talking to her a little about them, and expressed my hope of their having amused her. Her answer was, 'Oh dear yes, very much, very droll indeed, the opening of the house, and the striking up of the fiddles!' What she meant, poor woman, who shall say? I sought no farther. As soon as a whist party was formed, and a round table threatened, I made my mother an excuse and came away, leaving just as many for *their* round table as there were at Mrs Grant's.[*] I wish they might be as agreeable a set. My mother is very well, and finds great amusement in glove-knitting, and at present wants no other work. We quite run over with books. She has got Sir John Carr's *Travels in Spain*, and I am reading a Society octavo, an *Essay on the Military Police and Institutions of the British Empire*, by Capt. Pasley of the Engineers, a book which I protested against at first, but which upon trial I find delightfully written and highly

---

[*] At this time, February 1813, *Mansfield Park* was nearly finished.

entertaining. I am as much in love with the author as I ever was with Clarkson or Buchanan, or even the two Mr Smiths of the city. The first soldier I ever sighed for; but he does write with extraordinary force and spirit. Yesterday, moreover, brought us *Mrs Grant's Letters*, with Mr White's compliments; but I have disposed of them, compliments and all, to Miss P., and amongst so many readers or retainers of books as we have in Chawton, I dare say there will be no difficulty in getting rid of them for another fortnight, if necessary. I have disposed of Mrs Grant for the second fortnight to Mrs —. It can make no difference to *her* which of the twenty-six fortnights in the year the 3 vols lie on her table. I have been applied to for information as to the oath taken in former times of Bell, Book, and Candle, but have none to give. Perhaps you may be able to learn something of its origin where you now are. Ladies who read those enormous great stupid thick quarto volumes which one always sees in the breakfast parlour there must be acquainted with everything in the world. I detest a quarto. Capt. Pasley's book is too good for their society. They will not understand a man who condenses his thoughts into an octavo. I have learned from Sir J. Carr that there is no Government House at Gibraltar. I must alter it to the Commissioner's.

The following letter belongs to the same year, but treats of a different subject. It describes a journey from Chawton to London, in her brother's curricle, and shows how much could be seen and enjoyed in course of a long summer's day by leisurely travelling amongst scenery which the traveller in an express train now rushes through in little more than an hour, but scarcely sees at all:

Sloane Street, Thursday, May 20 (1813).
MY DEAR CASSANDRA – Before I say anything else, I claim a paper full of halfpence on the drawing-room mantel-piece; I put them there myself, and forgot to bring them with me. I cannot say that I have yet been in any distress for money, but I chuse to have my due, as well as the Devil. How lucky we were in our weather yesterday! This wet morning makes one more sensible of it. We had no rain of any consequence. The head of the curricle was put half up three or four times, but our share of the showers was very trifling, though they seemed to be heavy all round us, when we were on the Hog's-back, and I fancied it might then be raining so

hard at Chawton as to make you feel for us much more than we deserved. Three hours and a quarter took us to Guildford, where we staid barely two hours, and had only just time enough for all we had to do there; that is, eating a long and comfortable breakfast, watching the carriages, paying Mr Harrington, and taking a little stroll afterwards. From some views which that stroll gave us, I think most highly of the situation of Guildford. We wanted all our brothers and sisters to be standing with us in the bowling-green, and looking towards Horsham. I was very lucky in my gloves – got them at the first shop I went to, though I went into it rather because it was near than because it looked at all like a glove shop, and gave only four shillings for them; after which everybody at Chawton will be hoping and predicting that they cannot be good for anything, and their worth certainly remains to be proved; but I think they look very well. We left Guildford at twenty minutes before twelve (I hope somebody cares for these minutiae), and were at Esher in about two hours more. I was very much pleased with the country in general. Between Guildford and Ripley I thought it particularly pretty, also about Painshill; and from a Mr Spicer's grounds at Esher, which we walked into before dinner, the views were beautiful. I cannot say what we did not see, but I should think there could not be a wood, or a meadow, or palace, or remarkable spot in England that was not spread out before us on one side or other. Claremont is going to be sold: a Mr Ellis has it now. It is a house that seems never to have prospered. After dinner we walked forward to be overtaken at the coachman's time, and before he did overtake us we were very near Kingston. I fancy it was about half-past six when we reached this house – a twelve hours' business, and the horses did not appear more than reasonably tired. I was very tired too, and glad to get to bed early, but am quite well to-day. I am very snug in the front drawing-room all to myself, and would not say 'thank you' for any company but you. The quietness of it does me good. I have contrived to pay my two visits, though the weather made me a great while about it, and left me only a few minutes to sit with Charlotte Craven.* She looks very well, and her hair is done up with an elegance to do

* The present Lady Pollen, of Redenham, near Andover, then at a school in London.

credit to any education. Her manners are as unaffected and pleasing as ever. She had heard from her mother to-day. Mrs Craven spends another fortnight at Chilton. I saw nobody but Charlotte, which pleased me best. I was shewn upstairs into a drawing-room, where she came to me, and the appearance of the room, so totally unschool-like, amused me very much; it was full of modern elegancies.

Yours very affectly,

J. A.

The next letter, written in the following year, contains an account of another journey to London, with her brother Henry, and reading with him the manuscript of *Mansfield Park*:

Henrietta Street, Wednesday, March 2 (1814).

MY DEAR CASSANDRA – You were wrong in thinking of us at Guildford last night: we were at Cobham. On reaching G. we found that John and the horses were gone on. We therefore did no more than we had done at Farnham – sit in the carriage while fresh horses were put in, and proceeded directly to Cobham, which we reached by seven, and about eight were sitting down to a very nice roast fowl, &c. We had altogether a very good journey, and everything at Cobham was comfortable. I could not pay Mr Harrington! That was the only alas! of the business. I shall therefore return his bill, and my mother's £2, that you may try your luck. We did not begin reading till Bentley Green. Henry's approbation is hitherto even equal to my wishes. He says it is different from the other two, but does not appear to think it at all inferior. He has only married Mrs R. I am afraid he has gone through the most entertaining part. He took to Lady B. and Mrs N. most kindly, and gives great praise to the drawing of the characters. He understands them all, likes Fanny, and, I think, foresees how it will all be. I finished the *Heroine* last night, and was very much amused by it. I wonder James did not like it better. It diverted me exceedingly. We went to bed at ten. I was very tired, but slept to a miracle, and am lovely today, and at present Henry seems to have no complaint. We left Cobham at half-past eight, stopped to bait and breakfast at Kingston, and were in this house considerably before two. Nice smiling Mr Barlowe met us at the door and, in reply to enquiries after news, said that peace was generally expected. I have taken possession of my bedroom, unpacked my bandbox, sent Miss P.'s two letters to the twopenny post, been visited by Md. B., and am now writing by myself at the new table in the front room. It is snowing. We had some snowstorms yesterday, and a smart frost at night, which gave us a hard road from Cobham to Kingston; but as it was then getting dirty and heavy, Henry had a pair of leaders put on to the bottom of Sloane St. His own horses, therefore, cannot have had hard work. I watched for *veils* as we drove through the streets, and had the pleasure of seeing several upon vulgar heads. And now, how do you all do? – you in particular, after the worry of yesterday and the day before. I hope Martha had a pleasant visit again, and that you and my mother could eat your beef-pudding. Depend upon my thinking of the chimney-sweeper as soon as I wake to-morrow. Places are secured at Drury Lane for Saturday, but so great is the rage for seeing Kean that only a third and fourth row could be got; as it is in a front box, however, I hope we shall do pretty well – Shylock, a good play for Fanny – she cannot be much affected, I think. Mrs Perigord has just been here. She tells me that we owe her master for the silk-dyeing. My poor old muslin has never been dyed yet. It has been promised to be done several times. What wicked people dyers are. They begin with dipping their own souls in scarlet sin. It is evening. We have drank tea, and I have torn through the third vol. of the *Heroine*. I do not think it falls off. It is a delightful burlesque, particularly on the Radcliffe style. Henry is going on with *Mansfield Park*. He admires H. Crawford: I mean properly, as a clever, pleasant man. I tell you all the good I can, as I know how much you will enjoy it. We hear that Mr Kean is more admired than ever. There are no good places to be got in Drury Lane for the next fortnight, but Henry means to secure some for Saturday fortnight, when you are reckoned upon. Give my love to little Cass. I hope she found my bed comfortable last night. I have seen nobody in London yet with such a long chin as Dr Syntax, nor anybody quite so large as Gogmagolicus.

Yours affly,

J. AUSTEN.

*Seclusion from the literary world – Notice from the
Prince Regent – Correspondence with Mr Clarke –
Suggestions to alter her style of writing*

Jane Austen lived in entire seclusion from the literary world: neither
by correspondence, nor by personal intercourse was she known to
any contemporary authors. It is probable that she never was in
company with any person whose talents or whose celebrity equalled
her own; so that her powers never could have been sharpened by
collision with superior intellects, nor her imagination aided by their
casual suggestions. Whatever she produced was a genuine home-
made article. Even during the last two or three years of her life, when
her works were rising in the estimation of the public, they did not
enlarge the circle of her acquaintance. Few of her readers knew even
her name, and none knew more of her than her name. I doubt
whether it would be possible to mention any other author of note,
whose personal obscurity was so complete. I can think of none like
her, but of many to contrast with her in that respect. Fanny Burney,
afterwards Madame D'Arblay, was at an early age petted by Dr
Johnson, and introduced to the wits and scholars of the day at the
tables of Mrs Thrale and Sir Joshua Reynolds. Anna Seward, in her
self-constituted shrine at Lichfield, would have been miserable, had
she not trusted that the eyes of all lovers of poetry were devoutly
fixed on her. Joanna Baillie and Maria Edgeworth were indeed far
from courting publicity; they loved the privacy of their own families,
one with her brother and sister in their Hampstead villa, the other in
her more distant retreat in Ireland; but fame pursued them, and they
were the favourite correspondents of Sir Walter Scott. Crabbe, who
was usually buried in a country parish, yet sometimes visited London,
and dined at Holland House, and was received as a fellow-poet by
Campbell, Moore, and Rogers; and on one memorable occasion he
was Scott's guest at Edinburgh, and gazed with wondering eyes on
the incongruous pageantry with which George IV was entertained in

that city. Even those great writers who hid themselves amongst lakes and mountains associated with each other; and though little seen by the world were so much in its thoughts that a new term, 'Lakers', was coined to designate them. The chief part of Charlotte Brontë's life was spent in a wild solitude compared with which Steventon and Chawton might be considered to be in the gay world; and yet she attained to personal distinction which never fell to Jane's lot. When she visited her kind publisher in London, literary men and women were invited purposely to meet her: Thackeray bestowed upon her the honour of his notice; and once in Willis's Rooms,* she had to walk shy and trembling through an avenue of lords and ladies, drawn up for the purpose of gazing at the author of *Jane Eyre*. Miss Mitford, too, lived quietly in 'Our Village', devoting her time and talents to the benefit of a father scarcely worthy of her; but she did not live there unknown. Her tragedies gave her a name in London. She numbered Milman and Talfourd amongst her correspondents; and her works were a passport to the society of many who would not otherwise have sought her. Hundreds admired Miss Mitford on account of her writings for one who ever connected the idea of Miss Austen with the press. A few years ago, a gentleman visiting Winchester Cathedral desired to be shown Miss Austen's grave. The verger, as he pointed it out, asked, 'Pray, sir, can you tell me whether there was anything particular about that lady; so many people want to know where she was buried?' During her life the ignorance of the verger was shared by most people; few knew that 'there was anything particular about that lady'.

It was not till towards the close of her life, when the last of the works that she saw published was in the press, that she received the only mark of distinction ever bestowed upon her; and that was remarkable for the high quarter whence it emanated rather than for any actual increase of fame that it conferred. It happened thus. In the autumn of 1815 she nursed her brother Henry through a dangerous fever and slow convalescence at his house in Hans Place. He was attended by one of the Prince Regent's physicians. All attempts to keep her name secret had at this time ceased, and though it had never appeared on a title-page, all who cared to know might easily learn it: and the friendly physician was aware that his patient's nurse was the

* See Mrs Gaskell's *Life of Miss Brontë*, vol. ii, p. 215.

author of *Pride and Prejudice*. Accordingly he informed her one day that the Prince was a great admirer of her novels; that he read them often, and kept a set in every one of his residences; that he himself therefore had thought it right to inform His Royal Highness that Miss Austen was staying in London, and that the Prince had desired Mr Clarke, the librarian of Carlton House, to wait upon her. The next day Mr Clarke made his appearance, and invited her to Carlton House, saying that he had the Prince's instructions to show her the library and other apartments, and to pay her every possible attention. The invitation was of course accepted, and during the visit to Carlton House Mr Clarke declared himself commissioned to say that if Miss Austen had any other novel forthcoming she was at liberty to dedicate it to the Prince. Accordingly such a dedication was immediately prefixed to *Emma*, which was at that time in the press.

Mr Clarke was the brother of Dr Clarke, the traveller and mineralogist, whose life has been written by Bishop Otter. Jane found in him not only a very courteous gentleman, but also a warm admirer of her talents; though it will be seen by his letters that he did not clearly apprehend the limits of her powers, or the proper field for their exercise. The following correspondence took place between them.

Feeling some apprehension lest she should make a mistake in acting on the verbal permission which she had received from the Prince, Jane addressed the following letter to Mr Clarke:

Nov. 15, 1815.

Sir – I must take the liberty of asking you a question. Among the many flattering attentions which I received from you at Carlton House on Monday last was the information of my being at liberty to dedicate any future work to His Royal Highness the Prince Regent, without the necessity of any solicitation on my part. Such, at least, I believed to be your words; but as I am very anxious to be quite certain of what was intended, I entreat you to have the goodness to inform me how such a permission is to be understood, and whether it is incumbent on me to show my sense of the honour, by inscribing the work now in the press to His Royal Highness; I should be equally concerned to appear either presumptuous or ungrateful.

The following gracious answer was returned by Mr Clarke, together with a suggestion which must have been received with some surprise:

Carlton House, Nov. 16, 1815.

DEAR MADAM – It is certainly not *incumbent* on you to dedicate your work now in the press to His Royal Highness; but if you wish to do the Regent that honour either now or at any future period I am happy to send you that permission, which need not require any more trouble or solicitation on your part.

Your late works, Madam, and in particular *Mansfield Park*, reflect the highest honour on your genius and your principles. In every new work your mind seems to increase its energy and power of discrimination. The Regent has read and admired all your publications.

Accept my best thanks for the pleasure your volumes have given me. In the perusal of them I felt a great inclination to write and say so. And I also, dear Madam, wished to be allowed to ask you to delineate in some future work the habits of life, and character, and enthusiasm of a clergyman, who should pass his time between the metropolis and the country, who should be something like Beattie's Minstrel –

> Silent when glad, affectionate tho' shy,
>   And in his looks was most demurely sad;
> And now he laughed aloud, yet none knew why.

Neither Goldsmith, nor La Fontaine in his *Tableau de Famille*, have in my mind quite delineated an English clergyman, at least of the present day, fond of and entirely engaged in literature, no man's enemy but his own. Pray, dear Madam, think of these things.

Believe me at all times with sincerity and respect, your faithful and obliged servant,

J. S. CLARKE, *Librarian.*

The following letter, written in reply, will show how unequal the author of *Pride and Prejudice* felt herself to delineating an enthusiastic clergyman of the present day, who should resemble Beattie's Minstrel:

Dec. 11.

DEAR SIR – My *Emma* is now so near publication that I feel it right to assure you of my not having forgotten your kind recommendation of an early copy for Carlton House, and that I have Mr Murray's promise of its being sent to His Royal Highness, under cover to you, three days previous to the work being really out. I must make use of this opportunity to thank you, dear Sir, for the very high praise you bestow on my other novels. I am too vain to wish to convince you that you have praised them beyond their merits. My greatest anxiety at present is that this fourth work should not disgrace what was good in the others. But on this point I will do myself the justice to declare that, whatever may be my wishes for its success, I am strongly haunted with the idea that to those readers who have preferred *Pride and Prejudice* it will appear inferior in wit, and to those who have preferred *Mansfield Park* inferior in good sense. Such as it is, however, I hope you will do me the favour of accepting a copy. Mr Murray will have directions for sending one. I am quite honoured by your thinking me capable of drawing such a clergyman as you gave the sketch of in your note of Nov. 16th. But I assure you I am not. The comic part of the character I might be equal to, but not the good, the enthusiastic, the literary. Such a man's conversation must at times be on subjects of science and philosophy, of which I know nothing; or at least be occasionally abundant in quotations and allusions which a woman who, like me, knows only her own mother tongue, and has read little in that, would be totally without the power of giving. A classical education, or at any rate a very extensive acquaintance with English literature, ancient and modern, appears to me quite indispensable for the person who would do any justice to your clergyman; and I think I may boast myself to be, with all possible vanity, the most unlearned and uninformed female who ever dared to be an authoress.

Believe me, dear Sir,

Your obliged and faithful humbl Sert

JANE AUSTEN.*

Mr Clarke, however, was not to be discouraged from proposing another subject. He had recently been appointed chaplain and private English secretary to Prince Leopold, who was then about to be united to the Princess Charlotte; and when he again wrote to

---

* It was her pleasure to boast of greater ignorance than she had any just claim to. She knew more than her mother tongue, for she knew a good deal of French and a little of Italian.

express the gracious thanks of the Prince Regent for the copy of *Emma* which had been presented, he suggests that 'an historical romance illustrative of the august House of Cobourg would just now be very interesting', and might very properly be dedicated to Prince Leopold. This was much as if Sir William Ross had been set to paint a great battle-piece; and it is amusing to see with what grave civility she declined a proposal which must have struck her as ludicrous, in the following letter:

MY DEAR SIR – I am honoured by the Prince's thanks and very much obliged to yourself for the kind manner in which you mention the work. I have also to acknowledge a former letter forwarded to me from Hans Place. I assure you I felt very grateful for the friendly tenor of it, and hope my silence will have been considered, as it was truly meant, to proceed only from an unwillingness to tax your time with idle thanks. Under every interesting circumstance which your own talents and literary labours have placed you in, or the favour of the Regent bestowed, you have my best wishes. Your recent appointments I hope are a step to something still better. In my opinion, the service of a court can hardly be too well paid, for immense must be the sacrifice of time and feeling required by it.

You are very kind in your hints as to the sort of composition which might recommend me at present, and I am fully sensible that an historical romance, founded on the House of Saxe Cobourg, might be much more to the purpose of profit or popularity than such pictures of domestic life in country villages as I deal in. But I could no more write a romance than an epic poem. I could not sit seriously down to write a serious romance under any other motive than to save my life; and if it were indispensable for me to keep it up and never relax into laughing at myself or at other people, I am sure I should be hung before I had finished the first chapter. No, I must keep to my own style and go on in my own way; and though I may never succeed again in that, I am convinced that I should totally fail in any other.

I remain, my dear Sir,
Your very much obliged, and sincere friend,

J. AUSTEN.
Chawton, near Alton, April 1, 1816.

Mr Clarke should have recollected the warning of the wise man,

'Force not the course of the river.' If you divert it from the channel
in which nature taught it to flow, and force it into one arbitrarily cut
by yourself, you will lose its grace and beauty.

> But when his free course is not hindered,
> He makes sweet music with the enamelled stones,
> Giving a gentle kiss to every sedge
> He overtaketh in his pilgrimage:
> And so by many winding nooks he strays
> With willing sport.

All writers of fiction, who have genius strong enough to work out a
course of their own, resist every attempt to interfere with its
direction. No two writers could be more unlike each other than Jane
Austen and Charlotte Brontë; so much so that the latter was unable
to understand why the former was admired, and confessed that she
herself 'should hardly like to live with her ladies and gentlemen, in
their elegant but confined houses'; but each writer equally resisted
interference with her own natural style of composition. Miss Brontë,
in reply to a friendly critic, who had warned her against being too
melodramatic, and had ventured to propose Miss Austen's works to
her as a study, writes thus:

Whenever I *do* write another book, I think I will have nothing of
what you call 'melodrama'. I *think* so, but I am not sure. I *think*,
too, I will endeavour to follow the counsel which shines out of Miss
Austen's 'mild eyes', to finish more, and be more subdued; but
neither am I sure of that. When authors write best, or, at least,
when they write most fluently, an influence seems to waken in
them which becomes their master – which will have its way –
putting out of view all behests but its own, dictating certain words,
and insisting on their being used, whether vehement or measured
in their nature, new moulding characters, giving unthought of
turns to incidents, rejecting carefully elaborated old ideas, and
suddenly creating and adopting new ones. Is it not so? And should
we try to counteract this influence? Can we indeed counteract it?[*]

The playful raillery with which the one parries an attack on her
liberty, and the vehement eloquence of the other in pleading the

[*] Mrs Gaskell's *Life of Miss Brontë*, vol. ii, p. 53.

same cause and maintaining the independence of genius, are very characteristic of the minds of the respective writers.

The suggestions which Jane received as to the sort of story that she ought to write were, however, an amusement to her, though they were not likely to prove useful; and she has left amongst her papers one entitled, 'Plan of a novel according to hints from various quarters'. The names of some of those advisers are written on the margin of the manuscript opposite to their respective suggestions.

Heroine to be the daughter of a clergyman, who after having lived much in the world had retired from it, and settled on a curacy with a very small fortune of his own. The most excellent man that can be imagined, perfect in character, temper, and manner, without the smallest drawback or peculiarity to prevent his being the most delightful companion to his daughter from one year's end to the other. Heroine faultless in character, beautiful in person, and possessing every possible accomplishment. Book to open with father and daughter conversing in long speeches, elegant language, and a tone of high serious sentiment. The father induced, at his daughter's earnest request, to relate to her the past events of his life. Narrative to reach through the greater part of the first volume; as besides all the circumstances of his attachment to her mother, and their marriage, it will comprehend his going to sea as chaplain to a distinguished naval character about the court; and his going afterwards to court himself, which involved him in many interesting situations, concluding with his opinion of the benefits of tithes being done away with . . . From this outset the story will proceed, and contain a striking variety of adventures. Father an exemplary parish priest, and devoted to literature; but heroine and father never above a fortnight in one place: he being driven from his curacy by the vile arts of some totally unprincipled and heartless young man, desperately in love with the heroine, and pursuing her with unrelenting passion. No sooner settled in one country of Europe, than they are compelled to quit it, and retire to another, always making new acquaintance, and always obliged to leave them. This will of course exhibit a wide variety of character. The scene will be for ever shifting from one set of people to another, but there will be no mixture, all the good will be unexceptionable in every respect. There will be no foibles or weaknesses but with the wicked, who will be completely depraved and infamous, hardly a resemblance of humanity left in them. Early in her career, the heroine must meet with the hero: all perfection, of course, and only prevented from paying his addresses to her by some excess of refinement. Wherever she goes, somebody falls in love with her, and she receives repeated offers of marriage, which she refers wholly to her father, exceedingly angry that *he* should not be the first applied to. Often carried away by the anti-hero, but rescued either by her father or the hero. Often reduced to support herself and her father by her talents, and work for her bread; continually cheated, and defrauded of her hire; worn down to a skeleton, and now and then starved to death. At last, hunted out of civilised society, denied the poor shelter of the humblest cottage, they are compelled to retreat into Kamtschatka, where the poor father quite worn down, finding his end approaching, throws himself on the ground, and after four or five hours of tender advice and parental admonition to his miserable child, expires in a fine burst of literary enthusiasm, intermingled with invectives against the holders of tithes. Heroine inconsolable for some time, but afterwards crawls back towards her former country, having at least twenty narrow escapes of falling into the hands of anti-hero; and at last, in the very nick of time, turning a corner to avoid him, runs into the arms of the hero himself, who, having just shaken off the scruples which fettered him before, was at the very moment setting off in pursuit of her. The tenderest and completest *éclaircissement* takes place, and they are happily united. Throughout the whole work heroine to be in the most elegant society, and living in high style.

Since the first publication of this memoir, Mr Murray of Albemarle Street has very kindly sent to me copies of the following letters, which his father received from Jane Austen, when engaged in the publication of *Emma*. The increasing cordiality of the letters shows that the author felt that her interests were duly cared for, and was glad to find herself in the hands of a publisher whom she could consider as a friend.

Her brother had addressed to Mr Murray a strong complaint of the tardiness of a printer:

23 Hans Place, Thursday, November 23 (1815).

Sir – My brother's note last Monday has been so fruitless, that I am afraid there can be but little chance of my writing to any good effect; but yet I am so very much disappointed and vexed by the delays of the printers, that I cannot help begging to know whether there is no hope of their being quickened. Instead of the work being ready by the end of the present month, it will hardly, at the rate we now proceed, be finished by the end of the next; and as I expect to leave London early in December, it is of consequence that no more time should be lost. Is it likely that the printers will be influenced to greater dispatch and punctuality by knowing that the work is to be dedicated, by permission, to the Prince Regent? If you can make that circumstance operate, I shall be very glad. My brother returns *Waterloo* with many thanks for the loan of it. We have heard much of Scott's account of Paris.* If it be not incompatible with other arrangements, would you favour us with it, supposing you have any set already opened? You may depend upon its being in careful hands.

'I remain, Sir, your obt humble Set

J. Austen.

Hans Place, December 11 (1815).

Dear Sir – As I find that *Emma* is advertised for publication as early as Saturday next, I think it best to lose no time in settling all that remains to be settled on the subject, and adopt this method as involving the smallest tax on your time.

In the first place, I beg you to understand that I leave the terms on which the trade should be supplied with the work entirely to your judgment, entreating you to be guided in every such arrangement by your own experience of what is most likely to clear off the edition rapidly. I shall be satisfied with whatever you feel to be best. The title-page must be '*Emma*, dedicated by permission to H.R.H. the Prince Regent'. And it is my particular wish that one set should be completed and sent to H.R.H. two or three days before the work is generally public. It should be sent under cover to the Rev. J. S. Clarke, Librarian, Carlton House. I shall subjoin a list of those persons to whom I must trouble you to

---

* This must have been *Paul's Letters to his Kinsfolk*.

forward also a set each, when the work is out; all unbound, with 'From the Authoress' in the first page.

I return you, with very many thanks, the books you have so obligingly supplied me with. I am very sensible, I assure you, of the attention you have paid to my convenience and amusement. I return also *Mansfield Park*, as ready for a second edition, I believe, as I can make it. I am in Hans Place till the 16th. From that day inclusive, my direction will be Chawton, Alton, Hants.

I remain, dear Sir,

Yr faithful humb. Servt

J. AUSTEN.

I wish you would have the goodness to send a line by the bearer, stating *the day* on which the set will be ready for the Prince Regent.

Hans Place, December 11 (1815).

DEAR SIR – I am much obliged by yours, and very happy to feel everything arranged to our mutual satisfaction. As to my direction about the title-page, it was arising from my ignorance only, and from my having never noticed the proper place for a dedication. I thank you for putting me right. Any deviation from what is usually done in such cases is the last thing I should wish for. I feel happy in having a friend to save me from the ill effect of my own blunder.

Yours, dear Sir, &c.

J. AUSTEN.

Chawton, April 1, 1816.

DEAR SIR – I return you the *Quarterly Review* with many thanks. The Authoress of *Emma* has no reason, I think, to complain of her treatment in it, except in the total omission of *Mansfield Park*. I cannot but be sorry that so clever a man as the Reviewer of *Emma* should consider it as unworthy of being noticed. You will be pleased to hear that I have received the Prince's thanks for the *handsome* copy I sent him of *Emma*. Whatever he may think of *my* share of the work, yours seems to have been quite right.

In consequence of the late event in Henrietta Street, I must request that if you should at any time have anything to communicate by letter, you will be so good as to write by the post, directing to me (Miss J. Austen), Chawton, near Alton; and that for anything of a larger bulk, you will add to the same direction, by *Collier's Southampton coach*.

I remain, dear Sir,
Yours very faithfully,

J. AUSTEN.

About the same time the following letters passed between the Countess of Morley and the writer of *Emma*. I do not know whether they were personally acquainted with each other, nor in what this interchange of civilities originated:

The Countess of Morley to Miss J. Austen

Saltram, December 27 (1815).

MADAM – I have been most anxiously waiting for an introduction to *Emma*, and am infinitely obliged to you for your kind recollection of me, which will procure me the pleasure of her acquaintance some days sooner than I should otherwise have had it. I am already become intimate with the Woodhouse family, and feel that they will not amuse and interest me less than the Bennetts, Bertrams, Norrises, and all their admirable predecessors. I can give them no higher praise.

I am, Madam, your much obliged

F. MORLEY.

Miss J. Austen to the Countess of Morley

MADAM – Accept my thanks for the honour of your note, and for your kind disposition in favour of *Emma*. In my present state of doubt as to her reception in the world, it is particularly gratifying to me to receive so early an assurance of your Ladyship's approbation. It encourages me to depend on the same share of general good opinion which *Emma*'s predecessors have experienced, and to believe that I have not yet, as almost every writer of fancy does sooner or later, overwritten myself.

I am, Madam,
Your obliged and faithful Servt

J. AUSTEN.
December 31, 1815.

8

*Slow growth of her fame – Ill success of first attempts at
publication – Two Reviews of her works contrasted*

Seldom has any literary reputation been of such slow growth as that
of Jane Austen. Readers of the present day know the rank that is
generally assigned to her. They have been told by Archbishop
Whately, in his review of her works, and by Lord Macaulay, in his
review of Madame D'Arblay's, the reason why the highest place is to
be awarded to Jane Austen, as a truthful drawer of character, and
why she is to be classed with those who have approached nearest, in
that respect, to the great master Shakespeare. They see her safely
placed, by such authorities, in her niche, not indeed amongst the
highest orders of genius, but in one confessedly her own, in our
British temple of literary fame; and it may be difficult to make them
believe how coldly her works were at first received, and how few
readers had any appreciation of their peculiar merits. Sometimes a
friend or neighbour, who chanced to know of our connection with
the author, would condescend to speak with moderate approbation
of *Sense and Sensibility*, or *Pride and Prejudice*; but if they had known
that we, in our secret thoughts, classed her with Madame D'Arblay
or Miss Edgeworth, or even with some other novel writers of the
day whose names are now scarcely remembered, they would have
considered it an amusing instance of family conceit. To the
multitude her works appeared tame and commonplace,[*] poor in

---

[*] A greater genius than my aunt shared with her the imputation of being
commonplace. Lockhart, speaking of the low estimation in which Scott's
conversational powers were held in the literary and scientific society of
Edinburgh, says: 'I think the epithet most in vogue concerning it was
"commonplace".' He adds, however, that one of the most eminent of that
society was of a different opinion, 'who, when some glib youth chanced to
echo in his hearing the consolatory tenet of local mediocrity, answered
quietly, "I have the misfortune to think differently from you – in my
humble opinion Walter Scott's sense is a still more wonderful thing than
his genius." ' – Lockhart's *Life of Scott*, vol. iv, chap. v.

colouring, and sadly deficient in incident and interest. It is true that we were sometimes cheered by hearing that a different verdict had been pronounced by more competent judges: we were told how some great statesman or distinguished poet held these works in high estimation; we had the satisfaction of believing that they were most admired by the best judges, and comforted ourselves with Horace's 'satis est Equitem mihi plaudere'. So much was this the case, that one of the ablest men of my acquaintance[*] said, in that kind of jest which has much earnest in it, that he had established it in his own mind, as a new test of ability, whether people *could* or *could not* appreciate Miss Austen's merits.

But though such golden opinions were now and then gathered in, yet the wide field of public taste yielded no adequate return either in praise or profit. Her reward was not to be the quick return of the cornfield, but the slow growth of the tree which is to endure to another generation. Her first attempts at publication were very discouraging. In November, 1797, her father wrote the following letter to Mr Cadell:

> Sir – I have in my possession a manuscript novel, comprising 3 vols, about the length of Miss Burney's *Evelina*. As I am well aware of what consequence it is that a work of this sort shd make its first appearance under a respectable name, I apply to you. I shall be much obliged therefore if you will inform me whether you choose to be concerned in it, what will be the expense of publishing it at the author's risk, and what you will venture to advance for the property of it, if on perusal it is approved of. Should you give any encouragement, I will send you the work.
>
> 'I am, Sir, your humble Servant,
>
> GEORGE AUSTEN.
> *Steventon, near Overton, Hants, 1st Nov. 1797.*

This proposal was declined by return of post! The work thus summarily rejected must have been *Pride and Prejudice*.

The fate of *Northanger Abbey* was still more humiliating. It was sold, in 1803, to a publisher in Bath, for ten pounds, but it found so little favour in his eyes, that he chose to abide by his first loss rather than risk farther expense by publishing such a work. It seems to have

---

[*] The late Mr R. H. Cheney.

lain for many years unnoticed in his drawers; somewhat as the first chapters of *Waverley* lurked forgotten amongst the old fishing-tackle in Scott's cabinet. Tilneys, Thorpes, and Morlands consigned apparently to eternal oblivion! But when four novels of steadily increasing success had given the writer some confidence in herself, she wished to recover the copyright of this early work. One of her brothers undertook the negotiation. He found the purchaser very willing to receive back his money, and to resign all claim to the copyright. When the bargain was concluded and the money paid, but not till then, the negotiator had the satisfaction of informing him that the work which had been so lightly esteemed was by the author of *Pride and Prejudice*. I do not think that she was herself much mortified by the want of early success. She wrote for her own amusement. Money, though acceptable, was not necessary for the moderate expenses of her quiet home. Above all, she was blessed with a cheerful contented disposition, and an humble mind; and so lowly did she esteem her own claims, that when she received £150 from the sale of *Sense and Sensibility*, she considered it a prodigious recompense for that which had cost her nothing. It cannot be supposed, however, that she was altogether insensible to the superiority of her own workmanship over that of some contemporaries who were then enjoying a brief popularity. Indeed a few touches in the following extracts from two of her letters show that she was as quicksighted to absurdities in composition as to those in living persons.

Mr C.'s opinion is gone down in my list; but as my paper relates only to *Mansfield Park*, I may fortunately excuse myself from entering Mr D's. I will redeem my credit with him by writing a close imitation of *Self-Control*, as soon as I can. I will improve upon it. My heroine shall not only be wafted down an American river in a boat by herself. She shall cross the Atlantic in the same way; and never stop till she reaches Gravesend.

We have got *Rosanne* in our Society, and find it much as you describe it; very good and clever, but tedious. Mrs Hawkins' great excellence is on serious subjects. There are some very delightful conversations and reflections on religion: but on lighter topics I think she falls into many absurdities; and, as to love, her heroine has very comical feelings. There are a thousand improbabilities in the story. Do you remember the two Miss Ormsdens introduced just at last? Very flat and unnatural. Madelle Cossart is rather my passion.

Two notices of her works appeared in the *Quarterly Review*. One in October 1815, and another, more than three years after her death, in January 1821. The latter article is known to have been from the pen of Whately, afterwards Archbishop of Dublin.* They differ much from each other in the degree of praise which they award, and I think also it may be said, in the ability with which they are written. The first bestows some approval, but the other expresses the warmest admiration. One can scarcely be satisfied with the critical acumen of the former writer, who, in treating of *Sense and Sensibility*, takes no notice whatever of the vigour with which many of the characters are drawn, but declares that 'the interest and *merit* of the piece depends *altogether* upon the behaviour of the elder sister!' Nor is he fair when, in *Pride and Prejudice*, he represents Elizabeth's change of sentiments towards Darcy as caused by the sight of his house and grounds. But the chief discrepancy between the two reviewers is to be found in their appreciation of the commonplace and silly characters to be found in these novels. On this point the difference almost amounts to a contradiction, such as one sometimes sees drawn up in parallel columns, when it is desired to convict some writer or some statesman of inconsistency. The Reviewer, in 1815, says:

> The faults of these works arise from the minute detail which the author's plan comprehends. Characters of folly or simplicity, such as those of old Woodhouse and Miss Bates, are ridiculous when first presented, but if too often brought forward, or too long dwelt on, their prosing is apt to become as tiresome in fiction as in real society.

The Reviewer, in 1821, on the contrary, singles out the fools as especial instances of the writer's abilities, and declares that in this

---

* Lockhart had supposed that this article had been written by Scott, because it exactly accorded with the opinions which Scott had often been heard to express, but he learned afterwards that it had been written by Whately; and Lockhart, who became the Editor of the *Quarterly*, must have had the means of knowing the truth. (See Lockhart's *Life of Sir Walter Scott*, vol. v, p. 158.) I remember that, at the time when the review came out, it was reported in Oxford that Whately had written the article at the request of the lady whom he afterwards married.

respect she shows a regard to character hardly exceeded by Shakespeare himself. These are his words:

Like him (Shakespeare) she shows as admirable a discrimination in the character of fools as of people of sense; a merit which is far from common. To invent indeed a conversation full of wisdom or of wit requires that the writer should himself possess ability; but the converse does not hold good, it is no fool that can describe fools well; and many who have succeeded pretty well in painting superior characters have failed in giving individuality to those weaker ones which it is necessary to introduce in order to give a faithful representation of real life: they exhibit to us mere folly in the abstract, forgetting that to the eye of the skilful naturalist the insects on a leaf present as wide differences as exist between the lion and the elephant. Slender, and Shallow, and Aguecheek, as Shakespeare has painted them, though equally fools, resemble one another no more than Richard, and Macbeth, and Julius Caesar; and Miss Austen's[*] Mrs Bennet, Mr Rushworth, and Miss Bates are no more alike than her Darcy, Knightley, and Edmund Bertram. Some have complained indeed of finding her fools too much like nature, and consequently tiresome. There is no disputing about tastes; all we can say is, that such critics must (whatever deference they may outwardly pay to received opinions) find the *Merry Wives of Windsor* and *Twelfth Night* very tiresome; and that those who look with pleasure at Wilkie's pictures, or those of the Dutch school, must admit that excellence of imitation may confer attraction on that which would be insipid or disagreeable in the reality. Her minuteness of detail has also been found fault with; but even where it produces, at the time, a degree of tediousness, we know not whether that can justly be reckoned a blemish, which is absolutely essential to a very high excellence. Now it is absolutely impossible, without this, to produce that thorough acquaintance with the characters which is necessary to make the reader heartily interested in them. Let anyone cut out from the *Iliad* or from Shakespeare's plays everything (we are far from saying that either might not lose some parts with advantage, but let him reject

---

[*] In transcribing this passage I have taken the liberty so far to correct it as to spell her name properly with an 'e'.

everything) which is absolutely devoid of importance and interest
in itself; and he will find that what is left will have lost more than
half its charms. We are convinced that some writers have
diminished the effect of their works by being scrupulous to admit
nothing into them which had not some absolute and independent
merit. They have acted like those who strip off the leaves of a fruit
tree, as being of themselves good for nothing, with the view of
securing more nourishment to the fruit, which in fact cannot attain
its full maturity and flavour without them.

The world, I think, has endorsed the opinion of the later writer;
but it would not be fair to set down the discrepancy between the two
entirely to the discredit of the former. The fact is that, in the course
of the intervening five years, these works had been read and reread
by many leaders in the literary world. The public taste was forming
itself all this time, and 'grew by what it fed on'. These novels belong
to a class which gain rather than lose by frequent perusals, and it is
probable that each Reviewer represented fairly enough the
prevailing opinions of readers in the year when each wrote.

Since that time, the testimonies in favour of Jane Austen's works
have been continual and almost unanimous. They are frequently
referred to as models; nor have they lost their first distinction of
being especially acceptable to minds of the highest order. I shall
indulge myself by collecting into the next chapter instances of the
homage paid to her by such persons.

9

Into this list of the admirers of my Aunt's works, I admit those only whose eminence will be universally acknowledged. No doubt the number might have been increased.

Southey, in a letter to Sir Egerton Brydges, says:

> You mention Miss Austen. Her novels are more true to nature, and have, for my sympathies, passages of finer feeling than any others of this age. She was a person of whom I have heard so well and think so highly, that I regret not having had an opportunity of testifying to her the respect which I felt for her.

It may be observed that Southey had probably heard from his own family connections of the charm of her private character. A friend of hers, the daughter of Mr Bigge Wither, of Manydown Park near Basingstoke, was married to Southey's uncle, the Revd Herbert Hill, who had been useful to his nephew in many ways, and especially in supplying him with the means of attaining his extensive knowledge of Spanish and Portuguese literature. Mr Hill had been Chaplain to the British Factory at Lisbon, where Southey visited him and had the use of a library in those languages which his uncle had collected. Southey himself continually mentions his uncle Hill in terms of respect and gratitude.

S. T. Coleridge would sometimes burst out into high encomiums of Miss Austen's novels as being, 'in their way, perfectly genuine and individual productions'.

I remember Miss Mitford's saying to me: 'I would almost cut off one of my hands, if it would enable me to write like your aunt with the other.'

The biographer of Sir J. Mackintosh says:

> Something recalled to his mind the traits of character which are so delicately touched in Miss Austen's novels . . . He said that there

was genius in sketching out that new kind of novel . . . He was vexed for the credit of the *Edinburgh Review* that it had left her unnoticed* . . . The *Quarterly* had done her more justice . . . It was impossible for a foreigner to understand fully the merit of her works. Madame de Staël, to whom he had recommended one of her novels, found no interest in it; and in her note to him in reply said it was 'vulgaire': and yet, he said, nothing could be more true than what he wrote in answer: 'There is no book which that word would so little suit.' . . . Every village could furnish matter for a novel to Miss Austen. She did not need the common materials for a novel, strong emotions, or strong incidents.†

It was not, however, quite impossible for a foreigner to appreciate these works; for Mons. Guizot writes thus:

I am a great novel reader, but I seldom read German or French novels. The characters are too artificial. My delight is to read English novels, particularly those written by women. 'C'est toute une école de morale.' Miss Austen, Miss Ferrier, &c., form a school which in the excellence and profusion of its productions resembles the cloud of dramatic poets of the great Athenian age.

In the *Keepsake* of 1825 the following lines appeared, written by Lord Morpeth, afterwards seventh Earl of Carlisle, and Lord-Lieutenant of Ireland, accompanying an illustration of a lady reading a novel.

> Beats thy quick pulse o'er Inchbald's thrilling leaf,
> Brunton's high moral, Opie's deep wrought grief?
> Has the mild chaperon claimed thy yielding heart,
> Carroll's dark page, Trevelyan's gentle art?
> Or is it thou, all perfect Austen? Here
> Let one poor wreath adorn thy early bier,
> That scarce allowed thy modest youth to claim
> Its living portion of thy certain fame!
> Oh! Mrs Bennet! Mrs Norris too!
> While memory survives we'll dream of you.

* Incidentally she had received high praise in Lord Macaulay's Review of Madame D'Arblay's Works in the *Edinburgh*.
† *Life of Sir J. Mackintosh*, vol. ii, p. 472.

And Mr Woodhouse, whose abstemious lip
Must thin, but not too thin, his gruel sip.
Miss Bates, our idol, though the village bore;
And Mrs Elton, ardent to explore.
While the clear style flows on without pretence,
With unstained purity, and unmatched sense:
Or, if a sister e'er approached the throne,
She called the rich 'inheritance' her own.

The admiration felt by Lord Macaulay would probably have taken a very practical form, if his life had been prolonged. I have the authority of his sister, Lady Trevelyan, for stating that he had intended to undertake the task upon which I have ventured. He purposed to write a memoir of Miss Austen, with criticisms on her works, to prefix it to a new edition of her novels, and from the proceeds of the sale to erect a monument to her memory in Winchester Cathedral. Oh! that such an idea had been realised! That portion of the plan in which Lord Macaulay's success would have been most certain might have been almost sufficient for his object. A memoir written by him would have been a monument.

I am kindly permitted by Sir Henry Holland to give the following quotation from his printed but unpublished recollections of his past life:

I have the picture still before me of Lord Holland lying on his bed, when attacked with gout, his admirable sister, Miss Fox, beside him reading aloud, as she always did on these occasions, some one of Miss Austen's novels, of which he was never wearied. I well recollect the time when these charming novels, almost unique in their style of humour, burst suddenly on the world. It was sad that their writer did not live to witness the growth of her fame.

My brother-in-law, Sir Denis Le Marchant, has supplied me with the following anecdotes from his own recollections:

When I was a student at Trinity College, Cambridge, Mr Whewell, then a Fellow and afterwards Master of the College, often spoke to me with admiration of Miss Austen's novels. On one occasion I said that I had found *Persuasion* rather dull. He quite fired up in defence of it, insisting that it was the most beautiful of her works. This accomplished philosopher was deeply versed in works of fiction. I recollect his writing to me from Caernarvon, where he had the charge of some pupils, that he was weary of *his* stay, for he had read the circulating library twice through.

During a visit I paid to Lord Lansdowne, at Bowood, in 1846, one of Miss Austen's novels became the subject of conversation and of praise, especially from Lord Lansdowne, who observed that one of the circumstances of his life which he looked back upon with vexation was that Miss Austen should once have been living some weeks in his neighbourhood without his knowing it.

I have heard Sydney Smith, more than once, dwell with eloquence on the merits of Miss Austen's novels. He told me he should have enjoyed giving her the pleasure of reading her praises in the *Edinburgh Review*. Fanny Price was one of his prime favourites.

I close this list of testimonies, this long 'Catena Patrum', with the remarkable words of Sir Walter Scott, taken from his diary for March 14, 1826:*

Read again, for the third time at least, Miss Austen's finely written novel of *Pride and Prejudice*. That young lady had a talent for describing the involvements and feelings and characters of ordinary life, which is to me the most wonderful I ever met with. The big Bow-Wow strain I can do myself like any now going; but the exquisite touch which renders ordinary common-place things and characters interesting from the truth of the description and the sentiment is denied to me. What a pity such a gifted creature died so early!

The well-worn condition of Scott's own copy of these works attests that they were much read in his family. When I visited Abbotsford, a few years after Scott's death, I was permitted, as an unusual favour, to take one of these volumes in my hands. One cannot suppress the wish that she had lived to know what such men thought of her powers, and how gladly they would have cultivated a personal acquaintance with her. I do not think that it would at all have impaired the modest simplicity of her character; or that we should

* Lockhart's *Life of Scott*, vol. vi, chap. vii.

have lost our own dear 'Aunt Jane' in the blaze of literary fame.

It may be amusing to contrast with these testimonies from the great, the opinions expressed by other readers of more ordinary intellect. The author herself has left a list of criticisms which it had been her amusement to collect, through means of her friends. This list contains much of warm-hearted sympathising praise, interspersed with some opinions which may be considered surprising.

One lady could say nothing better of *Mansfield Park*, than that it was 'a mere novel'.

Another owned that she thought *Sense and Sensibility* and *Pride and Prejudice* downright nonsense; but expected to like *Mansfield Park* better, and having finished the first volume, hoped that she had got through the worst.

Another did not like *Mansfield Park*. Nothing interesting in the characters. Language poor.

One gentleman read the first and last chapters of *Emma*, but did not look at the rest because he had been told that it was not interesting.

The opinions of another gentleman about *Emma* were so bad that they could not be reported to the author.

Quot homines, tot sententiae.

Thirty-five years after her death there came also a voice of praise from across the Atlantic. In 1852 the following letter was received by her brother Sir Francis Austen:

Boston, Massachusetts, U.S.A., 6th Jan. 1852.
Since high critical authority has pronounced the delineations of character in the works of Jane Austen second only to those of Shakespeare, transatlantic admiration appears superfluous; yet it may not be uninteresting to her family to receive an assurance that the influence of her genius is extensively recognised in the American Republic, even by the highest judicial authorities. The late Mr Chief Justice Marshall, of the supreme Court of the United States, and his associate Mr Justice Story, highly estimated and admired Miss Austen, and to them we owe our introduction to her society. For many years her talents have brightened our daily path, and her name and those of her characters are familiar to us as 'household words'. We have long wished to express to

some of her family the sentiments of gratitude and affection she has inspired, and request more information relative to her life than is given in the brief memoir prefixed to her works.

Having accidentally heard that a brother of Jane Austen held a high rank in the British Navy, we have obtained his address from our friend Admiral Wormley, now resident in Boston, and we trust this expression of our feeling will be received by her relations with the kindness and urbanity characteristic of Admirals of *her creation*. Sir Francis Austen, or one of his family, would confer a great favour by complying with our request. The autograph of his sister, or a few lines in her handwriting, would be placed among our chief treasures.

The family who delight in the companionship of Jane Austen, and who present this petition, are of English origin. Their ancestor held a high rank among the first emigrants to New England, and his name and character have been ably represented by his descendants in various public stations of trust and responsibility to the present time in the colony and state of Massachusetts. A letter addressed to Miss Quincey, care of the Honble Josiah Quincey, Boston, Massachusetts, would reach its destination.

Sir Francis Austen returned a suitable reply to this application; and sent a long letter of his sister's, which, no doubt, still occupies the place of honour promised by the Quincey family.

Observations on the Novels

It is not the object of these memoirs to attempt a criticism on Jane Austen's novels. Those particulars only have been noticed which could be illustrated by the circumstances of her own life; but I now desire to offer a few observations on them, and especially on one point, on which my age renders me a competent witness – the fidelity with which they represent the opinions and manners of the class of society in which the author lived early in this century. They do this the more faithfully on account of the very deficiency with which they have been sometimes charged – namely, that they make no attempt to raise the standard of human life, but merely represent it as it was. They certainly were not written to support any theory or inculcate any particular moral, except indeed the great moral which is to be equally gathered from an observation of the course of actual life – namely, the superiority of high over low principles, and of greatness over littleness of mind. These writings are like photographs, in which no feature is softened; no ideal expression is introduced, all is the unadorned reflection of the natural object; and the value of such a faithful likeness must increase as time gradually works more and more changes in the face of society itself. A remarkable instance of this is to be found in her portraiture of the clergy. She was the daughter and the sister of clergymen, who certainly were not low specimens of their order: and she has chosen three of her heroes from that profession; but no one in these days can think that either Edmund Bertram or Henry Tilney had adequate ideas of the duties of a parish minister. Such, however, were the opinions and practice then prevalent among respectable and conscientious clergymen before their minds had been stirred, first by the Evangelical, and afterwards by the High Church movement which this century has witnessed. The country may be congratulated which, on looking back to such a fixed landmark, can find that it has been advancing instead of receding from it.

The long interval that elapsed between the completion of

Northanger Abbey in 1798, and the commencement of *Mansfield Park* in 1811, may sufficiently account for any difference of style which may be perceived between her three earlier and her three later productions. If the former showed quite as much originality and genius, they may perhaps be thought to have less of the faultless finish and high polish which distinguish the latter. The characters of the John Dashwoods, Mr Collins, and the Thorpes stand out from the canvas with a vigour and originality which cannot be surpassed; but I think that in her last three works are to be found a greater refinement of taste, a more nice sense of propriety, and a deeper insight into the delicate anatomy of the human heart, marking the difference between the brilliant girl and the mature woman. Far from being one of those who have over-written themselves, it may be affirmed that her fame would have stood on a narrower and less firm basis, if she had not lived to resume her pen at Chawton.

Some persons have surmised that she took her characters from individuals with whom she had been acquainted. They were so life-like that it was assumed that they must once have lived, and have been transferred bodily, as it were, into her pages. But surely such a supposition betrays an ignorance of the high prerogative of genius to create out of its own resources imaginary characters, who shall be true to nature and consistent in themselves. Perhaps, however, the distinction between keeping true to nature and servilely copying any one specimen of it is not always clearly apprehended. It is indeed true, both of the writer and of the painter, that he can use only such lineaments as exist, and as he has observed to exist, in living objects; otherwise he would produce monsters instead of human beings; but in both it is the office of high art to mould these features into new combinations, and to place them in the attitudes, and impart to them the expressions which may suit the purposes of the artist; so that they are nature, but not exactly the same nature which had come before his eyes; just as honey can be obtained only from the natural flowers which the bee has sucked; yet it is not a reproduction of the odour or flavour of any particular flower, but becomes something different when it has gone through the process of transformation which that little insect is able to effect. Hence, in the case of painters, arises the superiority of original compositions over portrait painting. Reynolds was exercising a higher faculty when he designed Comedy and Tragedy contending for Garrick, than when he merely took a likeness of that actor. The same difference exists in writings between the original conceptions of Shakespeare and some other creative geniuses, and such full-length likenesses of individual persons, *The Talking Gentleman* for instance, as are admirably drawn by Miss Mitford. Jane Austen's powers, whatever may be the degree in which she possessed them, were certainly of that higher order. She did not copy individuals, but she invested her own creations with individuality of character. A reviewer in the *Quarterly* speaks of an acquaintance who, ever since the publication of *Pride and Prejudice*, had been called by his friends Mr Bennet, but the author did not know him. Her own relations never recognised any individual in her characters; and I can call to mind several of her acquaintance whose peculiarities were very tempting and easy to be caricatured of whom there are no traces in her pages. She herself, when questioned on the subject by a friend, expressed a dread of what she called such an 'invasion of social proprieties'. She said that she thought it quite fair to note peculiarities and weaknesses, but that it was her desire to create, not to reproduce; 'besides', she added, 'I am too proud of my gentlemen to admit that they were only Mr A. or Colonel B.' She did not, however, suppose that her imaginary characters were of a higher order than are to be found in nature; for she said, when speaking of two of her great favourites, Edmund Bertram and Mr Knightley: 'They are very far from being what I know English gentlemen often are.'

She certainly took a kind of parental interest in the beings whom she had created, and did not dismiss them from her thoughts when she had finished her last chapter. We have seen, in one of her letters, her personal affection for Darcy and Elizabeth; and when sending a copy of *Emma* to a friend whose daughter had been lately born, she wrote thus: 'I trust you will be as glad to see my *Emma*, as I shall be to see your Jemima.' She was very fond of *Emma*, but did not reckon on her being a general favourite; for, when commencing that work, she said, 'I am going to take a heroine whom no one but myself will much like.' She would, if asked, tell us many little particulars about the subsequent career of some of her people. In this traditionary way we learned that Miss Steele never succeeded in catching the Doctor; that Kitty Bennet was satisfactorily married to a clergyman near Pemberley, while Mary obtained nothing higher than one of her uncle Philip's clerks, and was content to be considered a star in the society of Meriton; that the 'considerable sum' given by Mrs Norris to William Price was one pound; that Mr Woodhouse survived his daughter's marriage, and kept her and Mr Knightley from settling at Donwell, about two years; and that the letters placed by Frank Churchill before Jane Fairfax, which she swept away unread, contained the word 'pardon'. Of the good people in *Northanger Abbey* and *Persuasion* we know nothing more than what is written: for before those works were published their author had been taken away from us, and all such amusing communications had ceased for ever.

11

*Declining health of Jane Austen – Elasticity of her spirits –
Her resignation and humility – Her death*

Early in the year 1816 some family troubles disturbed the usually
tranquil course of Jane Austen's life; and it is probable that the inward
malady, which was to prove ultimately fatal, was already felt by her;
for some distant friends,* whom she visited in the spring of that year,
thought that her health was somewhat impaired, and observed that
she went about her old haunts, and recalled old recollections
connected with them in a particular manner, as if she did not expect
ever to see them again. It is not surprising that, under these circumstances, some of her letters were of a graver tone than had been
customary with her, and expressed resignation rather than cheerfulness. In reference to these troubles in a letter to her brother Charles,
after mentioning that she had been laid up with an attack of bilious
fever, she says: 'I live up stairs for the present and am coddled. I am
the only one of the party who has been so silly, but a weak body must
excuse weak nerves.' And again, to another correspondent: 'But I am
getting too near complaint; it has been the appointment of God,
however secondary causes may have operated.' But the elasticity of
her spirits soon recovered their tone. It was in the latter half of that
year that she addressed the two following lively letters to a nephew,
one while he was at Winchester School, the other soon after he had
left it:

Chawton, July 9, 1816.

My Dear E. – Many thanks. A thank for every line, and as many
to Mr W. Digweed for coming. We have been wanting very much
to hear of your mother, and are happy to find she continues to
mend, but her illness must have been a very serious one indeed.
When she is really recovered, she ought to try change of air, and
come over to us. Tell your father that I am very much obliged to

---

* The Fowles, of Kintbury, in Berkshire.

him for his share of your letter, and most sincerely join in the hope of her being eventually much the better for her present discipline. She has the comfort moreover of being confined in such weather as gives one little temptation to be out. It is really too bad, and has been too bad for a long time, much worse than anyone can bear, and I begin to think it will never be fine again. This is a *finesse* of mine, for I have often observed that if one writes about the weather, it is generally completely changed before the letter is read. I wish it may prove so now, and that when Mr W. Digweed reaches Steventon to-morrow, he may find you have had a long series of hot dry weather. We are a small party at present, only grandmamma, Mary Jane, and myself. Yalden's coach cleared off the rest yesterday. I am glad you recollected to mention your being come home.* My heart began to sink within me when I had got so far through your letter without its being mentioned. I was dreadfully afraid that you might be detained at Winchester by severe illness, confined to your bed perhaps, and quite unable to hold a pen, and only dating from Steventon in order, with a mistaken sort of tenderness, to deceive me. But now I have no doubt of your being at home. I am sure you would not say it so seriously unless it actually were so. We saw a countless number of post-chaises full of boys pass by yesterday morning† – full of future heroes, legislators, fools, and villains. You have never thanked me for my last letter, which went by the cheese. I cannot bear not to be thanked. You will not pay us a visit yet of course; we must not think of it. Your mother must get well first, and you must go to Oxford and *not* be elected; after that a little change of scene may be good for you, and your physicians I hope will order you to the sea, or to a house by the side of a very considerable pond.‡ Oh! it rains again. It beats against the window. Mary Jane and I have been wet through once already to-day; we set off in the donkey-carriage for Farringdon, as I wanted to see the improvement Mr Woolls is making, but we

---

* It seems that her young correspondent, after dating from his home, had been so superfluous as to state in his letter that he was returned home, and thus to have drawn on himself this banter.

† The road by which many Winchester boys returned home ran close to Chawton Cottage.

‡ There was, though it exists no longer, a pond close to Chawton Cottage, at the junction of the Winchester and Gosport roads.

were obliged to turn back before we got there, but not soon enough to avoid a pelter all the way home. We met Mr Woolls. I talked of its being bad weather for the hay, and he returned me the comfort of its being much worse for the wheat. We hear that Mrs S. does not quit Tangier: why and wherefore? Do you know that our Browning is gone? You must prepare for a William when you come, a good-looking lad, civil and quiet, and seeming likely to do. Good bye. I am sure Mr W. D.* will be astonished at my writing so much, for the paper is so thin that he will be able to count the lines if not to read them.

Yours affecly,

JANE AUSTEN.

In the next letter will be found her description of her own style of composition, which has already appeared in the notice prefixed to *Northanger Abbey* and *Persuasion*:

Chawton, Monday, Dec. 16th (1816).

MY DEAR E. – One reason for my writing to you now is, that I may have the pleasure of directing to you Esqre. I give you joy of having left Winchester. Now you may own how miserable you were there; now it will gradually all come out, your crimes and your miseries – how often you went up by the Mail to London and threw away fifty guineas at a tavern, and how often you were on the point of hanging yourself, restrained only, as some ill-natured aspersion upon poor old Winton has it, by the want of a tree within some miles of the city. Charles Knight and his companions passed through Chawton about 9 this morning; later than it used to be. Uncle Henry and I had a glimpse of his handsome face, looking all health and good humour. I wonder when you will come and see us. I know what I rather speculate upon, but shall say nothing. We think uncle Henry in excellent looks. Look at him this moment, and think so too, if you have not done it before; and we have the great comfort of seeing decided improvement in uncle Charles, both as to health, spirits, and appearance. And they are each of them so agreeable in their different way, and harmonise so well,

---

* Mr Digweed, who conveyed the letters to and from Chawton, was the gentleman named in page 32, as renting the old manor-house and the large farm at Steventon.

that their visit is thorough enjoyment. Uncle Henry writes very superior sermons. You and I must try to get hold of one or two, and put them into our novels: it would be a fine help to a volume; and we could make our heroine read it aloud on a Sunday evening, just as well as Isabella Wardour, in the *Antiquary*, is made to read the *History of the Hartz Demon* in the ruins of St Ruth, though I believe, on recollection, Lovell is the reader. By the bye, my dear E., I am quite concerned for the loss your mother mentions in her letter. Two chapters and a half to be missing is monstrous! It is well that *I* have not been at Steventon lately, and therefore cannot be suspected of purloining them: two strong twigs and a half towards a nest of my own would have been something. I do not think, however, that any theft of that sort would be really very useful to me. What should I do with your strong, manly, vigorous sketches, full of variety and glow? How could I possibly join them on to the little bit (two inches wide) of ivory on which I work with so fine a brush, as produces little effect after much labour?

You will hear from uncle Henry how well Anna is. She seems perfectly recovered. Ben was here on Saturday, to ask uncle Charles and me to dine with them, as to-morrow, but I was forced to decline it, the walk is beyond my strength (though I am otherwise very well), and this is not a season for donkey-carriages; and as we do not like to spare uncle Charles, he has declined it too.

Tuesday. Ah, ah! Mr E. I doubt your seeing uncle Henry at Steventon to-day. The weather will prevent your expecting him, I think. Tell your father, with aunt Cass's love and mine, that the pickled cucumbers are extremely good, and tell him also – 'tell him what you will'. No, don't tell him what you will, but tell him that grandmamma begs him to make Joseph Hall pay his rent, if he can.

You must not be tired of reading the word *uncle*, for I have not done with it. Uncle Charles thanks your mother for her letter; it was a great pleasure to him to know that the parcel was received and gave so much satisfaction, and he begs her to be so good as to give three shillings for him to Dame Staples, which shall be allowed for in the payment of her debt here.

Adieu, Amiable! I hope Caroline behaves well to you.

Yours affecly,

J. Austen.

I cannot tell how soon she was aware of the serious nature of her malady. By God's mercy it was not attended with much suffering; so that she was able to tell her friends as in the foregoing letter, and perhaps sometimes to persuade herself that, excepting want of strength, she was 'otherwise very well'; but the progress of the disease became more and more manifest as the year advanced. The usual walk was at first shortened, and then discontinued; and air was sought in a donkey-carriage. Gradually, too, her habits of activity within the house ceased, and she was obliged to lie down much. The sitting-room contained only one sofa, which was frequently occupied by her mother, who was more than seventy years old. Jane would never use it, even in her mother's absence; but she contrived a sort of couch for herself with two or three chairs, and was pleased to say that this arrangement was more comfortable to her than a real sofa. Her reasons for this might have been left to be guessed, but for the importunities of a little niece, which obliged her to explain that if she herself had shown any inclination to use the sofa, her mother might have scrupled being on it so much as was good for her.

It is certain, however, that the mind did not share in this decay of the bodily strength. *Persuasion* was not finished before the middle of August in that year; and the manner in which it was then completed affords proof that neither the critical nor the creative powers of the author were at all impaired. The book had been brought to an end in July; and the re-engagement of the hero and heroine effected in a totally different manner in a scene laid at Admiral Croft's lodgings. But her performance did not satisfy her. She thought it tame and flat, and was desirous of producing something better. This weighed upon her mind, the more so probably on account of the weak state of her health; so that one night she retired to rest in very low spirits. But such depression was little in accordance with her nature, and was soon shaken off. The next morning she awoke to more cheerful views and brighter inspirations: the sense of power revived; and imagination resumed its course. She cancelled the condemned chapter, and wrote two others, entirely different, in its stead. The result is that we possess the visit of the Musgrove party to Bath; the crowded and animated scenes at the White Hart Hotel; and the charming conversation between Capt. Harville and Anne Elliot, overheard by Capt. Wentworth, by which the two faithful lovers were at last led to understand each other's feelings. The tenth and eleventh chapters of *Persuasion* then, rather than the actual winding-up of the story, contain the latest of her printed compositions, her last contribution to the entertainment of the public. Perhaps it may be thought that she has seldom written anything more brilliant; and that, independent of the original manner in which the *dénouement* is brought about, the pictures of Charles Musgrove's good-natured boyishness and of his wife's jealous selfishness would have been incomplete without these finishing strokes. The cancelled chapter exists in manuscript. It is certainly inferior to the two which were substituted for it: but it was such as some writers and some readers might have been contented with; and it contained touches which scarcely any other hand could have given, the suppression of which may be almost a matter of regret.[*]

The following letter was addressed to her friend Miss Bigg, then staying at Streatham with her sister, the wife of the Reverend Herbert Hill, uncle of Robert Southey. It appears to have been written three days before she began her last work, which will be noticed in another chapter; and shows that she was not at that time aware of the serious nature of her malady:

Chawton, January 24, 1817.

MY DEAR ALETHEA – I think it time there should be a little writing between us, though I believe the epistolary debt is on *your* side, and I hope this will find all the Streatham party well, neither carried away by the flood, nor rheumatic through the damps. Such mild weather is, you know, delightful to *us*, and though we have a great many ponds, and a fine running stream through the meadows on the other side of the road, it is nothing but what beautifies us and does to talk of. *I* have certainly gained strength through the winter and am not far from being well; and I think I understand my own case now so much better than I did, as to be able by care to keep off any serious return of illness I am convinced that *bile* is at the bottom of all I have suffered, which makes it easy to know how to treat myself. You will be glad to hear thus much of me, I am sure. We have just had a few days' visit from Edward, who brought us a good account of his father, and

---

[*] This cancelled chapter is now printed, in compliance with the requests addressed to me from several quarters.

the very circumstance of his coming at all, of his father's being able to spare him, is itself a good account. He grows still, and still improves in appearance, at least in the estimation of his aunts, who love him better and better, as they see the sweet temper and warm affections of the boy confirmed in the young man: I tried hard to persuade him that he must have some message for William,* but in vain . . . This is not a time of year for donkey-carriages, and our donkeys are necessarily having so long a run of luxurious idleness that I suppose we shall find they have forgotten much of their education when we use them again. We do not use two at once however; don't imagine such excesses . . . Our own new clergy-man† is expected here very soon, perhaps in time to assist Mr Papillon on Sunday. I shall be very glad when the first hearing is over. It will be a nervous hour for our pew, though we hear that he acquits himself with as much ease and collectedness, as if he had been used to it all his life. We have no chance we know of seeing you between Streatham and Winchester: you go the other road and are engaged to two or three houses; if there should be any change, however, you know how welcome you would be . . . We have been reading the *Poet's Pilgrimage to Waterloo*, and generally with much approbation. Nothing will please all the world, you know; but parts of it suit me better than much that he has written before. The opening – *the proem* I believe he calls it – is very beautiful. Poor man! one cannot but grieve for the loss of the son so fondly described. Has he at all recovered it? What do Mr and Mrs Hill know about his present state?

Yours affly,

J. Austen.

The real object of this letter is to ask you for a receipt, but I thought it genteel not to let it appear early. We remember some excellent orange wine at Manydown, made from Seville oranges, entirely or chiefly. I should be very much obliged to you for the receipt, if you can command it within a few weeks.

On the day before, January 23rd, she had written to her niece in the same hopeful tone: 'I feel myself getting stronger than I was, and

* Miss Bigg's nephew, the present Sir William Heathcote, of Hursley.
† Her brother Henry, who had been ordained late in life.

can so perfectly walk *to* Alton, *or* back again without fatigue, that I hope to be able to do *both* when summer comes.'

Alas! summer came to her only on her deathbed. March 17th is the last date to be found in the manuscript on which she was engaged; and as the watch of the drowned man indicates the time of his death, so does this final date seem to fix the period when her mind could no longer pursue its accustomed course.

And here I cannot do better than quote the words of the niece to whose private records of her aunt's life and character I have been so often indebted:

I do not know how early the alarming symptoms of her malady came on. It was in the following March that I had the first idea of her being seriously ill. It had been settled that about the end of that month, or the beginning of April, I should spend a few days at Chawton, in the absence of my father and mother, who were just then engaged with Mrs Leigh Perrot in arranging her late husband's affairs; but Aunt Jane became too ill to have me in the house, and so I went instead to my sister Mrs Lefroy at Wyards'. The next day we walked over to Chawton to make enquiries after our aunt. She was then keeping her room, but said she would see us, and we went up to her. She was in her dressing gown, and was sitting quite like an invalid in an arm-chair, but she got up and kindly greeted us, and then, pointing to seats which had been arranged for us by the fire, she said, 'There is a chair for the married lady, and a little stool for you, Caroline.'* It is strange, but those trifling words were the last of hers that I can remember, for I retain no recollection of what was said by anyone in the conversation that ensued. I was struck by the alteration in herself. She was very pale, her voice was weak and low, and there was about her a general appearance of debility and suffering; but I have been told that she never had much acute pain. She was not equal to the exertion of talking to us, and our visit to the sick room was a very short one, Aunt Cassandra soon taking us away. I do not suppose we stayed a quarter of an hour; and I never saw Aunt Jane again.

In May 1817 she was persuaded to remove to Winchester, for the

* The writer was at that time under twelve years old.

sake of medical advice from Mr Lyford. The Lyfords have, for some generations, maintained a high character in Winchester for medical skill, and the Mr Lyford of that day was a man of more than provincial reputation, in whom great London practitioners expressed confidence. Mr Lyford spoke encouragingly. It was not, of course, his business to extinguish hope in his patient, but I believe that he had, from the first, very little expectation of a permanent cure. All that was gained by the removal from home was the satisfaction of having done the best that could be done, together with such alleviations of suffering as superior medical skill could afford.

Jane and her sister Cassandra took lodgings in College Street. They had two kind friends living in the Close, Mrs Heathcote and Miss Bigg, the mother and aunt of the present Sir Wm Heathcote of Hursley, between whose family and ours a close friendship has existed for several generations. These friends did all that they could to promote the comfort of the sisters, during that sad sojourn in Winchester, both by their society, and by supplying those little conveniences in which a lodging-house was likely to be deficient. It was shortly after settling in these lodgings that she wrote to a nephew the following characteristic letter, no longer, alas! in her former strong, clear hand.

Mrs David's, College St, Winton, Tuesday, May 27th.
There is no better way, my dearest E., of thanking you for your affectionate concern for me during my illness than by telling you myself, as soon as possible, that I continue to get better. I will not boast of my handwriting; neither that nor my face have yet recovered their proper beauty, but in other respects I gain strength very fast. I am now out of bed from 9 in the morning to 10 at night: upon the sofa, it is true, but I eat my meals with aunt Cassandra in a rational way, and can employ myself, and walk from one room to another. Mr Lyford says he will cure me, and if he fails, I shall draw up a memorial and lay it before the Dean and Chapter, and have no doubt of redress from that pious, learned, and disinterested body. Our lodgings are very comfortable. We have a neat little drawing-room with a bow window overlooking Dr Gabell's garden.* Thanks to the kindness of your father and

* It was the corner house in College Street, at the entrance to Commoners.

mother in sending me their carriage, my journey hither on Saturday was performed with very little fatigue, and had it been a fine day, I think I should have felt none; but it distressed me to see uncle Henry and Wm Knight, who kindly attended us on horseback, riding in the rain almost the whole way. We expect a visit from them to-morrow, and hope they will stay the night; and on Thursday, which is a confirmation and a holiday, we are to get Charles out to breakfast. We have had but one visit from *him*, poor fellow, as he is in sick-room, but he hopes to be out to-night. We see Mrs Heathcote every day, and William is to call upon us soon. God bless you, my dear E. If ever you are ill, may you be as tenderly nursed as I have been. May the same blessed alleviations of anxious, sympathising friends be yours: and may you possess, as I dare say you will, the greatest blessing of all in the consciousness of not being unworthy of their love. *I* could not feel this.

Your very affecte Aunt,

J. A.

The following extract from a letter which has been before printed, written soon after the former, breathes the same spirit of humility and thankfulness:

I will only say further that my dearest sister, my tender, watchful, indefatigable nurse, has not been made ill by her exertions. As to what I owe her, and the anxious affection of all my beloved family on this occasion, I can only cry over it, and pray God to bless them more and more.

Throughout her illness she was nursed by her sister, often assisted by her sister-in-law, my mother. Both were with her when she died. Two of her brothers, who were clergymen, lived near enough to Winchester to be in frequent attendance, and to administer the services suitable for a Christian's deathbed. While she used the language of hope to her correspondents, she was fully aware of her danger, though not appalled by it. It is true that there was much to attach her to life. She was happy in her family; she was just beginning to feel confidence in her own success; and, no doubt, the exercise of her great talents was an enjoyment in itself. We may well believe that she would gladly have lived longer; but she was enabled without dismay or complaint to prepare for death. She was a humble, believing Christian. Her life had been passed in the performance of home duties, and the cultivation of domestic affections, without any self-seeking or craving after applause. She had always sought, as it were by instinct, to promote the happiness of all who came within her influence, and doubtless she had her reward in the peace of mind which was granted her in her last days. Her sweetness of temper never failed. She was ever considerate and grateful to those who attended on her. At times, when she felt rather better, her playfulness of spirit revived, and she amused them even in their sadness. Once, when she thought herself near her end, she said what she imagined might be her last words to those around her, and particularly thanked her sister-in-law for being with her, saying: 'You have always been a kind sister to me, Mary.' When the end at last came, she sank rapidly, and on being asked by her attendants whether there was anything that she wanted, her reply was, '*Nothing but death*'. These were her last words. In quietness and peace she breathed her last on the morning of July 18, 1817.

On the 24th of that month she was buried in Winchester Cathedral, near the centre of the north aisle, almost opposite to the beautiful chantry tomb of William of Wykeham. A large slab of black marble in the pavement marks the place. Her own family only attended the funeral. Her sister returned to her desolated home, there to devote herself, for ten years, to the care of her aged mother; and to live much on the memory of her lost sister, till called many years later to rejoin her. Her brothers went back sorrowing to their several homes. They were very fond and very proud of her. They were attached to her by her talents, her virtues, and her engaging manners; and each loved afterwards to fancy a resemblance in some niece or daughter of his own to the dear sister Jane, whose perfect equal they yet never expected to see.

12

The Cancelled Chapter (Chap. 10) of Persuasion

With all this knowledge of Mr Elliot and this authority to impart it, Anne left Westgate Buildings, her mind deeply busy in revolving what she had heard, feeling, thinking, recalling, and foreseeing everything, shocked at Mr Elliot, sighing over future Kellynch, and pained for Lady Russell, whose confidence in him had been entire. The embarrassment which must be felt from this hour in his presence! How to behave to him? How to get rid of him? What to do by any of the party at home? Where to be blind? Where to be active? It was altogether a confusion of images and doubts – a perplexity, an agitation which she could not see the end of. And she was in Gay Street, and still so much engrossed that she started on being addressed by Admiral Croft, as if he were a person unlikely to be met there. It was within a few steps of his own door.

'You are going to call upon my wife,' said he. 'She will be very glad to see you.'

Anne denied it.

'No! she really had not time, she was in her way home'; but while she spoke the Admiral had stepped back and knocked at the door, calling out,

'Yes, yes; do go in; she is all alone; go in and rest yourself.'

Anne felt so little disposed at this time to be in company of any sort, that it vexed her to be thus constrained, but she was obliged to stop.

'Since you are so very kind,' said she, 'I will just ask Mrs Croft how she does, but I really cannot stay five minutes. You are sure she is quite alone?'

The possibility of Captain Wentworth had occurred; and most fearfully anxious was she to be assured – either that he was within, or that he was not – *which* might have been a question.

'Oh yes! quite alone, nobody but her mantua-maker with her, and they have been shut up together this half-hour, so it must be over soon.'

'Her mantua-maker! Then I am sure my calling now would be

most inconvenient. Indeed you must allow me to leave my card and be so good as to explain it afterwards to Mrs Croft.'

'No, no, not at all – not at all – she will be very happy to see you. Mind, I will not swear that she has not something particular to say to you, but that will all come out in the right place. I give no hints. Why, Miss Elliot, we begin to hear strange things of you (smiling in her face). But you have not much the look of it, as grave as a little judge!'

Anne blushed.

'Aye, aye, that will do now, it is all right. I thought we were not mistaken.'

She was left to guess at the direction of his suspicions; the first wild idea had been of some disclosure from his brother-in-law, but she was ashamed the next moment, and felt how far more probable it was that he should be meaning Mr Elliot. The door was opened, and the man evidently beginning to *deny* his mistress, when the sight of his master stopped him. The Admiral enjoyed the joke exceedingly. Anne thought his triumph over Stephen rather too long. At last, however, he was able to invite her up stairs, and stepping before her said, 'I will just go up with you myself and show you in. I cannot stay, because I must go to the Post-Office, but if you will only sit down for five minutes I am sure Sophy will come, and you will find nobody to disturb you – there is nobody but Frederick here,' opening the door as he spoke. Such a person to be passed over as nobody to *her*! After being allowed to feel quite secure, indifferent, at her ease, to have it burst on her that she was to be the next moment in the same room with him! No time for recollection! for planning behaviour or regulating manners! There was time only to turn pale before she had passed through the door, and met the astonished eyes of Captain Wentworth, who was sitting by the fire, pretending to read, and prepared for no greater surprise than the Admiral's hasty return.

Equally unexpected was the meeting on each side. There was nothing to be done, however, but to stifle feelings, and to be quietly polite, and the Admiral was too much on the alert to leave any troublesome pause. He repeated again what he had said before about his wife and everybody, insisted on Anne's sitting down and being perfectly comfortable – was sorry he must leave her himself, but was sure Mrs Croft would be down very soon, and would go upstairs and give her notice directly. Anne *was* sitting down, but now she arose, again to entreat him not to interrupt Mrs Croft and re-urge the wish of going away and calling another time. But the Admiral would not hear of it; and if she did not return to the charge with unconquerable perseverance, or did not with a more passive determination walk quietly out of the room (as certainly she might have done), may she not be pardoned? If she *had* no horror of a few minutes' tête-à-tête with Captain Wentworth, may she not be pardoned for not wishing to give him the idea that she had? She reseated herself, and the Admiral took leave, but on reaching the door, said, 'Frederick, a word with *you* if you please.'

Captain Wentworth went to him, and instantly, before they were well out of the room, the Admiral continued, 'As I am going to leave you together, it is but fair I should give you something to talk of; and so, if you please – '

Here the door was very firmly closed – she could guess by which of the two – and she lost entirely what immediately followed, but it was impossible for her not to distinguish parts of the rest, for the Admiral, on the strength of the door's being shut, was speaking without any management of voice, though she could hear his companion trying to check him. She could not doubt their being speaking of her. She heard her own name and Kellynch repeatedly. She was very much disturbed. She knew not what to do, or what to expect, and among other agonies felt the possibility of Captain Wentworth's not returning into the room at all, which, after her consenting to stay, would have been – too bad for language. They seemed to be talking of the Admiral's lease of Kellynch. She heard him say something of the lease being signed – or not signed – *that* was not likely to be a very agitating subject, but then followed – 'I hate to be at an uncertainty. I must know at once. Sophy thinks the same.'

Then in a lower tone Captain Wentworth seemed remonstrating, wanting to be excused, wanting to put something off.

'Phoo, phoo,' answered the Admiral, 'now is the time; if you will not speak, I will stop and speak myself.'

'Very well, sir, very well, sir,' followed with some impatience from his companion, opening the door as he spoke.

'You will then, you promise you will?' replied the Admiral in all the power of his natural voice, unbroken even by one thin door.

'Yes, sir, yes.' And the Admiral was hastily left, the door was closed, and the moment arrived in which Anne was alone with Captain Wentworth.

She could not attempt to see how he looked, but he walked immediately to a window as if irresolute and embarrassed, and for about the space of five seconds she repented what she had done – censured it as unwise, blushed over it as indelicate. She longed to be able to speak of the weather or the concert, but could only compass the relief of taking a newspaper in her hand.

The distressing pause was over, however; he turned round in half a minute, and coming towards the table where she sat, said in a voice of effort and constraint, 'You must have heard too much already, Madam, to be in any doubt of my having promised Admiral Croft to speak to you on a particular subject, and this conviction determines me to do so, however repugnant to my – to all my sense of propriety to be taking so great a liberty! You will acquit me of impertinence I trust, by considering me as speaking only for another, and speaking by necessity; and the Admiral is a man who can never be thought impertinent by one who knows him as you do. His intentions are always the kindest and the best, and you will perceive he is actuated by none other in the application which I am now, with – with very peculiar feelings – obliged to make.' He stopped, but merely to recover breath, not seeming to expect any answer. Anne listened as if her life depended on the issue of his speech.

He proceeded with a forced alacrity: 'The Admiral, Madam, was this morning confidently informed that you were – upon my soul, I am quite at a loss, ashamed (breathing and speaking quickly) – the awkwardness of *giving* information of this kind to one of the parties – you can be at no loss to understand me. It was very confidently said that Mr Elliot – that everything was settled in the family for a union between Mr Elliot and yourself. It was added that you were to live at Kellynch – that Kellynch was to be given up. This the Admiral knew could not be correct. But it occurred to him that it might be the *wish* of the parties. And my commission from him, Madam, is to say, that if the family wish is such, his lease of Kellynch shall be cancelled, and he and my sister will provide themselves with another home, without imagining themselves to be doing anything which under similar circumstances would not be done for *them*. This is all, Madam. A very few words in reply from you will be sufficient. That *I* should be the person commissioned on this subject is extraordinary! and believe me, Madam, it is no less painful. A very few words, however, will put an end to the awkwardness and distress we may *both* be feeling.'

Anne spoke a word or two, but they were unintelligible; and before she could command herself, he added, 'If you will only tell me that the Admiral may address a line to Sir Walter, it will be enough. Pronounce only the words, *he may*, and I shall immediately follow him with your message.'

'No, Sir,' said Anne; 'there is no message. You are misin – the Admiral is misinformed. I do justice to the kindness of his intentions, but he is quite mistaken. There is no truth in any such report.'

He was a moment silent. She turned her eyes towards him for the first time since his re-entering the room. His colour was varying, and he was looking at her with all the power and keenness which she believed no other eyes than his possessed.

'No truth in any such report?' he repeated. 'No truth in any *part* of it?'

'None.'

He had been standing by a chair, enjoying the relief of leaning on it, or of playing with it. He now sat down, drew it a little nearer to her, and looked with an expression which had something more than penetration in it – something softer. Her countenance did not discourage. It was a silent but a very powerful dialogue; on his supplication, on hers acceptance. Still a little nearer, and a hand taken and pressed; and 'Anne, my own dear Anne!' bursting forth in all the fulness of exquisite feeling, – and all suspense and indecision were over. They were re-united. They were restored to all that had been lost. They were carried back to the past with only an increase of attachment and confidence, and only such a flutter of present delight as made them little fit for the interruption of Mrs Croft when she joined them not long afterwards. *She*, probably, in the observations of the next ten minutes saw something to suspect; and though it was hardly possible for a woman of her description to wish the mantua-maker had imprisoned her longer, she might be very likely wishing for some excuse to run about the house, some storm to break the windows above, or a summons to the Admiral's shoemaker below. Fortune favoured them all, however, in another way, in a gentle, steady rain, just happily set in as the Admiral returned and Anne rose to go. She was earnestly invited to stay dinner. A note was despatched to Camden Place, and she staid – staid till ten at night; and during that time the husband and wife, either by the wife's contrivance, or by simply going on in their usual way, were frequently out of the room together – gone upstairs to hear a noise, or downstairs to settle their accounts, or upon the landing to trim the lamp. And these precious moments were turned to so good an account that all the most anxious feelings of the past were gone through. Before they parted at night, Anne had the felicity of being assured that in the first place (so far from being altered for the worse), she had gained inexpressibly in personal loveliness; and that as to character, hers was now fixed on his mind as *perfection* itself, maintaining the just medium of fortitude and gentleness – that he had never ceased to love and prefer her, though it had been only at Uppercross that he had learnt to do her justice, and only at Lyme that he had begun to understand his own feelings; that at Lyme he had received lessons of more than one kind – the passing admiration of Mr Elliot had at least *roused* him, and the scene on the Cobb, and at Captain Harville's, had fixed her superiority. In his preceding attempts to attach himself to Louisa Musgrove (the attempts of anger and pique), he protested that he had continually felt the impossibility of really caring for Louisa, though till *that day*, till the leisure for reflection which followed it, he had not understood the perfect excellence of the mind with which Louisa's could so ill bear comparison; or the perfect, the unrivalled hold it possessed over his own. There he had learnt to distinguish between the steadiness of principle and the obstinacy of self-will, between the darings of heedlessness and the resolution of a collected mind; there he had seen everything to exalt in his estimation the woman he had lost, and there had begun to deplore the pride, the folly, the madness of resentment, which had kept him from trying to regain her when thrown in his way. From that period to the present had his penance been the most severe. He had no sooner been free from the horror and remorse attending the first few days of Louisa's accident, no sooner had begun to feel himself alive again, than he had begun to feel himself, though alive, not at liberty.

He found that he was considered by his friend Harville an engaged man. The Harvilles entertained not a doubt of a mutual attachment between him and Louisa; and though this to a degree was contradicted instantly, it yet made him feel that perhaps by *her* family, by everybody, by *herself* even, the same idea might be held, and that he was not *free* in honour, though if such were to be the conclusion, too free alas! in heart. He had never thought justly on this subject before, and he had not sufficiently considered that his excessive intimacy at Uppercross must have its danger of ill consequence in many ways; and that while trying whether he could attach himself to either of the girls, he might be exciting unpleasant reports if not raising unrequited regard.

He found too late that he had entangled himself, and that precisely as he became thoroughly satisfied of his not *caring* for Louisa at all, he must regard himself as bound to her if her feelings for him were what the Harvilles supposed. It determined him to leave Lyme, and await her perfect recovery elsewhere. He would gladly weaken by any *fair* means whatever sentiment or speculations concerning them might exist; and he went therefore into Shropshire, meaning after a while to return to the Crofts at Kellynch, and act as he found requisite.

He had remained in Shropshire, lamenting the blindness of his own pride and the blunders of his own calculations, till at once released from Louisa by the astonishing felicity of her engagement with Benwick.

Bath – Bath had instantly followed in *thought*, and not long after in *fact*. To Bath – to arrive with hope, to be torn by jealousy at the first sight of Mr Elliot; to experience all the changes of each at the concert; to be miserable by the morning's circumstantial report, to be now more happy than language could express, or any heart but his own be capable of.

He was very eager and very delightful in the description of what he had felt at the concert; the evening seemed to have been made up of exquisite moments. The moment of her stepping forward in the octagon room to speak to him, the moment of Mr Elliot's appearing and tearing her away, and one or two subsequent moments, marked by returning hope or increasing despondency, were dwelt on with energy.

'To see you,' cried he, 'in the midst of those who could not be my well-wishers; to see your cousin close by you, conversing and smiling, and feel all the horrible eligibilities and proprieties of the match! To consider it as the certain wish of every being who could hope to influence you! Even if your own feelings were reluctant or indifferent, to consider what powerful support would be his! Was it not enough to make the fool of me which I appeared? How could I look on without agony? Was not the very sight of the friend who sat behind you; was not the recollection of what had been, the knowledge of her influence, the indelible, immovable impression of what persuasion had once done – was it not all against me?'

'You should have distinguished,' replied Anne. 'You should not have suspected me now; the case so different, and my age so different. If I was wrong in yielding to persuasion once, remember it was to persuasion exerted on the side of safety, not of risk. When I yielded, I thought it was to duty; but no duty could be called in aid here. In marrying a man indifferent to me, all risk would have been incurred, and all duty violated.'

'Perhaps I ought to have reasoned thus,' he replied; 'but I could not. I could not derive benefit from the late knowledge I had acquired of your character. I could not bring it into play; it was overwhelmed, buried, lost in those earlier feelings which I had been smarting under year after year. I could think of you only as one who had yielded, who had given me up, who had been influenced by anyone rather than by me. I saw you with the very person who had guided you in that year of misery. I had no reason to believe her of less authority now. The force of habit was to be added.'

'I should have thought,' said Anne, 'that my manner to yourself might have spared you much or all of this.'

'No, no! Your manner might be only the ease which your engagement to another man would give. I left you in this belief; and yet – I was determined to see you again. My spirits rallied with the morning, and I felt that I had still a motive for remaining here. The Admiral's news, indeed, was a revulsion; since that moment I have been divided what to do, and had it been confirmed, this would have been my last day in Bath.'

There was time for all this to pass, with such interruptions only as enhanced the charm of the communication, and Bath could hardly contain any other two beings at once so rationally and so rapturously happy as during that evening occupied the sofa of Mrs Croft's drawing-room in Gay Street.

Captain Wentworth had taken care to meet the Admiral as he returned into the house, to satisfy him as to Mr Elliot and Kellynch; and the delicacy of the Admiral's good-nature kept him from saying another word on the subject to Anne. He was quite concerned lest he might have been giving her pain by touching on a tender part – who could say? She might be liking her cousin better than he liked her; and, upon recollection, if they had been to marry at all, why should they have waited so long? When the evening closed, it is probable that the Admiral received some new ideas from his wife, whose particularly friendly manner in parting with her gave Anne the gratifying persuasion of her seeing and approving. It had been such a day to Anne; the hours which had passed since her leaving Camden Place had done so much! She was almost bewildered – almost too happy in looking back. It was necessary to sit up half the night, and lie awake the remainder, to comprehend with composure her present state, and pay for the overplus of bliss by headache and fatigue.

* * *

Then follows Chapter 11, *i.e.* 12 in the published book and at the end is written – '*Finis, July* 18, 1816.'

13

The Last Work

Jane Austen was taken from us: how much unexhausted talent perished with her, how largely she might yet have contributed to the entertainment of her readers, if her life had been prolonged, cannot be known; but it is certain that the mine at which she had so long laboured was not worked out, and that she was still diligently employed in collecting fresh materials from it. *Persuasion* had been finished in August 1816; some time was probably given to correcting it for the press; but on the 27th of the following January, according to the date on her own manuscript, she began a new novel, and worked at it up to the 17th of March. The chief part of this manuscript is written in her usual firm and neat hand, but some of the latter pages seem to have been first traced in pencil, probably when she was too weak to sit long at her desk, and written over in ink afterwards. The quantity produced does not indicate any decline of power or industry, for in those seven weeks twelve chapters had been completed. It is more difficult to judge of the quality of a work so little advanced. It had received no name; there was scarcely any indication what the course of the story was to be, nor was any heroine yet perceptible, who, like Fanny Price, or Anne Elliot, might draw round her the sympathies of the reader. Such an unfinished fragment cannot be presented to the public; but I am persuaded that some of Jane Austen's admirers will be glad to learn something about the latest creations which were forming themselves in her mind; and therefore, as some of the principal characters were already sketched in with a vigorous hand, I will try to give an idea of them, illustrated by extracts from the work.

The scene is laid at Sanditon, a village on the Sussex coast, just struggling into notoriety as a bathing-place, under the patronage of the two principal proprietors of the parish, Mr Parker and Lady Denham.

Mr Parker was an amiable man, with more enthusiasm than judgment, whose somewhat shallow mind overflowed with the one

idea of the prosperity of Sanditon, together with a jealous contempt
of the rival village of Brinshore, where a similar attempt was going
on. To the regret of his much-enduring wife, he had left his family
mansion, with all its ancestral comforts of gardens, shrubberies, and
shelter, situated in a valley some miles inland, and had built a new
residence – a Trafalgar House – on the bare brow of the hill
overlooking Sanditon and the sea, exposed to every wind that blows;
but he will confess to no discomforts, nor suffer his family to feel
any from the change. The following extract brings him before the
reader, mounted on his hobby:

> He wanted to secure the promise of a visit, and to get as many of
> the family as his own house would hold to follow him to Sanditon
> as soon as possible; and, healthy as all the Heywoods undeniably
> were, he foresaw that every one of them would be benefitted by
> the sea. He held it indeed as certain that no person, however
> upheld for the present by fortuitous aids of exercise and spirit in a
> semblance of health, could be really in a state of secure and
> permanent health without spending at least six weeks by the sea
> every year. The sea air and sea-bathing together were nearly
> infallible; one or other of them being a match for every disorder of
> the stomach, the lungs, or the blood. They were anti-spasmodic,
> anti-pulmonary, anti-bilious, and anti-rheumatic. Nobody could
> catch cold by the sea; nobody wanted appetite by the sea; nobody
> wanted spirits; nobody wanted strength. They were healing,
> softening, relaxing, fortifying, and bracing, seemingly just as was
> wanted; sometimes one, sometimes the other. If the sea breeze
> failed, the sea bath was the certain corrective; and when bathing
> disagreed, the sea breeze was evidently designed by nature for the
> cure. His eloquence, however, could not prevail. Mr and Mrs
> Heywood never left home . . . The maintenance, education, and
> fitting out of fourteen children demanded a very quiet, settled,
> careful course of life; and obliged them to be stationary and
> healthy at Willingden. What prudence had at first enjoined was
> now rendered pleasant by habit. They never left home, and they
> had a gratification in saying so.

Lady Denham's was a very different character. She was a rich
vulgar widow, with a sharp but narrow mind, who cared for the
prosperity of Sanditon only so far as it might increase the value of

her own property. She is thus described:

Lady Denham had been a rich Miss Brereton, born to wealth, but not to education. Her first husband had been a Mr Hollis, a man of considerable property in the country, of which a large share of the parish of Sanditon, with manor and mansion-house, formed a part. He had been an elderly man when she married him; her own age about thirty. Her motives for such a match could be little understood at the distance of forty years, but she had so well nursed and pleased Mr Hollis that at his death he left her everything – all his estates, and all at her disposal. After a widowhood of some years she had been induced to marry again. The late Sir Harry Denham, of Denham Park, in the neighbourhood of Sanditon, succeeded in removing her and her large income to his own domains; but he could not succeed in the views of permanently enriching his family which were attributed to him. She had been too wary to put anything out of her own power, and when, on Sir Harry's death, she returned again to her own house at Sanditon, she was said to have made this boast, 'that though she had *got* nothing but her title from the family, yet she had *given* nothing for it'. For the title it was to be supposed that she married.

Lady Denham was indeed a great lady, beyond the common wants of society; for she had many thousands a year to bequeath, and three distinct sets of people to be courted by: her own relations, who might very reasonably wish for her original thirty thousand pounds among them; the legal heirs of Mr Hollis, who might hope to be more indebted to *her* sense of justice than he had allowed them to be to *his*; and those members of the Denham family for whom her second husband had hoped to make a good bargain. By all these, or by branches of them, she had, no doubt, been long and still continued to be well attacked; and of these three divisions Mr Parker did not hesitate to say that Mr Hollis's kindred were the least in favour, and Sir Harry Denham's the most. The former, he believed, had done themselves irremediable harm by expressions of very unwise resentment at the time of Mr Hollis's death: the latter, to the advantage of being the remnant of a connection which she certainly valued, joined those of having been known to her from their childhood, and of being always at hand to pursue their interests by seasonable attentions. But another claimant was now to be taken into account: a young female relation whom Lady Denham had been induced to receive into her family. After having always protested against any such addition, and often enjoyed the repeated defeat she had given to every attempt of her own relations to introduce 'this young lady, or that young lady', as a companion at Sanditon House, she had brought back with her from London last Michaelmas a Miss Clara Brereton, who bid fair to vie in favour with Sir Edward Denham, and to secure for herself and her family that share of the accumulated property which they had certainly the best right to inherit.

Lady Denham's character comes out in a conversation which takes place at Mr Parker's tea-table.

The conversation turned entirely upon Sanditon, its present number of visitants, and the chances of a good season. It was evident that Lady Denham had more anxiety, more fears of loss than her co-adjutor. She wanted to have the place fill faster, and seemed to have many harassing apprehensions of the lodgings being in some instances underlet. To a report that a large boarding-school was expected she replies, 'Ah, well, no harm in that. They will stay their six weeks, and out of such a number who knows but some may be consumptive, and want asses' milk; and I have two milch asses at this very time. But perhaps the little Misses may hurt the furniture. I hope they will have a good sharp governess to look after them.' But she wholly disapproved of Mr Parker's wish to secure the residence of a medical man amongst them. 'Why, what should we do with a doctor here? It would only be encouraging our servants and the poor to fancy themselves ill, if there was a doctor at hand. Oh, pray let us have none of that tribe at Sanditon: we go on very well as we are. There is the sea, and the downs, and my milch asses: and I have told Mrs Whitby that if anybody enquires for a chamber horse, they may be supplied at a fair rate (poor Mr Hollis's chamber horse, as good as new); and what can people want more? I have lived seventy good years in the world, and never took physic, except twice: and never saw the face of a doctor in all my life on my own account; and I really believe if my poor dear Sir Harry had never seen one neither, he would have been alive now. Ten fees, one after another, did the men take who sent him out of the world. I beseech you, Mr Parker, no doctors here.'

This lady's character comes out more strongly in a conversation with Mr Parker's guest, Miss Charlotte Heywood. Sir Edward Denham with his sister Esther and Clara Brercton have just left them.

Charlotte accepted an invitation from Lady Denham to remain with her on the terrace, when the others adjourned to the library. Lady Denham, like a true great lady, talked, and talked only of her own concerns, and Charlotte listened. Taking hold of Charlotte's arm with the ease of one who felt that any notice from her was a favour, and communicative from the same sense of importance, or from a natural love of talking, she immediately said in a tone of great satisfaction, and with a look of arch sagacity: 'Miss Esther wants me to invite her and her brother to spend a week with me at Sanditon House, as I did last summer, but I shan't. She has been trying to get round me every way with her praise of this and her praise of that; but I saw what she was about. I saw through it all. I am not very easily taken in, my dear.'

Charlotte could think of nothing more harmless to be said than the simple enquiry of, 'Sir Edward and Miss Denham?'

'Yes, my dear; *my young folks*, as I call them, sometimes: for I take them very much by the hand, and had them with me last summer, about this time, for a week – from Monday to Monday – and very delighted and thankful they were. For they are very good young people, my dear. I would not have you think that I only notice them for poor dear Sir Harry's sake. No, no; they are very deserving themselves, or, trust me, they would not be so much in my company. I am not the woman to help anybody blindfold. I always take care to know what I am about, and who I have to deal with before I stir a finger. I do not think I was ever overreached in my life; and that is a good deal for a woman to say that has been twice married. Poor dear Sir Harry (between ourselves) thought at first to have got more, but (with a bit of a sigh) he is gone, and we must not find fault with the dead. Nobody could live happier together than us: and he was a very honourable man, quite the gentleman, of ancient family; and when he died I gave Sir Edward his gold watch.'

This was said with a look at her companion which implied its right to produce a great impression; and seeing no rapturous astonishment in Charlotte's countenance, she added quickly, 'He did not bequeath it to his nephew, my dear; it was no bequest; it was not in the will. He only told me, and *that* but *once*, that he should wish his nephew to have his watch; but it need not have been binding, if I had not chose it.'

'Very kind indeed, very handsome!' said Charlotte, absolutely forced to affect admiration.

'Yes, my dear; and it is not the only kind thing I have done by him. I have been a very liberal friend to Sir Edward; and, poor young man, he needs it bad enough. For, though I am only the dowager, my dear, and he is the heir, things do not stand between us in the way they usually do between those two parties. Not a shilling do I receive from the Denham estate. Sir Edward has no payments to make *me*. *He* don't stand uppermost, believe me; it is *I* that help *him*.'

'Indeed! he is a very fine young man, and particularly elegant in his address.'

This was said chiefly for the sake of saying something; but Charlotte directly saw that it was laying her open to suspicion, by Lady Denham's giving a shrewd glance at her, and replying, 'Yes, yes; he's very well to look at; and it is to be hoped that somebody of large fortune will think so; for Sir Edward *must* marry for money. He and I often talk that matter over. A handsome young man like him will go smirking and smiling about, and paying girls compliments, but he knows he *must* marry for money. And Sir Edward is a very steady young man, in the main, and has got very good notions.'

'Sir Edward Denham,' said Charlotte, 'with such personal advantages, may be almost sure of getting a woman of fortune, if he chooses it.'

This glorious sentiment seemed quite to remove suspicion.

'Aye, my dear, that is very sensibly said; and if we could but get a young heiress to Sanditon! But heiresses are monstrous scarce! I do not think we have had an heiress here, nor even a *Co.*, since Sanditon has been a public place. Families come after families, but, as far as I can learn, it is not one in a hundred of them that have any real property, landed or funded. An income, perhaps, but no property. Clergymen, may be, or lawyers from town, or half-pay officers, or widows with only a jointure; and what good can such people do to anybody? Except just as they take our empty houses, and (between ourselves) I think they are great fools for not staying at home. Now, if we could get a young heiress to be sent here for her health, and, as soon as she got well, have her fall in love with Sir Edward! And Miss Esther must marry somebody of fortune, too. She must get a rich husband. Ah! young ladies that have no money are very much to be pitied.' After a short pause: 'If Miss Esther thinks to talk me into inviting them to come and stay at Sanditon House, she will find herself mistaken. Matters are altered with me since last summer, you know: I have Miss Clara with me now, which makes a great difference. I should not choose to have my two housemaids' time taken up all the morning in dusting out bedrooms. They have Miss Clara's room to put to rights, as well as mine, every day. If they had hard work, they would want higher wages.'

Charlotte's feelings were divided between amusement and indignation. She kept her countenance, and kept a civil silence; but without attempting to listen any longer, and only conscious that Lady Denham was still talking in the same way, allowed her own thoughts to form themselves into such meditation as this: 'She is thoroughly mean; I had no expectation of anything so bad. Mr Parker spoke too mildly of her. He is too kind-hearted to see clearly, and their very connection misleads him. He has persuaded her to engage in the same speculation, and because they have so far the same object in view, he fancies that she feels like him in other things; but she is very, very mean. I can see no good in her. Poor Miss Brereton! And it makes everybody mean about her. This poor Sir Edward and his sister! how far nature meant them to be respectable I cannot tell; but they are obliged to be mean in their servility to her; and I am mean, too, in giving her my attention with the appearance of coinciding with her. Thus it is when rich people are sordid.'

Mr Parker has two unmarried sisters of singular character. They live together; Diana, the younger, always takes the lead, and the elder follows in the same track. It is their pleasure to fancy themselves invalids to a degree and in a manner never experienced by others; but, from a state of exquisite pain and utter prostration, Diana Parker can always rise to be officious in the concerns of all her acquaintance, and to make incredible exertions where they are not wanted.

It would seem that they must be always either very busy for the good of others, or else extremely ill themselves. Some natural delicacy of constitution, in fact, with an unfortunate turn for medicine, especially quack medicine, had given them an early tendency at various times to various disorders. The rest of their suffering was from their own fancy, the love of distinction, and the love of the wonderful. They had charitable hearts and many amiable feelings; but a spirit of restless activity, and the glory of doing more than anybody else, had a share in every exertion of benevolence, and there was vanity in all they did, as well as in all they endured.

These peculiarities come out in the following letter of Diana Parker to her brother:

MY DEAR TOM – We were much grieved at your accident, and if you had not described yourself as having fallen into such very good hands, I should have been with you at all hazards the day after receipt of your letter, though it found me suffering under a more severe attack than usual of my old grievance, spasmodic bile, and hardly able to crawl from my bed to the sofa. But how were you treated? Send me more particulars in your next. If indeed a simple sprain, as you denominate it, nothing would have been so judicious as friction – friction by the hand alone, supposing it could be applied *immediately*. Two years ago I happened to be calling on Mrs Sheldon, when her coachman sprained his foot, as he was cleaning the carriage, and could hardly limp into the house; but by the immediate use of friction alone, steadily persevered in (I rubbed his ancle with my own hands for four hours without intermission), he was well in three days . . . Pray never run into peril again in looking for an apothecary on our account; for had you the most experienced man in his line settled at Sanditon, it would be no recommendation to us. We have entirely done with the whole medical tribe. We have consulted physician after physician in vain, till we are quite convinced that they can do nothing for us, and that we must trust to our knowledge of our own wretched constitutions for any relief; but if you think it advisable for the interests of the *place* to get a medical man there, I will undertake the commission with pleasure, and have no doubt of succeeding. I could soon put the necessary irons in the fire. As for getting to Sanditon myself, it is an impossibility. I grieve to say that I cannot attempt it, but my feelings tell me too plainly that in my present state the sea-air would probably be the death of me; and in truth I doubt whether Susan's nerves would be equal to the effort. She has been suffering much from headache, and six leeches a day, for ten days together, relieved her so little that we thought it right to change our measures; and being convinced on examination that much of the evil lay in her gums, I persuaded her to attack the disorder there. She has accordingly had three teeth drawn, and is decidedly better; but her nerves are a good deal deranged, she can only speak in a whisper, and fainted away this morning on poor Arthur's trying to suppress a cough.

Within a week of the date of this letter, in spite of the impossibility of moving, and of the fatal effects to be apprehended from the sea-air, Diana Parker was at Sanditon with her sister. She had flattered herself that by her own indefatigable exertions, and by setting at work the agency of many friends, she had induced two large families to take houses at Sanditon. It was to expedite these politic views that she came; and though she met with some disappointment of her expectation, yet she did not suffer in health.

Such were some of the *dramatis personae*, ready dressed and prepared for their parts. They are at least original and unlike any that the author had produced before. The success of the piece must have depended on the skill with which these parts might be played; but few will be inclined to distrust the skill of one who had so often succeeded. If the author had lived to complete her work, it is probable that these personages might have grown into as mature an individuality of character, and have taken as permanent a place amongst our familiar acquaintance, as Mr Bennet, or John Thorp, Mary Musgrove, or Aunt Norris herself.

14

Postscript

When first I was asked to put together a memoir of my aunt, I saw reasons for declining the attempt. It was not only that, having passed the three score years and ten usually allotted to man's strength, and being unaccustomed to write for publication, I might well distrust my ability to complete the work, but that I also knew the extreme scantiness of the materials out of which it must be constructed. The grave closed over my aunt fifty-two years ago; and during that long period no idea of writing her life had been entertained by any of her family. Her nearest relatives, far from making provision for such a purpose, had actually destroyed many of the letters and papers by which it might have been facilitated. They were influenced, I believe, partly by an extreme dislike to publishing private details, and partly by never having assumed that the world would take so strong and abiding an interest in her works as to claim her name as public property. It was therefore necessary for me to draw upon recollections rather than on written documents for my materials; while the subject itself supplied me with nothing striking or prominent with which to arrest the attention of the reader. It has been said that the happiest individuals, like nations during their happiest periods, have no history. In the case of my aunt, it was not only that her course of life was unvaried, but that her own disposition was remarkably calm and even. There was in her nothing eccentric or angular; no ruggedness of temper; no singularity of manner; none of the morbid sensibility or exaggeration of feeling, which not unfrequently accompanies great talents, to be worked up into a picture. Hers was a mind well balanced on a basis of good sense, sweetened by an affectionate heart, and regulated by fixed principles; so that she was to be distinguished from many other amiable and sensible women only by that peculiar genius which shines out clearly enough in her works, but of which a biographer can make little use. The motive which at last induced me to make the attempt is exactly expressed in the passage prefixed to these pages. I thought that I saw something to be done: knew of no one who could do it but myself, and so was driven to the enterprise. I am glad that I have been able to finish my work. As a family record it can scarcely fail to be interesting to those relatives who must ever set a high value on their connection with Jane Austen, and to them I especially dedicate it; but as I have been asked to do so, I also submit it to the censure of the public, with all its faults both of deficiency and redundancy. I know that its value in their eyes must depend, not on any merits of its own, but on the degree of estimation in which my aunt's works may still be held; and indeed I shall esteem it one of the strongest testimonies ever borne to her talents, if for her sake an interest can be taken in so poor a sketch as I have been able to draw.

Bray Vicarage, Sept. 7, 1869.

Postscript printed at the end of the first edition; omitted from the second.
Since these pages were in type, I have read with astonishment the strange misrepresentation of my aunt's manners given by Miss Mitford in a letter which appears in her lately-published *Life*, vol. i, p. 305. Miss Mitford does not profess to have known Jane Austen herself, but to report what had been told her by her mother. Having stated that her mother '*before her marriage*' was well acquainted with Jane Austen and her family, she writes thus: 'Mamma says that she was *then* the prettiest, silliest, most affected, husband-hunting butterfly she ever remembers.' The editor of Miss Mitford's *Life* very properly observes in a note how different this description is from 'every other account of Jane Austen from whatever quarter'. Certainly it is so totally at variance with the modest simplicity of character which I have attributed to my aunt, that if it could be supposed to have a semblance of truth, it must be equally injurious to her memory and to my trustworthiness as her biographer. Fortunately I am not driven to put my authority in competition with that of Miss Mitford, nor to ask which ought to be considered the better witness in this case; because I am able to prove by a reference to dates that Miss Mitford must have been under a mistake, and that her mother could not possibly have known what she was supposed to have reported; inasmuch as Jane Austen, at the time referred to, was a little girl.

Mrs Mitford was the daughter of Dr Russell, Rector of Ashe, a parish adjoining Steventon, so that the families of Austen and

Russell must at that time have been known to each other. But the date assigned by Miss Mitford for the termination of the acquaintance is the time of her mother's marriage. This took place in October 1785, when Jane, who had been born in December 1775, was not quite ten years old. In point of fact, however, Miss Russell's opportunities of observing Jane Austen must have come to an end still earlier: for upon Dr Russell's death, in January 1783, his widow and daughter removed from the neighbourhood, so that all intercourse between the families ceased when Jane was little more than seven years old.

All persons who undertake to narrate from hearsay things which are supposed to have taken place before they were born are liable to error, and are apt to call in imagination to the aid of memory: and hence it arises that many a fancy piece has been substituted for genuine history.

I do not care to correct the inaccurate account of Jane Austen's manners in after life: because Miss Mitford candidly expresses a doubt whether she had not been misinformed on that point.

Nov. 17, 1869.

THE WATSONS

The Watsons

The first winter assembly in the town of D. in Surrey was to be held on Tuesday, October 13th and it was generally expected to be a very good one. A long list of county families was confidently run over as sure of attending, and sanguine hopes were entertained that the Osbornes themselves would be there. The Edwards' invitation to the Watsons followed, of course. The Edwards were people of fortune, who lived in the town and kept their coach. The Watsons inhabited a village about three miles distant, were poor, and had no close carriage; and ever since there had been balls in the place, the former were accustomed to invite the latter to dress, dine, and sleep at their house on every monthly return throughout the winter. On the present occasion, as only two of Mr Watson's children were at home, and one was always necessary as companion to himself, for he was sickly and had lost his wife, one only could profit by the kindness of their friends. Miss Emma Watson, who was very recently returned to her family from the care of an aunt who had brought her up, was to make her first public appearance in the neighbourhood, and her eldest sister, whose delight in a ball was not lessened by a ten years' enjoyment, had some merit in cheerfully undertaking to drive her and all her finery in the old chair to D. on the important morning.

As they splashed along the dirty lane, Miss Watson thus instructed and cautioned her inexperienced sister: 'I dare say it will be a very good ball, and among so many officers you will hardly want partners. You will find Mrs Edwards' maid very willing to help you, and I would advise you to ask Mary Edwards' opinion if you are at all at a loss, for she has very good taste. If Mr Edwards does not lose his money at cards, you will stay as late as you can wish for; if he does, he will hurry you home perhaps – but you are sure of some comfortable soup. I hope you will be in good looks. I should not be surprised if you were to be thought one of the prettiest girls in the room; there is a great deal in novelty. Perhaps Tom Musgrave may take notice of you; but I would advise you by all means not to give him any encouragement. He generally pays attention to every new girl; but he is a great flirt, and never means anything serious.'

'I think I have heard you speak of him before,' said Emma; 'who is he?'

'A young man of very good fortune, quite independent, and remarkably agreeable – a universal favourite wherever he goes. Most of the girls hereabouts are in love with him, or have been. I believe I am the only one among them that have escaped with a whole heart; and yet I was the first he paid attention to when he came into this country six years ago; and very great attention did he pay me. Some people say that he has never seemed to like any girl so well since, though he is always behaving in a particular way to one or another.'

'And how came *your* heart to be the only cold one?' said Emma, smiling.

'There was a reason for that,' replied Miss Watson, changing colour – 'I have not been very well used among them, Emma. I hope you will have better luck.'

'Dear sister, I beg your pardon if I have unthinkingly given you pain.'

'When first we knew Tom Musgrave,' continued Miss Watson, without seeming to hear her, 'I was very much attached to a young man of the name of Purvis, a particular friend of Robert's, who used to be with us a great deal. Everybody thought it would have been a match.'

A sigh accompanied these words, which Emma respected in silence; but her sister after a short pause went on.

'You will naturally ask why it did not take place, and why he is married to another woman, while I am still single. But you must ask her, not me – you must ask Penelope. Yes, Emma, Penelope was at the bottom of it all. She thinks everything fair for a husband. I trusted her; she set him against me, with a view of gaining him herself, and it ended in his discontinuing his visits, and soon after marrying somebody else. Penelope makes light of her conduct, but *I* think such treachery very bad. It has been the ruin of my happiness. I shall never love any man as I loved Purvis. I do not think Tom Musgrave should be named with him in the same day.'

'You quite shock me by what you say of Penelope,' said Emma. 'Could a sister do such a thing? Rivalry, treachery between sisters! I shall be afraid of being acquainted with her. But I hope it was not so; appearances were against her.'

'You do not know Penelope. There is nothing she would not do to get married. She would as good as tell you so herself. Do not trust her with any secrets of your own, take warning by me, do not trust her; she has her good qualities, but she has no faith, no honour, no scruples, if she can promote her own advantage. I wish with all my heart she was well married. I declare I had rather have her well married than myself.'

'Than yourself! yes, I can suppose so. A heart wounded like yours can have little inclination for matrimony.'

'Not much indeed – but you know we must marry. I could do very well single for my own part; a little company, and a pleasant ball now and then, would be enough for me, if one could be young forever; but my father cannot provide for us, and it is very bad to grow old and be poor and laughed at. I have lost Purvis, it is true; but very few people marry their first loves. I should not refuse a man because he was not Purvis. Not that I can ever quite forgive Penelope.'

Emma shook her head in acquiescence.

'Penelope, however, has had her troubles,' continued Miss Watson. 'She was sadly disappointed in Tom Musgrave, who afterwards transferred his attentions from me to her, and whom she was very fond of; but he never means anything serious, and when he had trifled with her long enough, he began to slight her for Margaret, and poor Penelope was very wretched. And since then she has been trying to make some match at Chichester – she won't tell us with whom; but I believe it is a rich old Dr Harding, uncle to the friend she goes to see; and she has taken a vast deal of trouble about him, and given up a great deal of time to no purpose as yet. When she went away the other day, she said it should be the last time. I suppose you did not know what her particular business was at Chichester, nor guess at the object which could take her away from Stanton just as you were coming home after so many years' absence.'

'No indeed, I had not the smallest suspicion of it. I considered her engagement to Mrs Shaw just at that time as very unfortunate for me. I had hoped to find all my sisters at home, to be able to make an immediate friend of each.'

'I suspect the Doctor to have had an attack of the asthma, and that she was hurried away on that account. The Shaws are quite on her side – at least, I believe so; but she tells me nothing. She professes to keep her own counsel; she says, and truly enough, that "Too many cooks spoil the broth".'

'I am sorry for her anxieties,' said Emma; 'but I do not like her plans or her opinions. I shall be afraid of her. She must have too masculine and bold a temper. To be so bent on marriage, to pursue a man merely for the sake of situation, is a sort of thing that shocks me; I cannot understand it. Poverty is a great evil; but to a woman of education and feeling it ought not, it cannot be the greatest. I would rather be teacher at a school (and I can think of nothing worse) than marry a man I did not like.'

'I would rather do anything than be teacher at a school,' said her sister. '*I* have been at school, Emma, and know what a life they lead; *you* never have. I should not like marrying a disagreeable man any more than yourself; but I do not think there *are* many very disagreeable men; I think I could like any good-humoured man with a comfortable income. I suppose my aunt brought you up to be rather refined.'

'Indeed I do not know. My conduct must tell you how I have been brought up. I am no judge of it myself. I cannot compare my aunt's method with any other person's, because I know no other.'

'But I can see in a great many things that you are very refined. I have observed it ever since you came home, and I am afraid it will not be for your happiness. Penelope will laugh at you very much.'

'*That* will not be for my happiness, I an sure. If my opinions are wrong, I must correct them; if they are above my situation, I must endeavour to conceal them; but I doubt whether ridicule – Has Penelope much wit?'

'Yes; she has great spirits, and never cares what she says.'

'Margaret is more gentle, I imagine?'

'Yes; especially in company. She is all gentleness and mildness when anybody is by; but she is a little fretful and perverse among ourselves. Poor creature! She is possessed with the notion of Tom Musgrave's being more seriously in love with her than he ever was with anybody else, and is always expecting him to come to the point. This is the second time within this twelvemonth that she has gone to spend a month with Robert and Jane on purpose to egg him on by her absence; but I am sure she is mistaken, and that he will no more follow her to Croydon now than he did last March. He will never marry unless he can marry somebody very great – Miss Osborne, perhaps, or something in that style.'

'Your account of this Tom Musgrave, Elizabeth, gives me very little inclination for his acquaintance.'

'You are afraid of him; I do not wonder at you.'

'No, indeed; I dislike and despise him.'

'Dislike and despise Tom Musgrave! No, *that* you never can. I defy you not to be delighted with him if he takes notice of you. I hope he will dance with you; and I dare say he will, unless the Osbornes come with a large party, and then he will not speak to anybody else.'

'He seems to have most engaging manners!' said Emma. 'Well, we shall see how irresistible Mr Tom Musgrave and I find each other. I suppose I shall know him as soon as I enter the ball-room; he *must* carry some of his charm in his face.'

'You will not find him in the ball-room, I can tell you; you will go early, that Mrs Edwards may get a good place by the fire, and he never comes till late; if the Osbornes are coming, he will wait in the passage and come in with them. I should like to look in upon you, Emma. If it was but a good day with my father, I would wrap myself up, and James should drive me over as soon as I had made tea for him; and I should be with you by the time the dancing began.'

'What! Would you come late at night in this chair?'

'To be sure I would. There, I said you were very refined, and *that*'s an instance of it.'

Emma for a moment made no answer. At last she said – 'I wish, Elizabeth, you had not made a point of my going to this ball; I wish you were going instead of me. Your pleasure would be greater than mine. I am a stranger here, and know nobody but the Edwards; my enjoyment, therefore, must be very doubtful. Yours, among all your acquaintance, would be certain. It is not too late to change. Very little apology could be requisite to the Edwards, who must be more glad of your company than of mine, and I should most readily return to my father; and should not be at all afraid to drive this quiet old creature home. Your clothes I would undertake to find means of sending to you.'

'My dearest Emma,' cried Elizabeth, warmly, 'do you think I would do such a thing? Not for the universe! But I shall never forget your good-nature in proposing it. You must have a sweet temper indeed! I never met with anything like it! And would you really give up the ball that I might be able to go to it? Believe me, Emma, I am not so selfish as that comes to. No; though I am nine years older than you are, I would not be the means of keeping you from being seen. You are very pretty, and it would be very hard that you should not have as fair a chance as we have all had to make your fortune. No, Emma, whoever stays at home this winter, it sha'n't be you. I am sure I should never have forgiven the person who kept me from a ball at nineteen.'

Emma expressed her gratitude, and for a few minutes they jogged on in silence. Elizabeth first spoke: –

'You will take notice who Mary Edwards dances with?'

'I will remember her partners, if I can; but you know they will be all strangers to me.'

'Only observe whether she dances with Captain Hunter more than once – I have my fears in that quarter. Not that her father or mother like officers; but if she does, you know, it is all over with poor Sam. And I have promised to write him word who she dances with.'

'Is Sam attached to Miss Edwards?'

'Did not you know *that*?'

'How should I know it? How should I know in Shropshire what is passing of that nature in Surrey? It is not likely that circumstances of such delicacy should have made any part of the scanty communication which passed between you and me for the last fourteen years.'

'I wonder I never mentioned it when I wrote. Since you have been at home, I have been so busy with my poor father and our great wash that I have had no leisure to tell you anything; but, indeed, I concluded you knew it all. He has been very much in love with her these two years, and it is a great disappointment to him that he cannot always get away to our balls; but Mr Curtis won't often spare him, and just now it is a sickly time at Guildford.'

'Do you suppose Miss Edwards inclined to like him?'

'I am afraid not: you know she is an only child, and will have at least ten thousand pounds.'

'But still she may like our brother.'

'Oh, no! The Edwards look much higher. Her father and mother would never consent to it. Sam is only a surgeon, you know. Sometimes I think she does like him. But Mary Edwards is rather prim and reserved; I do not always know what she would be at.'

'Unless Sam feels on sure grounds with the lady herself, it seems a pity to me that he should be encouraged to think of her at all.'

'A young man must think of somebody,' said Elizabeth, 'and why should not he be as lucky as Robert, who has got a good wife and six thousand pounds?'

'We must not all expect to be individually lucky,' replied Emma. 'The luck of one member of a family is luck to all.'

'Mine is all to come, I am sure,' said Elizabeth, giving another sigh to the remembrance of Purvis. 'I have been unlucky enough; and I cannot say much for you, as my aunt married again so foolishly. Well, you will have a good ball, I daresay. The next turning will bring us to the turnpike: you may see the church-tower over the hedge, and the White Hart is close by it. I shall long to know what you think of Tom Musgrave.'

Such were the last audible sounds of Miss Watson's voice, before they passed through the turnpike-gate, and entered on the pitching of the town, the jumbling and noise of which made farther conversation most thoroughly undesirable. The old mare trotted heavily on, wanting no direction of the reins to take the right turning, and making only one blunder, in proposing to stop at the milliner's before she drew up towards Mr Edwards' door. Mr Edwards lived in the best house in the street, and the best in the place, if Mr Tomlinson, the banker, might be indulged in calling his newly erected house at the end of the town, with a shrubbery and sweep, in the country.

Mr Edwards' house was higher than most of its neighbours, with four windows on each side the door, the windows guarded by posts and chains, and the door approached by a flight of stone steps.

'Here we are,' said Elizabeth, as the carriage ceased moving, 'safely arrived, and by the market clock we have been only five-and-thirty minutes coming; which *I* think is doing pretty well, though it would be nothing for Penelope. Is not it a nice town? The Edwards have a noble house, you see, and they live quite in style. The door will be opened by a man in livery, with a powdered head, I can tell you.'

Emma had seen the Edwardses only one morning at Stanton; they were therefore all but strangers to her; and though her spirits were by no means insensible to the expected joys of the evening, she felt a little uncomfortable in the thought of all that was to precede them. Her conversation with Elizabeth, too, giving her some very unpleasant feelings with respect to her own family, had made her more open to disagreeable impressions from any other cause, and increased her sense of the awkwardness of rushing into intimacy on so slight an acquaintance.

There was nothing in the manner of Mrs or Miss Edwards to give immediate change to these ideas. The mother, though a very friendly woman, had a reserved air, and a great deal of formal civility; and the daughter, a genteel-looking girl of twenty-two, with her hair in papers, seemed very naturally to have caught something of the style of her mother, who had brought her up. Emma was soon left to know what they could be, by Elizabeth's being obliged to hurry away; and some very languid remarks on the probable brilliancy of the ball were all that broke, at intervals, a silence of half an hour, before they were joined by the master of the house. Mr Edwards had a much easier and more communicative air than the ladies of the family; he was fresh from the street, and he came ready to tell whatever might interest.

After a cordial reception of Emma, he turned to his daughter with – 'Well, Mary, I bring you good news: the Osbornes will certainly be at the ball tonight. Horses for two carriages are ordered from the White Hart to be at Osborne Castle by nine.'

'I am glad of it,' observed Mrs Edwards, 'because their coming gives a credit to our assembly. The Osbornes being known to have been at the first ball, will dispose a great many people to attend the second. It is more than they deserve; for in fact, they add nothing to the pleasure of the evening: they come so late and go so early; but great people have always their charm.'

Mr Edwards proceeded to relate every other little article of news which his morning's lounge had supplied him with, and they chatted with greater briskness, till Mrs Edwards' moment for dressing arrived, and the young ladies were carefully recommended to lose no time. Emma was shown to a very comfortable apartment, and as soon as Mrs Edwards' civilities could leave her to herself, the happy occupation, the first bliss of a ball, began. The girls, dressing in some measure together, grew unavoidably better acquainted. Emma found in Miss Edwards the show of good sense, a modest unpretending mind, and a great wish of obliging; and when they returned to the parlour where Mrs Edwards was sitting, respectably attired in one of the two satin gowns which went through the winter, and a new cap from the milliner's, they entered it with much easier feelings and more natural smiles than they had taken away. Their dress was now to be examined: Mrs Edwards acknowledged herself too old-fashioned to approve of every modern extravagance, however sanctioned; and though complacently viewing her daughter's good looks, would give but a qualified admiration; and Mr Edwards, not less satisfied with Mary, paid some compliments of good-humoured gallantry to Emma at her expense. The discussion led to more intimate remarks, and Miss Edwards gently asked Emma if she were not often reckoned very like her youngest brother. Emma thought she could perceive a faint blush accompany the question, and there seemed something still more suspicious in the manner in which Mr Edwards took up the subject.

'You are paying Miss Emma no great compliment, I think, Mary,' said he, hastily. 'Mr Sam Watson is a very good sort of young man, and I dare say a very clever surgeon; but his complexion has been rather too much exposed to all weathers to make a likeness to him very flattering.'

Mary apologised, in some confusion – 'She had not thought a strong likeness at all incompatible with very different degrees of beauty. There might be resemblance in countenance, and the complexion and even the features be very unlike.'

'I know nothing of my brother's beauty,' said Emma, 'for I have not seen him since he was seven years old; but my father reckons us alike.'

'Mr Watson!' cried Mr Edwards; 'well, you astonish me. There is not the least likeness in the world; your brother's eyes are grey, yours are brown; he has a long face and a wide mouth. My dear, do *you* perceive the least resemblance?'

'Not the least. Miss Emma Watson puts me very much in mind of her eldest sister, and sometimes I see a look of Miss Penelope, and once or twice there has been a glance of Mr Robert, but I cannot perceive any likeness to Mr Samuel.'

'I see the likeness between her and Miss Watson,' replied Mr Edwards, 'very strongly, but I am not sensible of the others. I do not much think she is like any of the family *but* Miss Watson; but I am very sure there is no resemblance between her and Sam.'

This matter was settled, and they went to dinner.

'Your father, Miss Emma, is one of my oldest friends,' said Mr Edwards, as he helped her to wine, when they were drawn round the fire to enjoy their dessert. 'We must drink to his better health. It is a great concern to me, I assure you, that he should be such an invalid. I know nobody who likes a game of cards, in a social way, better than he does, and very few people that play a fairer rubber. It is a thousand pities that he should be so deprived of the pleasure. For now we have a quiet little Whist Club, that meets three times a week at the White Hart; and if he could but have his health, how much he would enjoy it!'

'I dare say he would, sir; and I wish, with all my heart, he were equal to it.'

'Your club would be better fitted for an invalid,' said Mrs Edwards, 'if you did not keep it up so late.'

This was an old grievance.

'So late, my dear! What are you talking of?' cried the husband, with sturdy pleasantry. 'We are always at home before midnight. They would laugh at Osborne Castle to hear you call *that* late; they are but just rising from dinner at midnight.'

'That is nothing to the purpose,' retorted the lady, calmly. 'The Osbornes are to be no rule for us. You had better meet every night, and break up two hours sooner.'

So far the subject was very often carried; but Mr and Mrs Edwards were so wise as never to pass that point; and Mr Edwards now turned to something else. He had lived long enough in the idleness of a town to become a little of a gossip, and having some anxiety to know more of the circumstances of his young guest than had yet reached him, he began with – 'I think, Miss Emma, I remember your aunt very well, about thirty years ago; I am pretty sure I danced with her in the old rooms at Bath, the year before I married. She was a very fine woman then; but like other people, I suppose, she is grown somewhat older since that time. I hope she is likely to be happy in her second choice.'

'I hope so; I believe so, sir,' said Emma, in some agitation.

'Mr Turner had not been dead a great while, I think?'

'About two years, sir.'

'I forget what her name is now.'

'O'Brien.'

'Irish! ah, I remember; and she is gone to settle in Ireland. I do not wonder that you should not wish to go with her into *that* country, Miss Emma; but it must be a great deprivation to her, poor lady!, after bringing you up like a child of her own.'

'I was not so ungrateful, sir,' said Emma, warmly, 'as to wish to be anywhere but with her. It did not suit them, it did not suit Captain O'Brien that I should be of the party.'

'Captain!' repeated Mrs Edwards. 'The gentleman is in the army then?'

'Yes, ma'am.'

'Aye, there is nothing like your officers for captivating the ladies, young or old. There is no resisting a cockade, my dear.'

'I hope there is,' said Mrs Edwards, gravely, with a quick glance at her daughter; and Emma had just recovered from her own perturbation in time to see a blush on Miss Edwards' cheek, and in remembering what Elizabeth had said of Captain Hunter, to wonder and waver between his influence and her brother's.

'Elderly ladies should be careful how they make a second choice,' observed Mr Edwards.

'Carefulness – discretion should not be confined to elderly ladies or to a second choice,' added his wife. 'They are quite as necessary to young ladies in their first.'

'Rather more so, my dear,' replied he; 'because young ladies are likely to feel the effects of it longer. When an old lady plays the fool, it is not in the course of nature that she should suffer from it many years.'

Emma drew her hand across her eyes; and Mrs Edwards, on perceiving it, changed the subject to one of less anxiety to all.

With nothing to do but to expect the hour of setting off, the afternoon was long to the two young ladies; and though Miss Edwards was rather discomposed at the very early hour which her mother always fixed for going, that early hour itself was watched for with some eagerness.

The entrance of the tea-things at seven o'clock was some relief; and luckily Mr and Mrs Edwards always drank a dish extraordinary and ate an additional muffin when they were going to sit up late, which lengthened the ceremony almost to the wished-for moment.

At a little before eight, the Tomlinsons' carriage was heard to go by – which was the constant signal for Mrs Edwards to order hers to the door; and in a very few minutes the party were transported from the quiet and warmth of a snug parlour to the bustle, noise, and draughts of air of the broad entrance passage of an inn. Mrs Edwards, carefully guarding her own dress, while she attended with yet greater solicitude to the proper security of her young charges' shoulders and throats, led the way up the wide staircase, while no sound of a ball but the first scrape of one violin blessed the ears of her followers; and

Miss Edwards, on hazarding the anxious inquiry of whether there were many people come yet, was told by the waiter, as she knew she should, that 'Mr Tomlinson's family were in the room'.

In passing along a short gallery to the assembly-room, brilliant in lights before them, they were accosted by a young man in a morning-dress and boots, who was standing in the doorway of a bed-chamber, apparently on purpose to see them go by.

'Ah! Mrs Edwards, how do you do? How do you do, Miss Edwards?' he cried, with an easy air. 'You are determined to be in good time, I see, as usual. The candles are but this moment lit.'

'I like to get a good seat by the fire, you know, Mr Musgrave,' replied Mrs Edwards.

'I am this moment going to dress,' said he. 'I am waiting for my stupid fellow. We shall have a famous ball. The Osbornes are certainly coming; you may depend upon *that*, for I was with Lord Osborne this morning.'

The party passed on. Mrs Edwards' satin gown swept along the clean floor of the ball-room to the fireplace at the upper end, where one party only were formally seated, while three or four officers were lounging together, passing in and out from the adjoining card-room. A very stiff meeting between these near neighbours ensued; and as soon as they were all duly placed again, Emma, in the low whisper which became the solemn scene, said to Miss Edwards – 'The gentleman we passed in the passage was Mr Musgrave, then; he is reckoned remarkably agreeable, I understand?'

Miss Edwards answered hesitatingly, 'Yes; he is very much liked by many people; but *we* are not very intimate.'

'He is rich, is not he?'

'He has about eight or nine hundred pounds a year, I believe. He came into possession of it when he was very young, and my father and mother think it has given him rather an unsettled turn. He is no favourite with them.'

The cold and empty appearance of the room and the demure air of the small cluster of females at one end of it, began soon to give way. The inspiriting sound of other carriages was heard, and continual accessions of portly chaperons and strings of smartly-dressed girls were received, with now and then a fresh gentleman straggler, who, if not enough in love to station himself near any fair creature, seemed glad to escape into the card-room.

Among the increasing number of military men, one now made his way to Miss Edwards with an air of *empressement* which decidedly said to her companion, 'I am Captain Hunter'; and Emma, who could not but watch her at such a moment, saw her looking rather distressed, but by no means displeased, and heard an engagement formed for the two first dances, which made her think her brother Sam's a hopeless case.

Emma in the meanwhile was not unobserved or unadmired herself. A new face, and a very pretty one, could not be slighted. Her name was whispered from one party to another; and no sooner had the signal been given by the orchestra's striking up a favourite air, which seemed to call the young to their duty and people the centre of the room, than she found herself engaged to dance with a brother officer, introduced by Captain Hunter.

Emma Watson was not more than of the middle height, well made and plump, with an air of healthy vigour. Her skin was very brown, but clear, smooth, and glowing, which, with a lively eye, a sweet smile, and an open countenance, gave beauty to attract, and expression to make that beauty improve on acquaintance. Having no reason to be dissatisfied with her partner, the evening began very pleasantly to her, and her feelings perfectly coincided with the reiterated observation of others, that it was an excellent ball. The two first dances were not quite over when the returning sound of carriages after a long interruption called general notice, and 'The Osbornes are coming! The Osbornes are coming!' was repeated round the room. After some minutes of extraordinary bustle without and watchful curiosity within, the important party, preceded by the attentive master of the inn to open a door which was never shut, made their appearance. They consisted of Lady Osborne; her son, Lord Osborne; her daughter, Miss Osborne; Miss Carr, her daughter's friend; Mr Howard, formerly tutor to Lord Osborne, now clergyman of the parish in which the castle stood; Mrs Blake, a widow sister who lived with him; her son, a fine boy of ten years old; and Mr Tom Musgrave, who probably, imprisoned within his own room, had been listening in bitter impatience to the sound of the music for the last half-hour. In their progress up the room, they paused almost immediately behind Emma to receive the compliments of some acquaintance; and she heard Lady Osborne observe that they had made a point of coming early for the gratification of Mrs Blake's little boy, who was uncommonly fond of dancing. Emma looked at them all as they passed, but chiefly and with most interest on Tom Musgrave, who was certainly a genteel, good-looking young man. Of the females, Lady Osborne had by much the finest person; though nearly fifty, she was very handsome, and had all the dignity of rank.

Lord Osborne was a very fine young man; but there was an air of coldness, of carelessness, even of awkwardness about him, which seemed to speak him out of his element in a ball-room. He came, in fact, only because it was judged expedient for him to please the borough; he was not fond of women's company, and he never danced. Mr Howard was an agreeable-looking man, a little more than thirty.

At the conclusion of the two dances, Emma found herself, she knew not how, seated amongst the Osborne set; and she was immediately struck with the fine countenance and animated gestures of the little boy, as he was standing before his mother, wondering when they should begin.

'You will not be surprised at Charles' impatience,' said Mrs Blake, a lively, pleasant-looking little woman of five or six and thirty, to a lady who was standing near her, 'when you know what a partner he is to have. Miss Osborne has been so very kind as to promise to dance the two first dances with him.'

'Oh, yes! we have been engaged this week,' cried the boy, 'and we are to dance down every couple.'

On the other side of Emma, Miss Osborne, Miss Carr, and a party of young men were standing engaged in very lively consultation; and soon afterwards she saw the smartest officer of the set walking off to the orchestra to order the dance, while Miss Osborne, passing before her to her little expecting partner, hastily said: 'Charles, I beg your pardon for not keeping my engagement, but I am going to dance these two dances with Colonel Berestord. I know you will excuse me, and I will certainly dance with you after tea'; and without staying for an answer, she turned again to Miss Carr, and in another minute was led by Colonel Beresford to begin the set. If the poor little boy's face had in its happiness been interesting to Emma, it was infinitely more so under this sudden reverse; he stood the picture of disappointment, with crimsoned cheeks, quivering lips, and eyes bent on the floor. His mother, stifling her own mortification, tried to soothe his with the prospect of Miss Osborne's second promise;

but though he contrived to utter, with an effort of boyish bravery, 'Oh, I do not mind it!' it was very evident, by the unceasing agitation of his features, that he minded it as much as ever.

Emma did not think or reflect; she felt and acted. 'I shall be very happy to dance with you, sir, if you like it,' said she, holding out her hand with the most unaffected good-humour. The boy, in one moment restored to all his first delight, looked joyfully at his mother; and stepping forwards with an honest and simple 'Thank you, ma'am,' was instantly ready to attend his new acquaintance. The thankfulness of Mrs Blake was more diffuse; with a look most expressive of unexpected pleasure and lively gratitude, she turned to her neighbour with repeated and fervent acknowledgements of so great and condescending a kindness to her boy. Emma, with perfect truth, could assure her that she could not be giving greater pleasure than she felt herself; and Charles being provided with his gloves and charged to keep them on, they joined the set which was now rapidly forming, with nearly equal complacency. It was a partnership which could not be noticed without surprise. It gained her a broad stare from Miss Osborne and Miss Carr as they passed her in the dance. 'Upon my word, Charles, you are in luck,' said the former, as she turned him; 'you have got a better partner than me'; to which the happy Charles answered 'Yes.'

Tom Musgrave, who was dancing with Miss Carr, gave her many inquisitive glances; and after a time Lord Osborne himself came, and under pretence of talking to Charles, stood to look at his partner. Though rather distressed by such observation, Emma could not repent what she had done, so happy had it made both the boy and his mother; the latter of whom was continually making opportunities of addressing her with the warmest civility. Her little partner, she found, though bent chiefly on dancing, was not unwilling to speak, when her questions or remarks gave him anything to say; and she learnt, by a sort of inevitable inquiry, that he had two brothers and a sister, that they and their mamma all lived with his uncle at Wickstead, that his uncle taught him Latin, that he was very fond of riding, and had a horse of his own given him by Lord Osborne; and that he had been out once already with Lord Osborne's hounds.

At the end of these dances, Emma found they were to drink tea; Miss Edwards gave her a caution to be at hand, in a manner which convinced her of Mrs Edwards' holding it very important to have them both close to her when she moved into the tea-room; and Emma was accordingly on the alert to gain her proper station. It was always the pleasure of the company to have a little bustle and crowd when they adjourned for refreshment. The tea-room was a small room within the card-room; and in passing through the latter, where the passage was straitened by tables, Mrs Edwards and her party were for a few moments hemmed in. It happened close by Lady Osborne's cassino table; Mr Howard, who belonged to it, spoke to his nephew; and Emma, on perceiving herself the object of attention both to Lady Osborne and him, had just turned away her eyes in time to avoid seeming to hear her young companion delightedly whisper aloud, 'Oh, uncle! do look at my partner; she is so pretty!' As they were immediately in motion again, however, Charles was hurried off without being able to receive his uncle's suffrage. On entering the tea-room, in which two long tables were prepared, Lord Osborne was to be seen quite alone at the end of one, as if retreating as far as he could from the ball, to enjoy his own thoughts and gape without restraint. Charles instantly pointed him out to Emma. 'There's Lord Osborne; let you and I go and sit by him.'

'No, no,' said Emma, laughing; 'you must sit with my friends.'

Charles was now free enough to hazard a few questions in his turn. 'What o'clock was it?'

'Eleven.'

'Eleven! and I am not at all sleepy. Mamma said I should be asleep before ten. Do you think Miss Osborne will keep her word with me, when tea is over?'

'Oh, yes! I suppose so'; though she felt that she had no better reason to give than that Miss Osborne had *not* kept it before.

'When shall you come to Osborne Castle?'

'Never, probably. I am not acquainted with the family.'

'But you may come to Wickstead and see mamma, and she can take you to the castle. There is a monstrous curious stuffed fox there, and a badger; anybody would think they were alive. It is a pity you should not see them.'

On rising from tea, there was again a scramble for the pleasure of being first out of the room, which happened to be increased by one or two of the card-parties having just broken up, and the players being disposed to move exactly the different way. Among these was

Mr Howard, his sister leaning on his arm; and no sooner were they within reach of Emma, than Mrs Blake, calling her notice by a friendly touch, said, 'Your goodness to Charles, my dear Miss Watson, brings all his family upon you. Give me leave to introduce my brother, Mr Howard.' Emma curtsied, the gentleman bowed, made a hasty request for the honour of her hand in the two next dances, to which as hasty an affirmative was given, and they were immediately impelled in opposite directions. Emma was very well pleased with the circumstance; there was a quietly cheerful, gentlemanlike air in Mr Howard which suited her; and in a few minutes afterwards the value of her engagement increased, when, as she was sitting in the card-room, somewhat screened by a door, she heard Lord Osborne, who was lounging on a vacant table near her, call Tom Musgrave towards him and say, 'Why do not you dance with that beautiful Emma Watson? I want you to dance with her, and I will come and stand by you.'

'I was determining on it this very moment, my lord; I'll be introduced and dance with her directly.'

'Aye, do; and if you find she does not want much talking to, you may introduce me by and by.'

'Very well, my lord; if she is like her sisters, she will only want to be listened to. I will go this moment. I shall find her in the tea-room. That stiff old Mrs Edwards has never done tea.'

Away he went, Lord Osborne after him; and Emma lost no time in hurrying from her corner exactly the other way, forgetting in her haste that she left Mrs Edwards behind.

'We had quite lost you,' said Mrs Edwards, who followed her with Mary in less than five minutes. 'If you prefer this room to the other, there is no reason why you should not be here; but we had better all be together.'

Emma was saved the trouble of apologising, by their being joined at the moment by Tom Musgrave, who requesting Mrs Edwards aloud to do him the honour of presenting him to Miss Emma Watson, left that good lady without any choice in the business, but that of testifying by the coldness of her manner that she did it unwillingly. The honour of dancing with her was solicited without loss of time; and Emma, however she might like to be thought a beautiful girl by lord or commoner, was so little disposed to favour Tom Musgrave himself that she had considerable satisfaction in avowing her previous engagement. He was evidently surprised and discomposed. The style of her last partner had probably led him to believe her not overpowered with applications.

'My little friend Charles Blake,' he cried, 'must not expect to engross you the whole evening. We can never suffer this. It is against the rules of the assembly, and I am sure it will never be patronised by our good friend here, Mrs Edwards; she is by much too nice a judge of decorum to give her licence to such a dangerous particularity – '

'I am not going to dance with Master Blake, sir!'

The gentleman, a little disconcerted, could only hope he might be fortunate another time, and seeming unwilling to leave her, though his friend Lord Osborne was waiting in the doorway for the result, as Emma with some amusement perceived, he began to make civil inquiries after her family.

'How comes it that we have not the pleasure of seeing your sisters here this evening? Our assemblies have been used to be so well treated by them that we do not know how to take this neglect.'

'My eldest sister is the only one at home, and she could not leave my father.'

'Miss Watson the only one at home! You astonish me! It seems but the day before yesterday that I saw them all three in this town. But I am afraid I have been a very sad neighbour of late. I hear dreadful complaints of my negligence wherever I go, and I confess it is a shameful length of time since I was at Stanton. But I shall *now* endeavour to make myself amends for the past.'

Emma's calm curtsey in reply must have struck him as very unlike the encouraging warmth he had been used to receive from her sisters, and gave him probably the novel sensation of doubting his own influence, and of wishing for more attention than she bestowed The dancing now recommenced; Miss Carr being impatient to *call*, everybody was required to stand up; and Tom Musgrave's curiosity was appeased on seeing Mr Howard come forward and claim Emma's hand.

'That will do as well for me,' was Lord Osborne's remark, when his friend carried him the news, and he was continually at Howard's elbow during the two dances.

The frequency of his appearance there was the only unpleasant part of the engagement, the only objection she could make to Mr

Howard. In himself, she thought him as agreeable as he looked; though chatting on the commonest topics, he had a sensible, unaffected way of expressing himself, which made them all worth hearing, and she only regretted that he had not been able to make his pupil's manners as unexceptionable as his own. The two dances seemed very short, and she had her partner's authority for considering them so. At their conclusion the Osbornes and their train were all on the move.

'We are off at last,' said his lordship to Tom. 'How much longer do *you* stay in this heavenly place – till sunrise?'

'No, faith! my lord; I have had quite enough of it. I assure you, I shall not show myself here again when I have had the honour of attending Lady Osborne to her carriage. I shall retreat in as much secrecy as possible to the most remote corner of the house, where I shall order a barrel of oysters, and be famously snug.'

'Let me see you soon at the castle, and bring me word how she looks by daylight.'

Emma and Mrs Blake parted as old acquaintances, and Charles shook her by the hand, and wished her 'good-bye' at least a dozen times. From Miss Osborne and Miss Carr she received something like a jerking curtsey as they passed her; even Lady Osborne gave her a look of complacency, and his lordship actually came back, after the others were out of the room, to 'beg her pardon', and look in the window-seat behind her for the gloves which were visibly compressed in his hand. As Tom Musgrave was seen no more, we may suppose his plan to have succeeded, and imagine him mortifying with his barrel of oysters in dreary solitude, or gladly assisting the landlady in her bar to make fresh negus for the happy dancers above. Emma could not help missing the party by whom she had been, though in some respects unpleasantly, distinguished; and the two dances which followed and concluded the ball were rather flat in comparison with the others. Mr Edwards having played with good luck, they were some of the last in the room.

'Here we are back again, I declare,' said Emma, sorrowfully, as she walked into the dining-room, where the table was prepared, and the neat upper maid was lighting the candles. 'My dear Miss Edwards, how soon it is at an end! I wish it could all come over again.'

A great deal of kind pleasure was expressed in her having enjoyed the evening so much; and Mr Edwards was as warm as herself in the praise of the fullness, brilliancy, and spirit of the meeting, though as he had been fixed the whole time at the same table in the same room, with only one change of chairs, it might have seemed a matter scarcely perceived; but he had won four rubbers out of five, and everything went well. His daughter felt the advantage of this gratified state of mind, in the course of the remarks and retrospections which now ensued over the welcome soup.

'How came you not to dance with either of the Mr Tomlinsons, Mary?' said her mother.

'I was always engaged when they asked me.'

'I thought you were to have stood up with Mr James the two last dances; Mrs Tomlinson told me he was gone to ask you, and I had heard you say two minutes before that you were *not* engaged.'

'Yes, but there was a mistake; I had misunderstood. I did not know I was engaged. I thought it had been for the two dances after, if we stayed so long; but Captain Hunter assured me it was for those very two.'

'So you ended with Captain Hunter, Mary, did you?' said her father. 'And whom did you begin with?'

'Captain Hunter,' was repeated in a very humble tone.

'Hum! That is being constant, however. But who else did you dance with?'

'Mr Norton and Mr Styles.'

'And who are they?'

'Mr Norton is a cousin of Captain Hunter's.'

'And who is Mr Styles?'

'One of his particular friends.'

'All in the same regiment,' added Mrs Edwards. 'Mary was surrounded by red-coats all the evening. I should have been better pleased to see her dancing with some of our old neighbours, I confess.'

'Yes, yes; we must not neglect our old neighbours. But if these soldiers are quicker than other people in a ball-room, what are young ladies to do?'

'I think there is no occasion for their engaging themselves so many dances beforehand, Mr Edwards.'

'No, perhaps not; but I remember, my dear, when you and I did the same.'

Mrs Edwards said no more, and Mary breathed again. A good deal of good-humoured pleasantry followed; and Emma went to bed in charming spirits, her head full of Osbornes, Blakes, and Howards.

*   *   *

The next morning brought a great many visitors. It was the way of the place always to call on Mrs Edwards the morning after a ball, and this neighbourly inclination was increased in the present instance by a general spirit of curiosity on Emma's account, as everybody wanted to look again at the girl who had been admired the night before by Lord Osborne. Many were the eyes, and various the degrees of approbation with which she was examined. Some saw no fault, and some no beauty. With some her brown skin was the annihilation of every grace, and others could never be persuaded that she was half so handsome as Elizabeth Watson had been ten years ago. The morning passed quickly away in discussing the merits of the ball with all this succession of company; and Emma was at once astonished by finding it two o'clock, and considering that she had heard nothing of her father's chair. After this discovery, she had walked twice to the window to examine the street, and was on the point of asking leave to ring the bell and make inquiries, when the light sound of a carriage driving up to the door set her heart at ease. She stepped again to the window, but instead of the convenient though very un-smart family equipage, perceived a neat curricle. Mr Musgrave was shortly afterwards announced, and Mrs Edwards put on her very stiffest look at the sound. Not at all dismayed, however, by her chilling air, he paid his compliments to each of the ladies with no unbecoming ease, and continuing to address Emma, presented her a note, which 'he had the honour of bringing from her sister, but to which he must observe a verbal postscript from himself would be requisite'.

The note, which Emma was beginning to read rather *before* Mrs Edwards had entreated her to use no ceremony, contained a few lines from Elizabeth importing that their father, in consequence of being unusually well, had taken the sudden resolution of attending the visitation that day, and that as his road lay quite wide from D., it was impossible for her to come home till the following morning, unless the Edwardses would send her, which was hardly to be expected, or she could meet with any chance conveyance, or did not mind walking so far. She had scarcely run her eye through the whole, before she found herself obliged to listen to Tom Musgrave's farther account.

'I received that note from the fair hands of Miss Watson only ten minutes ago,' said he; 'I met her in the village of Stanton, whither my good stars prompted me to turn my horses' heads. She was at that moment in quest of a person to employ on the errand, and I was fortunate enough to convince her that she could not find a more willing or speedy messenger than myself. Remember, I say nothing of my disinterestedness. My reward is to be the indulgence of conveying you to Stanton in my curricle. Though they are not written down, I bring your sister's orders for the same.'

Emma felt distressed; she did not like the proposal – she did not wish to be on terms of intimacy with the proposer; and yet, fearful of encroaching on the Edwardses, as well as wishing to go home herself, she was at a loss how entirely to decline what he offered. Mrs Edwards continued silent, either not understanding the case, or waiting to see how the young lady's inclination lay. Emma thanked him, but professed herself very unwilling to give him so much trouble. 'The trouble was of course honour, pleasure, delight – what had he or his horses to do?' Still she hesitated – 'She believed she must beg leave to decline his assistance; she was rather afraid of the sort of carriage. The distance was not beyond a walk.' Mrs Edwards was silent no longer. She inquired into the particulars, and then said, 'We shall be extremely happy, Miss Emma, if you can give us the pleasure of your company till tomorrow; but if you cannot conveniently do so, our carriage is quite at your service, and Mary will be pleased with the opportunity of seeing your sister.'

This was precisely what Emma had longed for, and she accepted the offer most thankfully, acknowledging that as Elizabeth was entirely alone, it was her wish to return home to dinner. The plan was warmly opposed by their visitor – 'I cannot suffer it, indeed. I must not be deprived of the happiness of escorting you. I assure you there is not a possibility of fear with my horses. You might guide them yourself. *Your sisters* all know how quiet they are; they have none of them the smallest scruple in trusting themselves with me, even on a race-course. Believe me,' added he, lowering his voice, '*you* are quite safe – the danger is only *mine*.'

Emma was not more disposed to oblige him for all this.

'And as to Mrs Edwards' carriage being used the day after a ball, it is a thing quite out of rule, I assure you – never heard of before. The old coachman will look as black as his horses – won't he Miss Edwards?'

No notice was taken. The ladies were silently firm, and the gentleman found himself obliged to submit.

'What a famous ball we had last night!' he cried, after a short pause. 'How long did you keep it up after the Osbornes and I went away?'

'We had two dances more.'

'It is making it too much of a fatigue, I think, to stay so late. I suppose your set was not a very full one.'

'Yes; quite as full as ever, except the Osbornes. There seemed no vacancy anywhere; and everybody danced with uncommon spirit to the very last.'

Emma said this, though against her conscience.

'Indeed! perhaps I might have looked in upon you again, if I had been aware of as much, for I am rather fond of dancing than not. Miss Osborne is a charming girl, is not she?'

'I do not think her handsome,' replied Emma, to whom all this was chiefly addressed.

'Perhaps she is not critically handsome, but her manners are delightful. And Fanny Carr is a most interesting little creature. You can imagine nothing more *naïve* or *piquante*; and what do you think of *Lord Osborne*, Miss Watson?'

'He would be handsome even though he were *not* a lord, and perhaps, better bred; more desirous of pleasing and showing himself pleased in a right place.'

'Upon my word, you are severe upon my friend! I assure you Lord Osborne is a very good fellow.'

'I do not dispute his virtues, but I do not like his careless air.'

'If it were not a breach of confidence,' replied Tom, with an important look, 'perhaps I might be able to win a more favourable opinion of poor Osborne.'

Emma gave him no encouragement, and he was obliged to keep his friend's secret. He was also obliged to put an end to his visit, for Mrs Edwards having ordered her carriage, there was no time to be lost on Emma's side in preparing for it. Miss Edwards accompanied her home; but as it was dinner-hour at Stanton, stayed with them only a few minutes.

'Now, my dear Emma,' said Miss Watson, as soon as they were

alone, 'you must talk to me all the rest of the day without stopping, or I shall not be satisfied; but, first of all, Nanny shall bring in the dinner. Poor thing! You will not dine as you did yesterday, for we have nothing but some fried beef. How nice Mary Edwards looks in her new pelisse! And now tell me how you like them all, and what I am to say to Sam. I have begun my letter, Jack Stokes is to call for it tomorrow, for his uncle is going within a mile of Guildford the next day.'

Nanny brought in the dinner.

'We will wait upon ourselves,' continued Elizabeth, 'and then we shall lose no time. And so, you would not come home with Tom Musgrave?'

'No, you had said so much against him that I could not wish either for the obligation or the intimacy which the use of his carriage must have created. I should not even have liked the appearance of it.'

'You did very right; though I wonder at your forbearance, and I do not think I could have done it myself. He seemed so eager to fetch you that I could not say no, though it rather went against me to be throwing you together, so well as I knew his tricks; but I did long to see you, and it was a clever way of getting you home. Besides, it won't do to be too nice. Nobody could have thought of the Edwards' letting you have their coach, after the horses being out so late. But what am I to say to Sam?'

'If you are guided by me, you will not encourage him to think of Miss Edwards. The father is decidedly against him, the mother shows him no favour, and I doubt his having any interest with Mary. She danced twice with Captain Hunter, and I think shows him in general as much encouragement as is consistent with her disposition and the circumstances she is placed in. She once mentioned Sam, and certainly with a little confusion; but that was perhaps merely owing to the consciousness of his liking her, which may very probably have come to her knowledge.'

'Oh, dear! yes. She has heard enough of that from us all. Poor Sam! he is out of luck as well as other people. For the life of me, Emma, I cannot help feeling for those that are crossed in love. Well, now begin, and give me an account of everything as it happened.'

Emma obeyed her, and Elizabeth listened with very little interruption till she heard of Mr Howard as a partner.

'Dance with Mr Howard! Good heavens! you don't say so! Why,

he is quite one of the great and grand ones. Did you not find him very high?'

'His manners are of a kind to give *me* much more ease and confidence than Tom Musgrave's.'

'Well, go on. I should have been frightened out of my wits to have had anything to do with the Osbornes' set.'

Emma concluded her narration.

'And so you really did not dance with Tom Musgrave at all; but you must have liked him – you must have been struck with him altogether.'

'I do *not* like him, Elizabeth. I allow his person and air to be good, and that his manners to a certain point – his address rather – is pleasing, but I see nothing else to admire in him. On the contrary, he seems very vain, very conceited, absurdly anxious for distinction, and absolutely contemptible in some of the measures he takes for becoming so. There is a ridiculousness about him that entertains me, but his company gives me no other agreeable emotion.'

'My dearest Emma! You are like nobody else in the world. It is well Margaret is not by. You do not offend *me*, though I hardly know how to believe you; but Margaret would never forgive such words.'

'I wish Margaret could have heard him profess his ignorance of her being out of the country; he declared it seemed only two days since he had seen her.'

'Aye, that is just like him; and yet this is the man she *will* fancy so desperately in love with her. He is no favourite of mine, as you well know, Emma; but you must think him agreeable. Can you lay your hand on your heart, and say you do not?'

'Indeed, I can, both hands, and spread to their widest extent.'

'I should like to know the man you *do* think agreeable.'

'His name is Howard.'

'Howard! Dear me; I cannot think of *him* but as playing cards with Lady Osborne, and looking proud. I must own, however, that it *is* a relief to me to find you can speak as you do of Tom Musgrave. My heart did misgive me that you would like him too well. You talked so stoutly beforehand, that I was sadly afraid your brag would be punished. I only hope it will last, and that he will not come on to pay you much attention. It is a hard thing for a woman to stand against the flattering ways of a man, when he is bent upon pleasing her.'

As their quietly sociable little meal concluded, Miss Watson could not help observing how comfortably it had passed.

'It is so delightful to me,' said she, 'to have things going on in peace and good-humour. Nobody can tell how much I hate quarrelling. Now, though we have had nothing but fried beef, how good it has all seemed! I wish everybody were as easily satisfied as you; but poor Margaret is very snappish, and Penelope owns she had rather have quarrelling going on than nothing at all.'

Mr Watson returned in the evening not the worse for the exertion of the day, and, consequently pleased with what he had done, and glad to talk of it over his own fireside. Emma had not foreseen any interest to herself in the occurrences of a visitation; but when she heard Mr Howard spoken of as the preacher, and as having given them an excellent sermon, she could not help listening with a quicker ear.

'I do not know when I have heard a discourse more to my mind,' continued Mr Watson, 'or one better delivered. He reads extremely well, with great propriety, and in a very impressive manner, and at the same time without any theatrical grimace or violence. I own I do not like much action in the pulpit; I do not like the studied air and artificial inflexions of voice which your very popular and most admired preachers generally have. A simple delivery is much better calculated to inspire devotion, and shows a much better taste. Mr Howard read like a scholar and a gentleman.'

'And what had you for dinner, sir?' said his eldest daughter.

He related the dishes, and told what he had ate himself.

'Upon the whole,' he added, 'I have had a very comfortable day. My old friends were quite surprised to see me amongst them, and I must say that everybody paid me great attention, and seemed to feel for me as an invalid. They would make me sit near the fire; and as the partridges were pretty high, Dr Richards would have them sent away to the other end of the table, "that they might not offend Mr Watson", which I thought very kind of him. But what pleased me as much as anything was Mr Howard's attention. There is a pretty steep flight of steps up to the room we dine in, which do not quite agree with my gouty foot; and Mr Howard walked by me from the bottom to the top, and would make me take his arm. It struck me as very becoming in so young a man; but I am sure I had no claim to expect it, for I never saw him before in my life. By the by, he inquired after one of my daughters; but I do not know which. I suppose you know among yourselves.'

*   *   *

On the third day after the ball, as Nanny, at five minutes before three, was beginning to bustle into the parlour with the tray and the knife-case, she was suddenly called to the front door by the sound of as smart a rap as the end of a riding-whip could give; and though charged by Miss Watson to let nobody in, returned in half a minute with a look of awkward dismay to hold the parlour door open for Lord Osborne and Tom Musgrave. The surprise of the young ladies may be imagined. No visitors would have been welcome at such a moment, but such visitors as these – such a one as Lord Osborne at least, a nobleman and a stranger – was really distressing.

He looked a little embarrassed himself, as, on being introduced by his easy, voluble friend, he muttered something of doing himself the honour of waiting upon Mr Watson. Though Emma could not but take the compliment of the visit to herself, she was very far from enjoying it. She felt all the inconsistency of such an acquaintance with the very humble style in which they were obliged to live; and having in her aunt's family been used to many of the elegancies of life, was fully sensible of all that must be open to the ridicule of richer people in her present home. Of the pain of such feelings, Elizabeth knew very little. Her simple mind, or juster reason, saved her from such mortification; and though shrinking under a general sense of inferiority, she felt no particular shame. Mr Watson, as the gentlemen had already heard from Nanny, was not well enough to be downstairs. With much concern they took their seats; Lord Osborne near Emma, and the convenient Mr Musgrave, in high spirits at his own importance, on the other side of the fireplace, with Elizabeth. *He* was at no loss for words; but when Lord Osborne had hoped that Emma had not caught cold at the ball, he had nothing more to say for some time, and could only gratify his eye by occasional glances at his fair neighbour. Emma was not inclined to give herself much trouble for his entertainment; and after hard labour of mind, he produced the remark of its being a very fine day, and followed it up with the question of, 'Have you been walking this morning?'

'No, my lord; we thought it too dirty.'

'You should wear half-boots.' After another pause: 'Nothing sets off a neat ankle more than a half-boot; nankeen galoshed with black looks very well. Do not you like half-boots?'

'Yes; but unless they are so stout as to injure their beauty, they are not fit for country walking.'

'Ladies should ride in dirty weather. Do you ride?'

'No, my lord.'

'I wonder every lady does not; a woman never looks better than on horseback.'

'But every woman may not have the inclination, or the means.'

'If they knew how much it became them, they would all have the inclination; and I fancy, Miss Watson, when once they had the inclination, the means would soon follow.'

'Your lordship thinks we always have our own way. *That* is a point on which ladies and gentlemen have long disagreed; but without pretending to decide it, I may say that there are some circumstances which even *women* cannot control. Female economy will do a great deal my lord: but it cannot turn a small income into a large one.'

Lord Osborne was silenced. Her manner had been neither sententious nor sarcastic; but there was a something in its mild seriousness, as well as in the words themselves, which made his lordship think; and when he addressed her again, it was with a degree of considerate propriety totally unlike the half-awkward, half-fearless style of his former remarks. It was a new thing with him to wish to please a woman; it was the first time that he had ever felt what was due to a woman in Emma's situation; but as he wanted neither in sense nor a good disposition, he did not feel it without effect.

'You have not been long in this country, I understand,' said he, in the tone of a gentleman. 'I hope you are pleased with it.'

He was rewarded by a gracious answer, and a more liberal full view of her face than she had yet bestowed. Unused to exert himself, and happy in contemplating her, he then sat in silence for some minutes longer, while Tom Musgrave was chattering to Elizabeth; till they were interrupted by Nanny's approach, who, half-opening the door and putting in her head, said – 'Please, ma'am, master wants to know why he ben't to have his dinner?'

The gentlemen, who had hitherto disregarded every symptom, however positive, of the nearness of that meal, now jumped up with apologies, while Elizabeth called briskly after Nanny 'to tell Betty to take up the fowls'.

'I am sorry it happens so,' she added, turning good-humouredly towards Musgrave, 'but you know what early hours we keep.'

Tom had nothing to say for himself; he knew it very well, and such honest simplicity, such shameless truth, rather bewildered him. Lord Osborne's parting compliments took some time, his inclination for speech seeming to increase with the shortness of the term for indulgence. He recommended exercise in defiance of dirt; spoke again in praise of half-boots; begged that his sister might be allowed to send Emma the name of her shoemaker; and concluded with saying, 'My hounds will be hunting this country next week. I believe they will throw off at Stanton Wood on Wednesday at nine o'clock. I mention this in hopes of your being drawn out to see what's going on. If the morning's tolerable, pray do us the honour of giving us your good wishes in person.'

The sisters looked on each other with astonishment when their visitors had withdrawn.

'Here's an unaccountable honour!' cried Elizabeth, at last. 'Who would have thought of Lord Osborne's coming to Stanton? He is very handsome; but Tom Musgrave looks all to nothing the smartest and most fashionable man of the two. I am glad he did not say anything to me; I would not have had to talk to such a great man for the world. Tom was very agreeable, was not he? But did you hear him ask where Miss Penelope and Miss Margaret were, when he first came in? It put me out of patience. I am glad Nanny had not laid the cloth, however – it would have looked so awkward; just the tray did not signify.' To say that Emma was not flattered by Lord Osborne's visit would be to assert a very unlikely thing, and describe a very odd young lady; but the gratification was by no means unalloyed: his coming was a sort of notice which might please her vanity, but did not suit her pride; and she would rather have known that he wished the visit without presuming to make it, than have seen him at Stanton.

Among other unsatisfactory feelings, it once occurred to her to wonder why Mr Howard had not taken the same privilege of coming, and accompanied his lordship; but she was willing to suppose that he had either known nothing about it, or had declined any share in a measure which carried quite as much impertinence in its form as good-breeding.

Mr Watson was very far from being delighted when he heard what had passed; a little peevish under immediate pain, and ill-disposed to be pleased, he only replied – 'Phoo! phoo! what occasion could there be for Lord Osborne's coming? I have lived here fourteen years without being noticed by any of the family. It is some foolery of that idle fellow, Tom Musgrave. I cannot return the visit. *I* would not if I could.' And when Tom Musgrave was met with again, he was commissioned with a message of excuse to Osborne Castle, on the too-sufficient plea of Mr Watson's infirm state of health.

A week or ten days rolled quietly away after this visit before any new bustle arose to interrupt even for half a day the tranquil and affectionate intercourse of the two sisters, whose mutual regard was increasing with the intimate knowledge of each other which such intercourse produced. The first circumstance to break in on this security was the receipt of a letter from Croydon to announce the speedy return of Margaret, and a visit of two or three days from Mr and Mrs Robert Watson, who undertook to bring her home, and wished to see their sister Emma.

It was an expectation to fill the thoughts of the sisters at Stanton, and to busy the hours of one of them at least; for as Jane had been a woman of fortune, the preparations for her entertainment were considerable; and as Elizabeth had at all times more goodwill than method in her guidance of the house, she could make no change without a bustle. An absence of fourteen years had made all her brothers and sisters strangers to Emma, but in her expectation of Margaret there was more than the awkwardness of such an alienation; she had heard things which made her dread her return; and the day which brought the party to Stanton seemed to her the probable conclusion of almost all that had been comfortable in the house.

Robert Watson was an attorney at Croydon, in a good way of business; very well satisfied with himself for the same, and for having married the only daughter of the attorney to whom he had been clerk, with a fortune of six thousand pounds. Mrs Robert was not less pleased with herself for having had that six thousand pounds, and for being now in possession of a very smart house in Croydon, where she gave genteel parties and wore fine clothes. In her person there was nothing remarkable; her manners were pert and conceited. Margaret was not without beauty; she had a slight pretty figure, and rather wanted countenance than good features; but the sharp and anxious expression of her face made her beauty in general little felt. On meeting her long-absent sister, as on every occasion of show, her manner was all affection and her voice all gentleness; continual smiles and a very slow articulation being her constant resource when determined on pleasing.

She was now so 'delighted to see dear, dear Emma', that she could hardly speak a word in a minute.

'I am sure we shall be great friends,' she observed with much sentiment, as they were sitting together. Emma scarcely knew how to answer such a proposition, and the manner in which it was spoken she could not attempt to equal. Mrs Robert Watson eyed her with much familiar curiosity and triumphant compassion: the loss of the aunt's fortune was uppermost in her mind at the moment of meeting; and she could not but feel how much better it was to be the daughter of a gentleman of property in Croydon than the niece of an old woman who threw herself away on an Irish captain. Robert was carelessly kind, as became a prosperous man and a brother; more intent on settling with the post-boy, inveighing against the exorbitant advance in posting, and pondering over a doubtful half-crown, than on welcoming a sister who was no longer likely to have any property for him to get the direction of.

'Your road through the village is infamous, Elizabeth,' said he; 'worse than ever it was. By Heaven! I would indict it if I lived near you. Who is surveyor now?'

There was a little niece at Croydon to be fondly inquired after by the kind-hearted Elizabeth, who regretted very much her not being of the party.

'You are very good,' replied her mother, 'and I assure you it went very hard with Augusta to have us come away without her. I was forced to say we were only going to church, and promise to come back for her directly. But you know it would not do to bring her without her maid, and I am as particular as ever in having her properly attended to.'

'Sweet little darling!' cried Margaret. 'It quite broke my heart to leave her.'

'Then why was you in such a hurry to run away from her?' cried Mrs Robert. 'You are a sad, shabby girl. I have been quarrelling with you all the way we came, have not I? Such a visit as this, I never heard of! You know how glad we are to have any of you with us, if it be for months together; and I am sorry' (with a witty smile) 'we have not been able to make Croydon agreeable this autumn.'

'My dearest Jane, do not overpower me with your raillery. You know what inducements I had to bring me home. Spare me, I entreat you. I am no match for your arch sallies.'

'Well, I only beg you will not set your neighbours against the place. Perhaps Emma may be tempted to go back with us and stay till Christmas, if you don't put in your word.'

Emma was greatly obliged. 'I assure you we have very good society at Croydon. I do not much attend the balls, they are rather too mixed; but our parties are very select and good. I had seven tables last week in my drawing-room. Are you fond of the country? How do you like Stanton?'

'Very much,' replied Emma, who thought a comprehensive answer most to the purpose. She saw that her sister-in-law despised her immediately. Mrs Robert Watson was indeed wondering what sort of a home Emma could possibly have been used to in Shropshire, and setting it down as certain that the aunt could never have had six thousand pounds.

'How charming Emma is,' whispered Margaret to Mrs Robert, in her most languishing tone. Emma was quite distressed by such behaviour; and she did not like it better when she heard Margaret five minutes afterwards say to Elizabeth in a sharp, quick accent, totally unlike the first, 'Have you heard from Pen since she went to Chichester? I had a letter the other day. I don't find she is likely to make anything of it. I fancy she'll come back "Miss Penelope", as she went.'

Such, she feared, would be Margaret's common voice when the novelty of her own appearance were over; the tone of artificial sensibility was not recommended by the idea. The ladies were invited upstairs to prepare for dinner.

'I hope you will find things tolerably comfortable, Jane,' said Elizabeth, as she opened the door of the spare bedchamber.

'My good creature,' replied Jane, 'use no ceremony with me, I entreat you. I am one of those who always take things as they find them. I hope I can put up with a small apartment for two or three nights without making a piece of work. I always wish to be treated quite *en famille* when I come to see you. And now I do hope you have not been getting a great dinner for us. Remember, we never eat suppers.'

'I suppose,' said Margaret, rather quickly to Emma, 'you and I are to be together; Elizabeth always takes care to have a room to herself.'

'No. Elizabeth gives me half hers.'

'Oh!' in a softened voice, and rather mortified to find that she was not ill-used, 'I am sorry I am not to have the pleasure of your company, especially as it makes me nervous to be much alone.'

Emma was the first of the females in the parlour again; on entering it she found her brother alone.

'So, Emma,' said he, 'you are quite a stranger at home. It must seem odd enough for you to be here. A pretty piece of work your Aunt Turner has made of it! By Heaven! a woman should never be trusted with money. I always said she ought to have settled something on you, as soon as her husband died.'

'But that would have been trusting *me* with money,' replied Emma; 'and *I* am a woman too.'

'It might have been secured to your future use, without your having any power over it now. What a blow it must have been upon you! To find yourself, instead of heiress of £8,000 or £9,000, sent back a weight upon your family, without a sixpence. I hope the old woman will smart for it.'

'Do not speak disrespectfully of her; she was very good to me, and if she has made an imprudent choice, she will suffer more from it herself than *I* can possibly do.'

'I do not mean to distress you, but you know everybody must think her an old fool. I thought Turner had been reckoned an extraordinarily sensible, clever man. How the devil came he to make such a will?'

'My uncle's sense is not at all impeached in my opinion by his attachment to my aunt. She had been an excellent wife to him. The most liberal and enlightened minds are always the most confiding. The event has been unfortunate; but my uncle's memory is, if possible, endeared to me by such a proof of tender respect for my aunt.'

'That's odd sort of talking. He might have provided decently for his widow, without leaving everything that he had to dispose of, or any part of it, at her mercy.'

'My aunt may have erred,' said Emma, warmly; 'she *has* erred, but my uncle's conduct was faultless. I was her own niece, and he left to herself the power and the pleasure of providing for me.'

'But unluckily she has left the pleasure of providing for you to your father, and without the power. That's the long and short of the business. After keeping you at a distance from your family for such a length of time as must do away all natural affection among us, and breeding you up (I suppose) in a superior style, you are returned upon their hands without a sixpence.'

'You know,' replied Emma, struggling with her tears, 'my uncle's melancholy state of health. He was a greater invalid than my father. He could not leave home.'

'I do not mean to make you cry,' said Robert, rather softened – and after a short silence, by way of changing the subject, he added: 'I am just come from my father's room; he seems very indifferent. It will be a sad break up when he dies. Pity you can none of you get married! You must come to Croydon as well as the rest, and see what you can do there. I believe if Margaret had had a thousand or fifteen hundred pounds, there was a young man who would have thought of her.'

Emma was glad when they were joined by the others; it was better to look at her sister-in-law's finery than listen to Robert, who had equally irritated and grieved her. Mrs Robert, exactly as smart as she had been at her own party, came in with apologies for her dress.

'I would not make you wait,' said she; 'so I put on the first thing I met with. I am afraid I am a sad figure. My dear Mr W.,' (to her husband) 'you have not put any fresh powder in your hair.'

'No, I do not intend it. I think there is powder enough in my hair for my wife and sisters.'

'Indeed, you ought to make some alteration in your dress before dinner when you are out visiting, though you do not at home.'

'Nonsense.'

'It is very odd you should not like to do what other gentlemen do. Mr Marshall and Mr Hemmings change their dress every day of their lives before dinner. And what was the use of my putting up your last new coat, if you are never to wear it?'

'Do be satisfied with being fine yourself, and leave your husband alone.'

To put an end to this altercation and soften the evident vexation of her sister-in-law, Emma (though in no spirits to make such nonsense easy), began to admire her gown. It produced immediate complacency.

'Do you like it?' said she. 'I am very happy. It has been excessively admired; but sometimes I think the pattern too large. I shall wear one tomorrow that I think you will prefer to this. Have you seen the one I gave Margaret?'

Dinner came, and except when Mrs Robert looked at her husband's head, she continued gay and flippant, chiding Elizabeth for the profusion on the table, and absolutely protesting against the entrance of the roast turkey, which formed the only exception to 'You see your dinner.' 'I do beg and entreat that no turkey may be seen today. I am really frightened out of my wits with the number of dishes we have already. Let us have no turkey, I beseech you.'

'My dear,' replied Elizabeth, 'the turkey is roasted, and it may just as well come in as stay in the kitchen. Besides, if it is cut, I am in hopes my father may be tempted to eat a bit, for it is rather a favourite dish.'

'You may have it in, my dear; but I assure you I sha'n't touch it.'

Mr Watson had not been well enough to join the party at dinner, but was prevailed on to come down and drink tea with them.

'I wish we may be able to have a game of cards tonight,' said Elizabeth to Mrs Robert, after seeing her father comfortably seated in his arm-chair.

'Not on my account, my dear, I beg. You know I am no card-player. I think a snug chat infinitely better. I always say cards are very well sometimes to break a formal circle, but one never wants them among friends.'

'I was thinking of its being something to amuse my father,' said Elizabeth, 'if it was not disagreeable to you. He says his head won't bear whist, but perhaps if we make a round game he may be tempted to sit down with us.'

'By all means, my dear creature. I am quite at your service; only do not oblige me to choose the game, that's all. *Speculation* is the only round game at Croydon now, but I can play anything. When there is only one or two of you at home, you must be quite at a loss to amuse him. Why do you not get him to play at cribbage? Margaret and I have played at cribbage most nights that we have not been engaged.'

A sound like a distant carriage was at this moment caught; everybody listened; it became more decided; it certainly drew nearer. It was an unusual sound for Stanton at any time of the day, for the village was on no very public road, and contained no gentleman's family but the rector's. The wheels rapidly approached; in two minutes the general expectation was answered; they stopped beyond a doubt at the garden-gate of the parsonage. 'Who could it be? It was certainly a postchaise. Penelope was the only creature to be thought of; she might perhaps have met with some unexpected opportunity of returning.' A pause of suspense ensued. Steps were distinguished along the paved foot-way, which led under the windows of the house to the front door, and then within the passage. They were the steps of a man. It could not be Penelope. It must be Samuel. The door opened, and displayed Tom Musgrave in the wrap of a traveller. He had been in London, and was now on his way home, and he had come half-a-mile out of his road merely to call for ten minutes at Stanton. He loved to take people by surprise with sudden visits at extraordinary seasons, and, in the present instance, had had the additional motive of being able to tell the Miss Watsons, whom he depended on finding sitting quietly employed after tea, that he was going home to an eight-o'clock dinner.

As it happened, however, he did not give more surprise than he received, when, instead of being shown into the usual little sitting-room, the door of the best parlour (a foot larger each way than the other) was thrown open, and he beheld a circle of smart people whom he could not immediately recognise arranged, with all the honours of visiting, round the fire, and Miss Watson seated at the best Pembroke table, with the best tea-things before her. He stood a few seconds in silent amazement. 'Musgrave!' ejaculated Margaret, in a tender voice. He recollected himself, and came forward, delighted to find such a circle of friends, and blessing his good fortune for the unlooked-for indulgence. He shook hands with Robert, bowed and smiled to the ladies, and did everything very prettily, but as to any particularity of address or emotion towards Margaret, Emma, who closely observed him, perceived nothing that did not justify Elizabeth's opinion, though Margaret's modest smiles imported that she meant to take the visit to herself. He was persuaded without much difficulty to throw off his great-coat and drink tea with them. For 'whether he dined at eight or nine,' as he observed, 'was a matter of very little consequence;' and without seeming to seek, he did not turn away from the chair close by Margaret, which she was assiduous in providing him. She had thus secured him from her sisters, but it was not immediately in her power to preserve him from her brother's claims; for as he came avowedly from London, and had left it only four hours ago, the last current report as to public news, and the general opinion of the day, must be understood before Robert could let his attention be yielded to the less national and important demands of the women. At last, however, he was at liberty to hear Margaret's soft address, as she spoke her fears of his having had a most terrible cold, dark, dreadful journey.

'Indeed, you should not have set out so late.'

'I could not be earlier,' he replied. 'I was detained chatting at the Bedford by a friend. All hours are alike to me. How long have you been in the country, Miss Margaret?'

'We only came this morning; my kind brother and sister brought me home this very morning. 'Tis singular, is not it?'

'You were gone a great while, were not you? A fortnight, I suppose?'

'*You* may call a fortnight a great while, Mr Musgrave,' said Mrs Robert, sharply; 'but *we* think a month very little. I assure you we bring her home at the end of a month much against our will.'

'A month! Have you really been gone a month? 'Tis amazing how time flies.'

'You may imagine,' said Margaret, in a sort of whisper, 'what are my sensations in finding myself once more at Stanton; you know what a sad visitor I make. And I was so excessively impatient to see Emma; I dreaded the meeting, and at the same time longed for it. Do you not comprehend the sort of feeling?'

'Not at all,' cried he, aloud: 'I could never dread a meeting with Miss Emma Watson – or any of her sisters.'

It was lucky that he added that finish.

'Were you speaking to me?' said Emma, who had caught her own name.

'Not absolutely,' he answered; 'but I was thinking of you, as many at a greater distance are probably doing at this moment. Fine open weather, Miss Emma, charming season for hunting.'

'Emma is delightful, is not she?' whispered Margaret; 'I have found her more than answer my warmest hopes. Did you ever see anything more perfectly beautiful? I think even *you* must be a convert to a brown complexion.'

He hesitated. Margaret was fair herself, and he did not particularly want to compliment her; but Miss Osborne and Miss Carr were likewise fair, and his devotion to them carried the day.

'Your sister's complexion,' said he, at last, 'is as fine as a dark complexion can be; but I still profess my preference of a white skin. You have seen Miss Osborne? She is my model for a truly feminine complexion, and she is very fair.'

'Is she fairer than me?'

Tom made no reply. 'Upon my honour, ladies,' said he, giving a glance over his own person, 'I am highly indebted to your con-descension for admitting me in such *déshabille* into your drawing-room. I really did not consider how unfit I was to be here, or I hope I should have kept my distance. Lady Osborne would tell me that I were growing as careless as her son, if she saw me in this condition.'

The ladies were not wanting in civil returns, and Robert Watson, stealing a view of his own head in an opposite glass, said with equal civility – 'You cannot be more in *déshabille* than myself. We got here so late that I had not time even to put a little fresh powder in my hair.'

Emma could not help entering into what she supposed her sister-in-law's feelings at the moment.

When the tea-things were removed, Tom began to talk of his carriage; but the old card-table being set out, and the fish and counters, with a tolerably clean pack, brought forward from the buffet by Miss Watson, the general voice was so urgent with him to join their party that he agreed to allow himself another quarter of an hour. Even Emma was pleased that he would stay, for she was beginning to feel that a family party might be the worst of all parties; and the others were delighted.

'What's your game?' cried he, as they stood round the table.

'Speculation, I believe,' said Elizabeth. 'My sister recommends it, and I fancy we all like it. I know *you* do, Tom.'

'It is the only round game played at Croydon now,' said Mrs Robert; 'we never think of any other. I am glad it is a favourite with you.'

'Oh, me!' said Tom. 'Whatever you decide on will be a favourite with *me*. I have had some pleasant hours at speculation in my time, but I have not been in the way of it now for a long while. Vingt-un is the game at Osborne Castle. I have played nothing but vingt-un of late. You would be astonished to hear the noise we make there – the fine old lofty drawing-room rings again. Lady Osborne sometimes declares she cannot hear herself speak. Lord Osborne enjoys it famously, and he makes the best dealer without exception that I ever beheld – such quickness and spirit, he lets nobody dream over their cards. I wish you could see him overdraw himself on both his own cards. It is worth anything in the world!'

'Dear me!' cried Margaret, 'why should not we play at vingt-un? I think it is a much better game than speculation. I cannot say I am very fond of speculation.'

Mrs Robert offered not another word in support of the game. She was quite vanquished, and the fashions of Osborne Castle carried it over the fashions of Croydon.

'Do you see much of the parsonage family at the castle, Mr Musgrave?' said Emma, as they were taking their seats.

'Oh, yes; they are almost always there. Mrs Blake is a nice little good-humoured woman; she and I are sworn friends; and Howard's a very gentlemanlike, good sort of fellow! You are not forgotten, I assure you, by any of the party. I fancy you must have a little cheek-glowing now and then, Miss Emma. Were not you rather warm last Saturday about nine or ten o'clock in the evening? I will tell you how it was – I see you are dying to know. Says Howard to Lord Osborne – '

At this interesting moment he was called on by the others to regulate the game, and determine some disputable point; and his attention was so totally engaged in the business, and afterwards by the course of the game, as never to revert to what he had been saying before; and Emma, though suffering a good deal from curiosity, dared not remind him.

He proved a very useful addition to their table. Without him, it would have been a party of such very near relations as could have felt little interest, and perhaps maintained little complaisance; but his presence gave variety and secured good manners. He was, in fact, excellently qualified to shine at a round game, and few situations made him appear to greater advantage. He played with spirit, and had a great deal to say; and, though no wit himself, could sometimes make use of the wit of an absent friend, and had a lively way of retailing a common-place or saying a mere nothing, that had great effect at a card-table. The ways and good jokes of Osborne Castle were now added to his ordinary means of entertainment. He repeated the smart sayings of one lady, detailed the oversights of another, and indulged them even with a copy of Lord Osborne's style of overdrawing himself on both cards.

The clock struck nine while he was thus agreeably occupied; and when Nanny came in with her master's basin of gruel, he had the pleasure of observing to Mr Watson that he should leave him at supper while he went home to dinner himself. The carriage was ordered to the door, and no entreaties for his staying longer could now avail; for he well knew that if he stayed he must sit down to supper in less than ten minutes, which to a man whose heart had been long fixed on calling his next meal a dinner, was quite insupportable. On finding him determined to go, Margaret began to wink and nod at Elizabeth to ask him to dinner for the following day, and Elizabeth at last not able to resist hints which her own hospitable, social temper more than half seconded, gave the invitation: 'Would he give Robert the meeting, they should be very happy?'

'With the greatest pleasure' was his first reply. In a moment afterwards, 'That is, if I can possibly get here in time; but I shoot with Lord Osborne, and therefore must not engage. You will not think of me unless you see me.' And so he departed, delighted with the uncertainty in which he had left it.

*   *   *

Margaret, in the joy of her heart under circumstances which she chose to consider as peculiarly propitious, would willingly have made a confidante of Emma when they were alone for a short time the next morning, and had proceeded so far as to say, 'The young man who was here last night, my dear Emma, and returns today, is more interesting to me than perhaps you may be aware – '; but Emma, pretending to understand nothing extraordinary in the words, made some very inapplicable reply, and jumping up, ran away from a subject which was odious to her feelings. As Margaret would not allow a doubt to be repeated of Musgrave's coming to dinner, preparations were made for his entertainment much exceeding what had been deemed necessary the day before; and taking the office of superintendence entirely from her sister, she was half the morning in the kitchen herself, directing and scolding.

After a great deal of indifferent cooking and anxious suspense, however, they were obliged to sit down without their guest. Tom

Musgrave never came; and Margaret was at no pains to conceal her vexation under the disappointment, or repress the peevishness of her temper. The peace of the party for the remainder of that day and the whole of the next, which comprised the length of Robert's and Jane's visit, was continually invaded by her fretful displeasure and querulous attacks. Elizabeth was the usual object of both. Margaret had just respect enough for her brother's and sister's opinion to behave properly by *them*, but Elizabeth and the maids could never do anything right; and Emma, whom she seemed no longer to think about, found the continuance of the gentle voice beyond her calculation short. Eager to be as little among them as possible, Emma was delighted with the alternative of sitting above with her father, and warmly entreated to be his constant companion each evening; and as Elizabeth loved company of any kind too well not to prefer being below at all risks; as she had rather talk of Croydon with Jane, with every interruption of Margaret's perverseness, than sit with only her father, who frequently could not endure talking at all – the affair was so settled, as soon as she could be persuaded to believe it no sacrifice on her sister's part. To Emma, the change was most acceptable and delightful. Her father, if ill, required little more than gentleness and silence, and being a man of sense and education, was, if able to converse, a welcome companion. In *his* chamber Emma was at peace from the dreadful mortifications of unequal society and family discord; from the immediate endurance of hard-hearted prosperity, low-minded conceit, and wrong-headed folly, engrafted on an untoward disposition. She still suffered from them in the contemplation of their existence, in memory and in prospect; but for the moment, she ceased to be tortured by their effects. She was at leisure; she could read and think, though her situation was hardly such as to make reflection very soothing. The evils arising from the loss of her uncle were neither trifling nor likely to lessen; and when thought had been freely indulged, in contrasting the past and the present, the employment of mind and dissipation of unpleasant ideas which only reading could produce made her thankfully turn to a book.

The change in her home, society, and style of life, in consequence of the death of one friend and the imprudence of another, had indeed been striking. From being the first object of hope and solicitude to an uncle who had formed her mind with the care of a parent, and of tenderness to an aunt whose amiable temper had delighted to give her every indulgence; from being the life and spirit of a house where all had been comfort and elegance, and the expected heiress of an easy independence, she was become of importance to no one – a burden on those whose affections she could not expect, an addition in a house already overstocked, surrounded by inferior minds, with little chance of domestic comfort, and as little hope of future support. It was well for her that she was naturally cheerful, for the change had been such as might have plunged weak spirits in despondence.

She was very much pressed by Robert and Jane to return with them to Croydon, and had some difficulty in getting a refusal accepted, as they thought too highly of their own kindness and situation to suppose the offer could appear in a less advantageous light to anybody else. Elizabeth gave them her interest, though evidently against her own, in privately urging Emma to go.

'You do not know what you refuse, Emma,' said she, 'nor what you have to bear at home. I would advise you by all means to accept the invitation; there is always something lively going on at Croydon. You will be in company almost every day, and Robert and Jane will be very kind to you. As for me, I shall be no worse off without you than I have been used to be; but poor Margaret's disagreeable ways are new to *you*, and they would vex you more than you think for, if you stay at home.'

Emma was of course uninfluenced, except to greater esteem for Elizabeth, by such representations, and the visitors departed without her.

LADY SUSAN

Lady Susan

Letter 1

Langford, December

MY DEAR BROTHER – I can no longer refuse myself the pleasure of profiting by your kind invitation when we last parted of spending some weeks with you at Churchhill, and, therefore, if quite convenient to you and Mrs Vernon to receive me at present, I shall hope within a few days to be introduced to a sister whom I have so long desired to be acquainted with. My kind friends here are most affectionately urgent with me to prolong my stay, but their hospitable and cheerful dispositions lead them too much into society for my present situation and state of mind; and I impatiently look forward to the hour when I shall be admitted into your delightful retirement. I long to be made known to your dear little children, in whose hearts I shall be very eager to secure an interest. I shall soon have need for all my fortitude, as I am on the point of separation from my own daughter. The long illness of her dear father prevented my paying her that attention which duty and affection equally dictated, and I have too much reason to fear that the governess to whose care I consigned her was unequal to the charge. I have therefore resolved on placing her at one of the best private schools in town, where I shall have an opportunity of leaving her myself in my way to you. I am determined, you see, not to be denied admittance at Churchhill. It would indeed give me most painful sensations to know that it were not in your power to receive me.

Your most obliged and affectionate sister,

S. VERNON

Letter 2

Langford

You were mistaken, my dear Alicia, in supposing me fixed at this place for the rest of the winter: it grieves me to say how greatly you were mistaken, for I have seldom spent three months more agreeably than those which have just flown away. At present, nothing goes smoothly; the females of the family are united against me. You foretold how it would be when I first came to Langford, and Mainwaring is so uncommonly pleasing that I was not without apprehensions for myself. I remember saying to myself, as I drove to the house, 'I like this man, pray Heaven no harm come of it!' But I was determined to be discreet, to bear in mind my being only four months a widow, and to be as quiet as possible: and I have been so, my dear creature; I have admitted no one's attentions but Mainwaring's. I have avoided all general flirtation whatever; I have distinguished no creature besides, of all the numbers resorting hither, except Sir James Martin, on whom I bestowed a little notice, in order to detach him from Miss Mainwaring; but if the world could know my motive *there* they would honour me. I have been called an unkind mother, but it was the sacred impulse of maternal affection, it was the advantage of my daughter that led me on; and if that daughter were not the greatest simpleton on earth, I might have been rewarded for my exertions as I ought. Sir James did make proposals to me for Frederica; but Frederica, who was born to be the torment of my life, chose to set herself so violently against the match that I thought it better to lay aside the scheme for the present. I have more than once repented that I did not marry him myself; and were he but one degree less contemptibly weak I certainly should: but I must own myself rather romantic in that respect, and that riches only will not satisfy me. The event of all this is very provoking: Sir James is gone, Maria highly incensed, and Mrs Mainwaring insupportably jealous; so jealous, in short, and so enraged against me, that, in the fury of her temper, I should not be surprised at her appealing to her guardian, if she had the liberty of addressing him: but there your husband stands my friend; and the kindest, most amiable action of his life was his throwing her off for ever on her marriage. Keep up his resentment, therefore, I charge you. We are now in a sad state; no house was ever more altered; the whole party are at war, and Mainwaring scarcely dares speak to me. It is time for me to be gone; I have therefore determined on leaving them, and shall spend, I hope, a comfortable day with you in town within this week. If I am as little in favour with Mr Johnson as ever, you must come to me at 10 Wigmore Street; but I hope this may not be the case, for as Mr Johnson, with all his faults, is a man to whom that great word 'respectable' is always given, and I am known to be so intimate with his wife, his slighting me has an awkward look. I take London in my way to that insupportable spot, a country village; for I am really going to Churchhill. Forgive me, my dear friend, it is my last resource. Were there another place in England open to me I would prefer it. Charles Vernon is my aversion; and I am afraid of his wife. At Churchhill, however, I must remain till I have something better in view. My young lady accompanies me to town, where I shall deposit her under the care of Miss Summers, in Wigmore Street, till she becomes a little more reasonable. She will make good connections there, as the girls are all of the best families. The price is immense, and much beyond what I can ever attempt to pay. Adieu, I will send you a line as soon as I arrive in town.

Yours ever,

S. VERNON

Letter 3

MRS VERNON TO LADY DE COURCY

Churchhill

MY DEAR MOTHER – I am very sorry to tell you that it will not be in our power to keep our promise of spending our Christmas with you; and we are prevented that happiness by a circumstance which is not likely to make us any amends. Lady Susan, in a letter to her brother-in-law, has declared her intention of visiting us almost immediately; and as such a visit is in all probability merely an affair of convenience, it is impossible to conjecture its length. I was by no means prepared for such an event, nor can I now account for her ladyship's conduct; Langford appeared so exactly the place for her in every respect, as well from the elegant and expensive style of living there, as from her particular attachment to Mr Mainwaring, that I was very far from expecting so speedy a distinction, though I always imagined from her increasing friendship for us since her husband's death that we should, at some future period, be obliged to receive her. Mr Vernon, I think, was a great deal too kind to her when he was in Staffordshire; her behaviour to him, independent of her general character, has been so inexcusably artful and ungenerous since our marriage was first in agitation that no one less amiable and mild than himself could have overlooked it all; and though, as his brother's widow, and in narrow circumstances, it was proper to render her pecuniary assistance, I cannot help thinking his pressing invitation to her to visit us at Churchhill perfectly unnecessary. Disposed, however, as he always is to think the best of everyone, her display of grief, and professions of regret, and general resolutions of prudence, were sufficient to soften his heart and make him really confide in her sincerity; but, as for myself, I am still unconvinced, and plausibly as her ladyship has now written, I cannot make up my mind till I better understand her real meaning in coming to us. You may guess, therefore, my dear madam, with what feelings I look forward to her arrival. She will have occasion for all those attractive powers for which she is celebrated to gain any share of my regard; and I shall certainly endeavour to guard myself against their influence, if not accompanied by something more substantial. She expresses a most eager desire of being acquainted with me, and makes very gracious mention of my children but I am not quite weak enough to suppose a woman who has behaved with inattention, if not with unkindness, to her own child, should be attached to any of mine. Miss Vernon is to be placed at a school in London before her mother comes to us which I am glad of, for her sake and my own. It must be to her advantage to be separated from her mother, and a girl of sixteen who has received so wretched an education could not be a very desirable companion here. Reginald has long wished, I know, to see the captivating Lady Susan, and we shall depend on his joining our party soon.

I am glad to hear that my father continues so well; and am, with best love, &c.,

CATHERINE VERNON

Letter 4

Parklands

My dear Sister – I congratulate you and Mr Vernon on being about to receive into your family the most accomplished coquette in England. As a very distinguished flirt I have always been taught to consider her, but it has lately fallen in my way to hear some particulars of her conduct at Langford which prove that she does not confine herself to that sort of honest flirtation which satisfies most people, but aspires to the more delicious gratification of making a whole family miserable. By her behaviour to Mr Mainwaring she gave jealousy and wretchedness to his wife, and by her attentions to a young man previously attached to Mr Mainwaring's sister deprived an amiable girl of her lover. I learnt all this from Mr Smith, now in this neighbourhood (I have dined with him, at Hurst and Wilford), who is just come from Langford where he was a fortnight with her ladyship, and who is therefore well qualified to make the communication.

What a woman she must be! I long to see her, and shall certainly accept your kind invitation, that I may form some idea of those bewitching powers which can do so much – engaging at the same time, and in the same house, the affections of two men, who were neither of them at liberty to bestow them – and all this without the charm of youth! I am glad to find Miss Vernon does not accompany her mother to Churchhill, as she has not even manners to recommend her; and, according to Mr Smith's account, is equally dull and proud. Where pride and stupidity unite there can be no dissimulation worthy notice, and Miss Vernon shall be consigned to unrelenting contempt; but by all that I can gather, Lady Susan possesses a degree of captivating deceit which it must be pleasing to witness and detect. I shall be with you very soon, and am ever,

Your affectionate brother,

R. De Courcy

Letter 5

Churchhill

I received your note, my dear Alicia, just before I left town, and rejoice to be assured that Mr Johnson suspected nothing of your engagement the evening before. It is undoubtedly better to deceive him entirely, and since he will be stubborn he must be tricked. I arrived here in safety, and have no reason to complain of my reception from Mr Vernon; but I confess myself not equally satisfied with the behaviour of his lady. She is perfectly well-bred, indeed, and has the air of a woman of fashion, but her manners are not such as can persuade me of her being prepossessed in my favour. I wanted her to be delighted at seeing me. I was as amiable as possible on the occasion, but all in vain. She does not like me. To be sure when we consider that I *did* take some pains to prevent my brother-in-law's marrying her, this want of cordiality is not very surprising, and yet it shows an illiberal and vindictive spirit to resent a project which influenced me six years ago, and which never succeeded at last. I am sometimes disposed to repent that I did not let Charles buy Vernon Castle, when we were obliged to sell it; but it was a trying circumstance, especially as the sale took place exactly at the time of his marriage; and everybody ought to respect the delicacy of those feelings which could not endure that my husband's dignity should be lessened by his younger brother's having possession of the family estate. Could matters have been so arranged as to prevent the necessity of our leaving the castle, could we have lived with Charles and kept him single, I should have been very far from persuading my husband to dispose of it elsewhere; but Charles was on the point of marrying Miss De Courcy, and the event has justified me. Here are children in abundance, and what benefit could have accrued to me from his purchasing Vernon? My having prevented it may perhaps have given his wife an unfavourable impression, but where there is a disposition to dislike, a motive will never be wanting; and as to money matters it has not withheld him from being very useful to me. I really have a regard for him, he is so easily imposed upon!

The house is a good one, the furniture fashionable, and everything announces plenty and elegance. Charles is very rich, I am sure; when a man has once got his name in a banking-house he rolls in money; but they do not know what to do with it, keep very little company, and never go to London but on business. We shall be as stupid as possible. I mean to win my sister-in-law's heart through the children; I know all their names already, and am going to attach myself with the greatest sensibility to one in particular, a young Frederic, whom I take on my lap and sigh over for his dear uncle's sake.

Poor Mainwaring! I need not tell you how much I miss him, how perpetually he is in my thoughts. I found a dismal letter from him on my arrival here, full of complaints of his wife and sister, and lamentations on the cruelty of his fate. I passed off the letter as his wife's, to the Vernons, and when I write to him it must be under cover to you.

Ever yours,

S. VERNON

Letter 6

MRS VERNON TO MR DE COURCY

Churchhill

Well, my dear Reginald, I have seen this dangerous creature, and must give you some description of her, though I hope you will soon be able to form your own judgement. She is really excessively pretty; however you may choose to question the allurements of a lady no longer young, I must, for my own part, declare that I have seldom seen so lovely a woman as Lady Susan. She is delicately fair, with fine grey eyes and dark eyelashes; and from her appearance one would not suppose her more than five-and-twenty, though she must in fact be ten years older. I was certainly not disposed to admire her, though always hearing she was beautiful; but I cannot help feeling that she possesses an uncommon union of symmetry, brilliancy, and grace. Her address to me was so gentle, frank, and even affectionate, that, if I had not known how much she has always disliked me for marrying Mr Vernon, and that we had never met before, I should have imagined her an attached friend. One is apt, I believe, to connect assurance of manner with coquetry, and to expect that an impudent address will naturally attend an impudent mind; at least I was myself prepared for an improper degree of confidence in Lady Susan; but her countenance is absolutely sweet, and her voice and manner winningly mild. I am sorry it is so, for what is this but deceit? Unfortunately, one knows her too well. She is clever and agreeable, has all that knowledge of the world which makes conversation easy, and talks very well, with a happy command of language, which is too often used, I believe, to make black appear white. She has already almost persuaded me of her being warmly attached to her daughter, though I have been so long convinced to the contrary. She speaks of her with so much tenderness and anxiety, lamenting so bitterly the neglect of her education, which she represents however as wholly unavoidable, that I am forced to recollect how many successive springs her ladyship spent in town, while her daughter was left in Staffordshire to the care of servants, or a governess very little better, to prevent my believing what she says.

If her manners have so great an influence on my resentful heart, you may judge how much more strongly they operate on Mr Vernon's generous temper. I wish I could be as well satisfied as he is that it was really her choice to leave Langford for Churchhill; and if she had not stayed there for months before she discovered that her friends' manner of living did not suit her situation or feelings, I might have believed that concern for the loss of such a husband as Mr Vernon, to whom her own behaviour was far from unexceptionable, might for a time make her wish for retirement. But I cannot forget the length of her visit to the Mainwarings, and when I reflect on the different mode of life which she led with them from that to which she must now submit, I can only suppose that the wish of establishing her reputation by following, though late, the path of propriety, occasioned her removal from a family where she must in reality have been particularly happy. Your friend Mr Smith's story, however, cannot be quite correct, as she corresponds regularly with Mrs Mainwaring. At any rate it must be exaggerated. It is scarcely possible that two men should be so grossly deceived by her at once.

Yours, &c.,

S. VERNON

Letter 7

Churchhill

MY DEAR ALICIA – You are very good in taking notice of Frederica, and I am grateful for it as a mark of your friendship; but as I cannot have any doubt of the warmth of your affection, I am far from exacting so heavy a sacrifice. She is a stupid girl, and has nothing to recommend her. I would not, therefore, on my account, have you encumber one moment of your precious time by sending for her to Edward Street, especially as every visit is so much deducted from the grand affair of education, which I really wish to have attended to while she remains at Miss Summers's. I want her to play and sing with some portion of taste and a good deal of assurance, as she has *my* hand and arm and a tolerable voice. *I* was so much indulged in my infant years that I was never obliged to attend to anything, and consequently am without the accomplishments which are now necessary to finish a pretty woman. Not that I am an advocate for the prevailing fashion of acquiring a perfect knowledge of all languages, arts, and sciences. It is throwing time away to be mistress of French, Italian, and German; music, singing, drawing, &c., will gain a woman some applause, but will not add one lover to her list. Grace and manner, after all, are of the greatest importance. I do not mean, therefore, that Frederica's acquirements should be more than superficial, and I flatter myself that she will not remain long enough at school to understand anything thoroughly. I hope to see her the wife of Sir James within a twelvemonth. You know on what I ground my hope, and it is certainly a good foundation, for school must be very humiliating to a girl of Frederica's age. And, by the by, you had better not invite her any more on that account, as I wish her to find her situation as unpleasant as possible. I am sure of Sir James at any time, and could make him renew his application by a line. I shall trouble you meanwhile to prevent his forming any other attachment when he comes to town. Ask him to your house occasionally, and talk to him of Frederica, that he may not forget her.

Upon the whole, I commend my own conduct in this affair extremely, and regard it as a very happy instance of circumspection and tenderness. Some mothers would have insisted on their daughter's accepting so good an offer on the first overture; but I could not reconcile it to myself to force Frederica into a marriage from which her heart revolted, and instead of adopting so harsh a measure merely propose to make it her own choice by rendering her thoroughly uncomfortable till she does accept him – but enough of this tiresome girl.

You may well wonder how I contrive to pass my time here, and for the first week it was insufferably dull. Now, however, we begin to mend; our party is enlarged by Mrs Vernon's brother, a handsome young man, who promises me some amusement. There is something about him which rather interests me, a sort of sauciness and familiarity which I shall teach him to correct. He is lively, and seems clever, and when I have inspired him with greater respect for me than his sister's kind offices have implanted, he may be an agreeable flirt. There is exquisite pleasure in subduing an insolent spirit, in making a person predetermined to dislike acknowledge one's superiority. I have disconcerted him already by my calm reserve, and it shall be my endeavour to humble the pride of these self-important De Courcys still lower, to convince Mrs Vernon that her sisterly cautions have been bestowed in vain, and to persuade Reginald that she has scandalously belied me. This project will serve at least to amuse me, and prevent my feeling so acutely this dreadful separation from you and all whom I love.

Yours ever,

S. VERNON

Letter 8

MRS VERNON TO LADY DE COURCY

Churchhill

MY DEAR MOTHER – You must not expect Reginald back again for some time. He desires me to tell you that the present open weather induces him to accept Mr Vernon's invitation to prolong his stay in Sussex that they may have some hunting together. He means to send for his horses immediately, and it is impossible to say when you may see him in Kent. I will not disguise my sentiments on this change from you, my dear mother, though I think you had better not communicate them to my father, whose excessive anxiety about Reginald would subject him to an alarm which might seriously affect his health and spirits. Lady Susan has certainly contrived, in the space of a fortnight, to make my brother like her. In short, I am persuaded that his continuing here beyond the time originally fixed for his return is occasioned as much by a degree of fascination towards her as by the wish of hunting with Mr Vernon, and of course I cannot receive that pleasure from the length of his visit which my brother's company would otherwise give me. I am, indeed, provoked at the artifice of this unprincipled woman; what stronger proof of her dangerous abilities can be given than this perversion of Reginald's judgement, which when he entered the house was so decidedly against her! In his last letter he actually gave me some particulars of her behaviour at Langford, such as he received from a gentleman who knew her perfectly well, which, if true, must raise abhorrence against her, and which Reginald himself was entirely disposed to credit. His opinion of her, I am sure, was as low as of any woman in England; and when he first came it was evident that he considered her as one entitled neither to delicacy nor respect, and that he felt she would be delighted with the attentions of any man inclined to flirt with her.

Her behaviour, I confess, has been calculated to do away with such an idea; I have not detected the smallest impropriety in it – nothing of vanity, of pretension, of levity; and she is altogether so attractive that I should not wonder at his being delighted with her, had he known nothing of her previous to this personal acquaintance; but, against reason, against conviction, to be so well pleased with her as I am sure he is, does really astonish me. His admiration was at first very strong, but no more than was natural, and I did not wonder at his being much struck by the gentleness and delicacy of her manners; but when he has mentioned her of late it has been in terms of more extraordinary praise; and yesterday he actually said that he could not be surprised at any effect produced on the heart of man by such loveliness and such abilities; and when I lamented, in reply, the badness of her disposition, he observed that whatever might have been her errors they were to be imputed to her neglected education and early marriage, and that she was altogether a wonderful woman.

This tendency to excuse her conduct or to forget it, in the warmth of admiration, vexes me; and if I did not know that Reginald is too much at home at Churchhill to need an invitation for lengthening his visit, I should regret Mr Vernon's giving him any.

Lady Susan's intentions are of course those of absolute coquetry, or a desire of universal admiration; I cannot for a moment imagine that she has anything more serious in view; but it mortifies me to see a young man of Reginald's sense duped by her at all.

I am, &c.,

CATHERINE VERNON

Letter 9

MRS JOHNSON TO LADY S. VERNON

Edward Street

MY DEAREST FRIEND – I congratulate you on Mr De Courcy's arrival, and I advise you by all means to marry him; his father's estate is, we know, considerable, and I believe certainly entailed. Sir Reginald is very infirm, and not likely to stand in your way long. I hear the young man well spoken of, and though no one can really deserve you, my dearest Susan, Mr De Courcy may be worth having. Mainwaring will storm of course, but you may easily pacify him; besides, the most scrupulous point of honour could not require you to wait for *his* emancipation. I have seen Sir James; he came to town for a few days last week, and called several times in Edward Street. I talked to him about you and your daughter, and he is so far from having forgotten you, that I am sure he would marry either of you with pleasure. I gave him hopes of Frederica's relenting, and told him a great deal of her improvements. I scolded him for making love to Maria Mainwaring; he protested that he had been only in joke, and we both laughed heartily at her disappointment, and in short were very agreeable. He is as silly as ever.

Yours faithfully,

ALICIA

Letter 10

Churchhill

I am much obliged to you, my dear friend, for your advice respecting Mr De Courcy, which I know was given with the full conviction of its expediency, though I am not quite determined on following it. I cannot easily resolve on anything so serious as marriage; especially as I am not at present in want of money, and might perhaps, till the old gentleman's death, be very little benefited by the match. It is true that I am vain enough to believe it within my reach. I have made him sensible of my power, and can now enjoy the pleasure of triumphing over a mind prepared to dislike me, and prejudiced against all my past actions. His sister, too, is, I hope, convinced how little the ungenerous representations of anyone to the disadvantage of another will avail when opposed by the immediate influence of intellect and manner. I see plainly that she is uneasy at my progress in the good opinion of her brother, and conclude that nothing will be wanting on her part to counteract me; but having once made him doubt the justice of her opinion of me, I think I may defy her. It has been delightful to me to watch his advances towards intimacy, especially to observe his altered manner in consequence of my repressing by the cool dignity of my deportment his insolent approach to direct familiarity. My conduct has been equally guarded from the first, and I never behaved less like a coquette in the whole course of my life, though perhaps my desire of dominion was never more decided. I have subdued him entirely by sentiment and serious conversation, and made him, I may venture to say, at least *half* in love with me, without the semblance of the most commonplace flirtation. Mrs Vernon's consciousness of deserving every sort of revenge that it can be in my power to inflict for her ill-offices could alone enable her to perceive that I am actuated by any design in behaviour so gentle and unpretending. Let her think and act as she chooses, however. I have never yet found that the advice of a sister could prevent a young man's being in love if he chose. We are advancing now to some kind of confidence, and in short are likely to be engaged in a sort of platonic friendship. On *my* side you may be sure of its never being more, for if I were not already attached to another person as much as I can be to anyone, I should make a point of not bestowing my affection on a man who had dared to think so meanly of me.

Reginald has a good figure and is not unworthy the praise you have heard given him, but is still greatly inferior to our friend at Langford. He is less polished, less insinuating than Mainwaring, and is comparatively deficient in the power of saying those delightful things which put one in good humour with oneself and all the world. He is quite agreeable enough, however, to afford me amusement, and to make many of those hours pass very pleasantly which would otherwise be spent in endeavouring to overcome my sister-in-law's reserve, and listening to the insipid talk of her husband.

Your account of Sir James is most satisfactory, and I mean to give Miss Frederica a hint of my intentions very soon.

Yours, &c.,

S. VERNON

Letter 11

MRS VERNON TO LADY DE COURCY

Churchhill

I really grow quite uneasy, my dearest mother, about Reginald, from witnessing the very rapid increase of Lady Susan's influence. They are now on terms of the most particular friendship, frequently engaged in long conversations together; and she has contrived by the most artful coquetry to subdue his judgement to her own purposes. It is impossible to see the intimacy between them so very soon established without some alarm, though I can hardly suppose that Lady Susan's plans extend to marriage. I wish you could get Reginald home again on any plausible pretence; he is not at all disposed to leave us, and I have given him as many hints of my father's precarious state of health as common decency will allow me to do in my own house. Her power over him must now be boundless, as she has entirely effaced all his former ill-opinion, and persuaded him not merely to forget but to justify her conduct. Mr Smith's account of her proceedings at Langford, where he accused her of having made Mr Mainwaring and a young man engaged to Miss Mainwaring distractedly in love with her, which Reginald firmly believed when he came here, is now, he is persuaded, only a scandalous invention. He has told me so with a warmth of manner which spoke his regret at having believed the contrary himself.

How sincerely do I grieve that she ever entered this house! I always looked forward to her coming with uneasiness; but very far was it from originating in anxiety for Reginald. I expected a most disagreeable companion for myself, but could not imagine that my brother would be in the smallest danger of being captivated by a woman with whose principles he was so well acquainted, and whose character he so heartily despised. If you can get him away it will be a good thing.

Yours, &c.,

CATHERINE VERNON

Letter 12

SIR REGINALD DE COURCY TO HIS SON

Parklands

I know that young men in general do not admit of any enquiry even from their nearest relations into affairs of the heart, but I hope, my dear Reginald, that you will be superior to such as allow nothing for a father's anxiety, and think themselves privileged to refuse him their confidence and slight his advice. You must be sensible that as an only son, and the representative of an ancient family, your conduct in life is most interesting to your connections; and in the very important concern of marriage especially, there is everything at stake – your own happiness, that of your parents, and the credit of your name. I do not suppose that you would deliberately form an absolute engagement of that nature without acquainting your mother and myself, or at least without being convinced that we should approve of your choice; but I cannot help fearing that you may be drawn in, by the lady who has lately attached you, to a marriage which the whole of your family, far and near, must highly reprobate.

Lady Susan's age is itself a material objection, but her want of character is one so much more serious that the difference of even twelve years becomes in comparison of small account. Were you not blinded by a sort of fascination, it would be ridiculous in me to repeat the instances of great misconduct on her side so very generally known. Her neglect of her husband, her encouragement of other men, her extravagance and dissipation, were so gross and notorious that no one could be ignorant of them at the time, nor can now have forgotten them. To our family she has always been represented in softened colours by the benevolence of Mr Charles Vernon, and yet, in spite of his generous endeavours to excuse her, we know that she did, from the most selfish motives, take all possible pains to prevent his marriage with Catherine.

My years and increasing infirmities make me very desirous of seeing you settled in the world. To the fortune of a wife, the goodness of my own will make me indifferent, but her family and character must be equally unexceptionable. When your choice is fixed so that no objection can be made to either, then I can promise you a ready and cheerful consent; but it is my duty to oppose a match which deep art only could render possible, and must in the end make wretched.

It is possible her behaviour may arise only from vanity, or the wish of gaining the admiration of a man whom she must imagine to be particularly prejudiced against her; but it is more likely that she should aim at something further. She is poor, and may naturally seek an alliance which must be advantageous to herself; you know your own rights, and that it is out of my power to prevent your inheriting the family estate. My ability of distressing you during my life would be a species of revenge to which I could hardly stoop under any circumstances. I honestly tell you my sentiments and intentions: I do not wish to work on your fears, but on your sense and affection. It would destroy every comfort of my life to know that you were married to Lady Susan Vernon; it would be the death of that honest pride with which I have hitherto considered my son; I should blush to see him, to hear of him, to think of him.

I may perhaps do no good but that of relieving my own mind by this letter, but I felt it my duty to tell you that your partiality for Lady Susan is no secret to your friends, and to warn you against her. I should be glad to hear your reasons for disbelieving Mr Smith's intelligence; you had no doubt of its authenticity a month ago.

If you can give me your assurance of having no design beyond enjoying the conversation of a clever woman for a short period, and of yielding admiration only to her beauty and abilities, without being blinded by them to her faults, you will restore me to happiness; but if you cannot do this, explain to me, at least, what has occasioned so great an alteration in your opinion of her.

I am, &c., &c,

REGINALD DE COURCY

Letter 13

LADY DE COURCY TO MRS VERNON

Parklands

MY DEAR CATHERINE – Unluckily I was confined to my room when your last letter came, by a cold which affected my eyes so much as to prevent my reading it myself, so I could not refuse your father when he offered to read it to me, by which means he became acquainted, to my great vexation, with all your fears about your brother. I had intended to write to Reginald myself as soon as my eyes would let me, to point out, as well as I could, the danger of an intimate acquaintance with so artful a woman as Lady Susan to a young man of his age and high expectations. I meant, moreover, to have reminded him of our being quite alone now, and very much in need of him to keep up our spirits these long winter evenings. Whether it would have done any good can never be settled now, but I am excessively vexed that Sir Reginald should know anything of a matter which we foresaw would make him so uneasy. He caught all your fears the moment he had read your letter, and I am sure he has not had the business out of his head since. He wrote by the same post to Reginald a long letter full of it all, and particularly asking an explanation of what he may have heard from Lady Susan to contradict the late shocking reports. His answer came this morning, which I shall enclose to you, as I think you will like to see it. I wish it was more satisfactory, but it seems written with such a determination to think well of Lady Susan that his assurances as to marriage, &c., do not set my heart at ease. I say all I can, however, to satisfy your father, and he is certainly less uneasy since Reginald's letter. How provoking it is, my dear Catherine, that this unwelcome guest of yours should not only prevent our meeting this Christmas, but be the occasion of so much vexation and trouble! Kiss the dear children for me.

Your affectionate mother,

C. De Courcy

Letter 14

Mr De Courcy to Sir Reginald

Churchhill

My dear Sir – I have this moment received your letter, which has given me more astonishment than I ever felt before. I am to thank my sister, I suppose, for having represented me in such a light as to injure me in your opinion, and give you all this alarm. I know not why she should choose to make herself and her family uneasy by apprehending an event which no one but herself, I can affirm, would ever have thought possible. To impute such a design to Lady Susan would be taking from her every claim to that excellent understanding which her bitterest enemies have never denied her; and equally low must sink my pretensions to common sense if I am suspected of matrimonial views in my behaviour to her. Our difference of age must be an insuperable objection, and I entreat you, my dear father, to quiet your mind, and no longer harbour a suspicion which cannot be more injurious to your own peace than to our understandings.

I can have no other view in remaining with Lady Susan than to enjoy for a short time (as you have yourself expressed it) the conversation of a woman of high intellectual powers. If Mrs Vernon would allow something to my affection for herself and her husband in the length of my visit, she would do more justice to us all; but my sister is unhappily prejudiced beyond the hope of conviction against Lady Susan. From an attachment to her husband, which in itself does honour to both, she cannot forgive the endeavours at preventing their union, which have been attributed to selfishness in Lady Susan; but in this case, as well as in many others, the world has most grossly injured that lady by supposing the worst where the motives of her conduct have been doubtful.

Lady Susan had heard something so materially to the disadvantage of my sister as to persuade her that the happiness of Mr Vernon, to whom she was always much attached, would be wholly destroyed by the marriage. And this circumstance, while it explains the true motives of Lady Susan's conduct, and removes all the blame which has been so lavished on her, may also convince us how little the general report of anyone ought to be credited; since no character, however upright, can escape the malevolence of slander. If my sister, in the security of retirement, with as little opportunity as inclination to do evil, could not avoid censure, we must not rashly condemn those who, living in the world and surrounded with temptations, should be accused of errors which they are known to have the power of committing.

I blame myself severely for having so easily believed the slanderous tales invented by Charles Smith to the prejudice of Lady Susan, as I am now convinced how greatly they have traduced her. As to Mrs Mainwaring's jealousy, it was totally his own invention, and his account of her attaching Miss Mainwaring's lover was scarcely better founded. Sir James Martin had been drawn in by that young lady to pay her some attention; and as he is a man of fortune, it was easy to see *her* views extended to marriage. It is well known that Miss M. is absolutely on the catch for a husband, and no one therefore can pity her for losing, by the superior attractions of another woman, the chance of being able to make a worthy man completely wretched. Lady Susan was far from intending such a conquest, and on finding how warmly Miss Mainwaring resented her lover's defection, determined, in spite of Mr and Mrs Mainwaring's most urgent entreaties, to leave the family. I have reason to imagine she did receive serious proposals from Sir James, but her removing to Langford immediately on the discovery of his attachment must acquit her on that article with any mind of common candour. You will, I am sure, my dear Sir, feel the truth of this, and will hereby learn to do justice to the character of a very injured woman.

I know that Lady Susan in coming to Churchhill was governed only by the most honourable and amiable intentions; her prudence and economy are exemplary, her regard for Mr Vernon equal even to *his* deserts, and her wish of obtaining my sister's good opinion merits a better return than it has received. As a mother she is unexceptionable; her solid affection for her child is shown by placing her in hands where her education will be properly attended to; but because she has not the blind and weak partiality of most mothers, she is accused of wanting maternal tenderness. Every person of sense, however, will know how to value and commend her well-directed affection, and will join me in wishing that Frederica Vernon may prove more worthy than she has yet done of her mother's tender care.

I have now, my dear father, written my real sentiments of Lady Susan; you will know from this letter how highly I admire her abilities, and esteem her character; but if you are not equally convinced by my full and solemn assurance that your fears have been most idly created, you will deeply mortify and distress me.

I am, &c., &c.,

R. DE COURCY

Letter 15

MRS VERNON TO LADY DE COURCY

Churchhill

MY DEAR MOTHER – I return you Reginald's letter, and rejoice with all my heart that my father is made easy by it: tell him so, with my congratulations; but, between ourselves, I must own it has only convinced *me* of my brother's having no *present* intention of marrying Lady Susan, not that he is in no danger of doing so three months hence. He gives a very plausible account of her behaviour at Langford; I wish it may be true, but his intelligence must come from herself, and I am less disposed to believe it than to lament the degree of intimacy subsisting between them implied by the discussion of such a subject.

I am sorry to have incurred his displeasure, but can expect nothing better while he is so very eager in Lady Susan's justification. He is very severe against me indeed, and yet I hope I have not been hasty in my judgement of her. Poor woman! though I have reasons enough for my dislike, I cannot help pitying her at present, as she is in real distress, and with too much cause. She had this morning a letter from the lady with whom she has placed her daughter, to request that Miss Vernon might be immediately removed, as she had been detected in an attempt to run away. Why, or whither she intended to go, does not appear; but as her situation seems to have been unexceptionable, it is a sad thing and of course highly distressing to Lady Susan.

Frederica must be as much as sixteen, and ought to know better; but from what her mother insinuates, I am afraid she is a perverse girl. She has been sadly neglected, however, and her mother ought to remember it.

Mr Vernon set off for London as soon as she had determined what should be done. He is, if possible, to prevail on Miss Summers to let Frederica continue with her; and if he cannot succeed, to bring her to Churchhill for the present, till some other situation can be found for her. Her ladyship is comforting herself meanwhile by strolling along the shrubbery with Reginald, calling forth all his tender feelings, I suppose, on this distressing occasion. She has been talking a great deal about it to me. She talks vastly well; I am afraid of being ungenerous, or I should say, *too* well to feel so very deeply; but I will not look for her faults; she may be Reginald's wife! Heaven forbid it! but why should I be quicker-sighted than anyone else? Mr Vernon declares that he never saw deeper distress than hers, on the receipt of the letter – and is his judgement inferior to mine?

She was very unwilling that Frederica should be allowed to come to Churchhill, and justly enough, as it seems a sort of reward to behaviour deserving very differently; but it was impossible to take her anywhere else, and she is not to remain here long.

'It will be absolutely necessary,' said she, 'as you, my dear sister, must be sensible, to treat my daughter with some severity while she is here; a most painful necessity, but I will *endeavour* to submit to it. I am afraid I have often been too indulgent, but my poor Frederica's temper could never bear opposition well: you must support and encourage me; you must urge the necessity of reproof if you see me too lenient.'

All this sounds very reasonable. Reginald is so incensed against the poor silly girl. Surely it is not to Lady Susan's credit that he should be so bitter against her daughter; his idea of her must be drawn from the mother's description.

Well, whatever may be his fate, we have the comfort of knowing that we have done our utmost to save him. We must commit the event to a higher power.

Yours ever, &c.,

CATHERINE VERNON

Letter 16

Churchhill

Never, my dearest Alicia, was I so provoked in my life as by a letter this morning from Miss Summers. That horrid girl of mine has been trying to run away. I had not a notion of her being such a little devil before, she seemed to have all the Vernon milkiness; but on receiving the letter in which I declared my intention about Sir James, she actually attempted to elope; at least, I cannot otherwise account for her doing it. She meant, I suppose, to go to the Clarkes in Staffordshire, for she has no other acquaintances. But she *shall* be punished, she *shall* have him. I have sent Charles to town to make matters up if he can, for I do not by any means want her here. If Miss Summers will not keep her, you must find me out another school, unless we can get her married immediately. Miss S— writes word that she could not get the young lady to assign any cause for her extraordinary conduct, which confirms me in my own previous explanation of it.

Frederica is too shy, I think, and too much in awe of me to tell tales, but if the mildness of her uncle *should* get anything out of her, I am not afraid. I trust I shall be able to make my story as good as hers. If I am vain of anything, it is of my eloquence. Consideration and esteem as surely follow command of language as admiration waits on beauty, and here I have opportunity enough for the exercise of my talent, as the chief of my time is spent in conversation. Reginald is never easy unless we are by ourselves, and when the weather is tolerable, we pace the shrubbery for hours together. I like him on the whole very well; he is clever and has a good deal to say, but he is sometimes impertinent and troublesome. There is a sort of ridiculous delicacy about him which requires the fullest explanation of whatever he may have heard to my disadvantage, and is never satisfied till he thinks he has ascertained the beginning and end of everything.

This is *one* sort of love, but I confess it does not particularly recommend itself to me. I infinitely prefer the tender and liberal spirit of Mainwaring, which, impressed with the deepest conviction of my merit, is satisfied that whatever I do must be right; and look with a degree of contempt on the inquisitive and doubtful fancies of that heart which seems always debating on the reasonableness of its emotions. Mainwaring is indeed, beyond all compare, superior to Reginald – superior in everything but the power of being with me! Poor fellow! he is quite distracted by jealousy, which I am not sorry for, as I know no better support of love. He has been teasing me to allow of his coming into this country, and lodging somewhere near me *incog.* – but I forbid anything of the kind. Those women are inexcusable who forget what is due to themselves, and the opinion of the world.

Yours ever,

S. VERNON

Letter 17

MRS VERNON TO LADY DE COURCY

Churchhill

MY DEAR MOTHER – Mr Vernon returned on Thursday night, bringing his niece with him. Lady Susan had received a line from him by that day's post, informing her that Miss Summers had absolutely refused to allow of Miss Vernon's continuance in her academy; we were therefore prepared for her arrival, and expected them impatiently the whole evening. They came while we were at tea, and I never saw any creature look so frightened as Frederica when she entered the room.

Lady Susan, who had been shedding tears before, and showing great agitation at the idea of the meeting, received her with perfect self-command, and without betraying the least tenderness of spirit. She hardly spoke to her, and on Frederica's bursting into tears as soon as we were seated, took her out of the room, and did not return for some time. When she did, her eyes looked very red and she was as much agitated as before. We saw no more of her daughter.

Poor Reginald was beyond measure concerned to see his fair friend in such distress, and watched her with so much tender solicitude, that I, who occasionally caught her observing his countenance with exultation, was quite out of patience. This pathetic representation lasted the whole evening, and so ostentatious and artful a display has entirely convinced me that she did in fact feel nothing.

I am more angry with her than ever since I have seen her daughter; the poor girl looks so unhappy that my heart aches for her. Lady Susan is surely too severe, for Frederica does not seem to have the sort of temper to make severity necessary. She looks perfectly timid, dejected, and penitent.

She is very pretty, though not so handsome as her mother, nor at all like her. Her complexion is delicate, but neither so fair nor so blooming as Lady Susan's, and she has quite the Vernon cast of countenance, the oval face and mild dark eyes, and there is peculiar sweetness in her look when she speaks either to her uncle or me, for as we behave kindly to her we have of course engaged her gratitude. Her mother has insinuated that her temper is intractable, but I never saw a face less indicative of any evil disposition than hers; and from what I can see of the behaviour of each to the other, the invariable severity of Lady Susan and the silent dejection of Frederica, I am led to believe as heretofore that the former has no real love for her daughter, and has never done her justice or treated her affectionately.

I have not yet been able to have any conversation with my niece; she is shy, and I think I can see that some pains are taken to prevent her being much with me. Nothing satisfactory transpires as to her reason for running away. Her kind-hearted uncle, you may be sure, was too fearful of distressing her to ask many questions as they travelled. I wish it had been possible for me to fetch her instead of him. I think I should have discovered the truth in the course of a thirty-mile journey.

The small pianoforte has been removed within these few days, at Lady Susan's request, into her dressing-room, and Frederica spends great part of the day there, *practising* as it is called; but I seldom hear any noise when I pass that way; what she does with herself there I do not know. There are plenty of books, but it is not every girl who has been running wild the first fifteen years of her life, that can or will read. Poor creature! the prospect from her window is not very instructive, for that room overlooks the lawn, you know, with the shrubbery on one side, where she may see her mother walking for an hour together in earnest conversation with Reginald. A girl of Frederica's age must be childish indeed if such things do not strike her. Is it not inexcusable to give such an example to a daughter? Yet Reginald still thinks Lady Susan the best of mothers, and still condemns Frederica as a worthless girl! He is convinced that her attempt to run away proceeded from no justifiable cause, and had no provocation. I am sure I cannot say that it *had*, but while Miss Summers declares that Miss Vernon showed no signs of obstinacy or perverseness during her whole stay in Wigmore Street, till she was detected in this scheme, I cannot so readily credit what Lady Susan has made him and wants to make me believe, that it was merely an impatience of restraint and a desire of escaping from the tuition of masters which brought on the plan of an elopement. O Reginald, how is your judgement enslaved! He scarcely dares even allow her to be handsome, and when I speak of her beauty, replies only that her eyes have no brilliancy!

Sometimes he is sure she is deficient in understanding, and at others that her temper only is in fault. In short, when a person is always to deceive, it is impossible to be consistent. Lady Susan finds it necessary that Frederica should be to blame, and probably has sometimes judged it expedient to excuse her of ill-nature and sometimes to lament her want of sense. Reginald is only repeating after her ladyship.

I remain, &c., &c.,

CATHERINE VERNON

Letter 18

FROM THE SAME TO THE SAME

Churchhill

MY DEAR MOTHER – I am very glad to find that my description of Frederica Vernon has interested you, for I do believe her truly deserving of your regard; and when I have communicated a notion which has recently struck me, your kind impressions in her favour will, I am sure, be heightened. I cannot help fancying that she is growing partial to my brother. I so very often see her eyes fixed on his face with a remarkable expression of pensive admiration. He is certainly very handsome; and yet more, there is an openness in his manner that must be highly prepossessing, and I am sure she feels it so. Thoughtful and pensive in general, her countenance always brightens into a smile when Reginald says anything amusing; and, let the subject be ever so serious that he may be conversing on, I am much mistaken if a syllable of his uttering escapes her.

I want to make *him* sensible of all this, for we know the power of gratitude on such a heart as his; and could Frederica's artless affection detach him from her mother, we might bless the day which brought her to Churchhill. I think, my dear mother, you would not disapprove of her as a daughter. She is extremely young, to be sure, and has had a wretched education and a dreadful example of levity in her mother; but yet I can pronounce her disposition to be excellent, and her natural abilities very good.

Though totally without accomplishments, she is by no means so ignorant as one might expect to find her, being fond of books and spending the chief of her time in reading. Her mother leaves her more to herself than she did, and I have her with me as much as possible, and have taken great pains to overcome her timidity. We are very good friends, and though she never opens her lips before her mother, she talks enough when alone with me to make it clear that, if properly treated by Lady Susan, she would always appear to much greater advantage. There cannot be a more gentle, affectionate heart, or more obliging manners, when acting without restraint, and her little cousins are all very fond of her.

Your affectionate daughter,

C. VERNON

Letter 19

LADY SUSAN TO MRS JOHNSON

Churchhill

You will be eager, I know, to hear something further of Frederica, and perhaps may think me negligent for not writing before. She arrived with her uncle last Thursday fortnight, when, of course, I lost no time in demanding the cause of her behaviour; and soon found myself to have been perfectly right in attributing it to my own letter. The purport of it frightened her so thoroughly, that, with a mixture of true girlish perverseness and folly, without considering that she could not escape my authority by running away from Wigmore Street, she resolved on getting out of the house and proceeding directly by the stage to her friends, the Clarkes; and had really got as far as the length of two streets in her journey when she was fortunately missed, pursued, and overtaken.

Such was the first distinguished exploit of Miss Frederica Susanna Vernon; and, if we consider that it was achieved at the tender age of sixteen, we shall have room for the most flattering prognostics of her future renown. I am excessively provoked, however, at the parade of propriety which prevented Miss Summers from keeping the girl; and it seems so extraordinary a piece of nicety, considering my daughter's family connections, that I can only suppose the lady to be governed by the fear of never getting her money. Be that as it may, however, Frederica is returned on my hands; and, having nothing else to employ her, is busy in pursuing the plan of romance begun at Langford. She is actually falling in love with Reginald De Courcy! To disobey her mother by refusing an unexceptionable offer is not enough; her affections must also be given without her mother's approbation. I never saw a girl of her age bid fairer to be the sport of mankind. Her feelings are tolerably acute, and she is so charmingly artless in their display as to afford the most reasonable hope of her being ridiculous, and despised by every man who sees her.

Artlessness will never do in love matters; and that girl is born a simpleton who has it either by nature or affectation. I am not yet certain that Reginald sees what she is about, nor is it of much consequence. She is now an object of indifference to him, and she would be one of contempt were he to understand her emotions. Her beauty is much admired by the Vernons, but it has no effect on him. She is in high favour with her aunt altogether, because she is so little like myself, of course. She is exactly the companion for Mrs Vernon, who dearly loves to be firm, and to have all the sense and all the wit of the conversation to herself: Frederica will never eclipse her. When she first came I was at some pains to prevent her seeing much of her aunt; but I have relaxed, as I believe I may depend on her observing the rules I have laid down for their discourse.

But do not imagine that with all this lenity I have for a moment given up my plan of her marriage. No; I am unalterably fixed on this point, though I have not yet quite decided on the manner of bringing it about. I should not choose to have the business brought on here, and canvassed by the wise heads of Mr and Mrs Vernon; and I cannot just now afford to go to town. Miss Frederica must therefore wait a little.

Yours ever,

S. Vernon

Letter 20

Mrs Vernon to Lady De Courcy

Churchhill

We have a very unexpected guest with us at present, my dear mother: he arrived yesterday. I heard a carriage at the door, as I was sitting with my children while they dined, and supposing I should be wanted, left the nursery soon afterwards, and was halfway downstairs, when Frederica, as pale as ashes, came running up, and rushed by me into her own room. I instantly followed, and asked her what was the matter. 'Oh!' said she, 'he is come – Sir James is come, and what shall I do?' This was no explanation; I begged her to tell me what she meant. At that moment we were interrupted by a knock at the door: it was Reginald, who came, by Lady Susan's direction, to call Frederica down. 'It is Mr De Courcy!' said she, colouring violently. 'Mamma has sent for me; I must go.'

We all three went down together; and I saw my brother examining the terrified face of Frederica with surprise. In the breakfast-room we found Lady Susan, and a young man of gentlemanlike appearance, whom she introduced by the name of Sir James Martin – the very person, as you may remember, whom it was said she had been at pains to detach from Miss Mainwaring; but the conquest, it seems, was not designed for herself, or she has since transferred it to her daughter; for Sir James is now desperately in love with Frederica, and with full encouragement from mamma. The poor girl, however, I am sure, dislikes him; and though his person and address are very well, he appears, both to Mr Vernon and me, a very weak young man.

Frederica looked so shy, so confused, when we entered the room, that I felt for her exceedingly. Lady Susan behaved with great attention to her visitor; and yet I thought I could perceive that she had no particular pleasure in seeing him. Sir James talked a great deal, and made many civil excuses to me for the liberty he had taken in coming to Churchhill – mixing more frequent laughter with his discourse than the subject required – said many things over and over again, and told Lady Susan three times that he had seen Mrs Johnson a few evenings before. He now and then addressed Frederica, but more frequently her mother. The poor girl sat all this time without opening her lips – her eyes cast down, and her colour varying every instant – while Reginald observed all that passed in perfect silence.

At length Lady Susan, weary, I believe, of her situation, proposed walking; and we left the two gentlemen together to put on our pelisses.

As we went upstairs Lady Susan begged permission to attend me for a few moments in my dressing-room, as she was anxious to speak with me in private. I led her thither accordingly, and as soon as the door was closed, she said: 'I was never more surprised in my life than by Sir James's arrival, and the suddenness of it requires some apology to *you*, my dear sister, though to *me*, as a mother, it is highly flattering. He is so extremely attached to my daughter that he could not exist longer without seeing her. Sir James is a young man of an amiable disposition and excellent character; a little too much of the *rattle*, perhaps, but a year or two will rectify *that*; and he is in other respects so very eligible a match for Frederica, that I have always observed his attachment with the greatest pleasure; and am persuaded that you and my brother will give the alliance your hearty approbation. I have never before mentioned the likelihood of its taking place to anyone, because I thought that whilst Frederica continued at school it had better not be known to exist; but now, as I am convinced that Frederica is too old ever to submit to school confinement, and have, therefore, begun to consider her union with Sir James as not very distant, I had intended within a few days to acquaint yourself and Mr Vernon with the whole business. I am sure, my dear sister, you will excuse my remaining silent so long, and agree with me that such circumstances, while they continue from any cause in suspense, cannot be too cautiously concealed. When you have the happiness of bestowing your sweet little Catherine, some years hence, on a man who in connection and character is alike unexceptionable, you will know what I feel now;

though, thank Heaven, you cannot have all my reasons for rejoicing in such an event. Catherine will be amply provided for, and not, like my Frederica, indebted to a fortunate establishment for the comforts of life.'

She concluded by demanding my congratulations. I gave them somewhat awkwardly, I believe; for, in fact, the sudden disclosure of so important a matter took from me the power of speaking with any clearness, She thanked me, however, most affectionately, for my kind concern in the welfare of herself and daughter; and then said: 'I am not apt to deal in professions, my dear Mrs Vernon, and I never had the convenient talent of affecting sensations foreign to my heart; and therefore I trust you will believe me when I declare that much as I had heard in your praise before I knew you, I had no idea that I should ever love you as I now do; and I must further say that your friendship towards me is more particularly gratifying because I have reason to believe that some attempts were made to prejudice you against me. I only wish that they, whoever they are, to whom I am indebted for such kind intentions, could see the terms on which we now are together, and understand the real affection we feel for each other; but I will not detain you any longer. God bless you for your goodness to me and my girl, and continue to you all your present happiness.'

What can one say of such a woman, my dear mother? Such earnestness, such solemnity of expression! and yet I cannot help suspecting the truth of everything she says.

As for Reginald, I believe he does not know what to make of the matter. When Sir James came, he appeared all astonishment and perplexity; the folly of the young man and the confusion of Frederica entirely engrossed him; and though a little private discourse with Lady Susan has since had its effect, he is still hurt, I am sure, at her allowing of such a man's attentions to her daughter.

Sir James invited himself with great composure to remain here a few days – hoped we would not think it odd, was aware of its being very impertinent, but he took the liberty of a relation; and concluded by wishing, with a laugh, that he might be really one very soon. Even Lady Susan seemed a little disconcerted by this forwardness; in her heart I am persuaded she sincerely wishes him gone.

But something must be done for this poor girl, if her feelings are such as both I and her uncle believe them to be. She must not be sacrificed to policy or ambition, and she must not be left to suffer from the dread of it. The girl whose heart can distinguish Reginald De Courcy, deserves, however he may slight her, a better fate than to be Sir James Martin's wife. As soon as I can get her alone, I will discover the real truth; but she seems to wish to avoid me. I hope this does not proceed from anything wrong, and that I shall not find out I have thought too well of her. Her behaviour to Sir James certainly speaks the greatest consciousness and embarrassment, but I see nothing in it more like encouragement.

Adieu, my dear mother.

Yours, &c.,

C. VERNON

Letter 21

MISS VERNON TO MR DE COURCY

SIR – I hope you will excuse this liberty; I am forced upon it by the greatest distress, or I should be ashamed to trouble you. I am very miserable about Sir James Martin, and have no other way in the world of helping myself but by writing to you, for I am forbidden even speaking to my uncle and aunt on the subject; and this being the case, I am afraid my applying to you will appear no better than equivocation, and as if I attended to the letter and not the spirit of mamma's commands. But if *you* do not take my part and persuade her to break it off, I shall be half-distracted, for I cannot bear him. No human being but *you* could have any chance of prevailing with her. If you will, therefore, have the unspeakably great kindness of taking my part with her, and persuading her to send Sir James away, I shall be more obliged to you than it is possible for me to express. I always disliked him from the first: it is not a sudden fancy, I assure you, sir; I always thought him silly and impertinent and disagreeable, and now he is grown worse than ever. I would rather work for my bread than marry him. I do not know how to apologise enough for this letter; I know it is taking so great a liberty. I am aware how dreadfully angry it will make mamma, but I must run the risk.

I am, sir, your most humble servant,

F. S. V.

Letter 22

Churchhill

This is insufferable! My dearest friend, I was never so enraged before, and must relieve myself by writing to you, who I know will enter into all my feelings. Who should come on Tuesday but Sir James Martin! Guess my astonishment, and vexation – for, as you well know, I never wished him to be seen at Churchhill. What a pity that you should not have known his intentions! Not content with coming, he actually invited himself to remain here a few days. I could have poisoned him! I made the best of it, however, and told my story with great success to Mrs Vernon, who, whatever might be her real sentiments, said nothing in opposition to mine. I made a point also of Frederica's behaving civilly to Sir James, and gave her to understand that I was absolutely determined on her marrying him. She said something of her misery, but that was all. I have for some time been more particularly resolved on the match from seeing the rapid increase of her affection for Reginald, and from not feeling secure that a knowledge of such affection might not in the end awaken a return. Contemptible as a regard founded only on compassion must make them both in my eyes, I felt by no means assured that such might not be the consequence. It is true that Reginald has not in any degree grown cool towards me; but yet he has lately mentioned Frederica spontaneously and unnecessarily, and once said something in praise of her person.

He was all astonishment at the appearance of my visitor, and at first observed Sir James with an attention which I was pleased to see not unmixed with jealousy, but unluckily it was impossible for me really to torment him, as Sir James, though extremely gallant to me, very soon made the whole party understand that his heart was devoted to my daughter.

I had no great difficulty in convincing De Courcy, when we were alone, that I was perfectly justified, all things considered, in desiring the match; and the whole business seemed most comfortably arranged. They could none of them help perceiving that Sir James was no Solomon; but I had positively forbidden Frederica complaining to Charles Vernon or his wife, and they had therefore no pretence for interference; though my impertinent sister, I believe, wanted only opportunity for doing so.

Everything, however, was going on calmly and quietly; and, though I counted the hours of Sir James's stay, my mind was entirely satisfied with the posture of affairs. Guess, then, what I must feel at the sudden disturbance of all my schemes; and that, too, from a quarter where I had least reason to expect it. Reginald came this morning into my dressing-room, with a very unusual solemnity of countenance, and after some preface informed me in so many words that he wished to reason with me on the impropriety and unkindness of allowing Sir James Martin to address my daughter, contrary to *her* inclinations. I was all amazement. When I found that he was not to be laughed out of his design, I calmly begged an explanation, and desired to know by what he was impelled, and by whom commissioned, to reprimand me. He then told me, mixing in his speech a few insolent compliments and ill-timed expressions of tenderness, to which I listened with perfect indifference, that my daughter had acquainted him with some circumstances, concerning herself, Sir James and me, which had given him great uneasiness.

In short, I found that she had in the first place actually written to him to request his interference, and that, on receiving her letter, he had conversed with her on the subject of it, in order to understand the particulars, and to assure himself of her real wishes.

I have not a doubt but that the girl took this opportunity of making downright love to him. I am convinced of it by the manner in which he spoke of her. Much good may such love do him! I shall ever despise the man who can be gratified by the passion which he never wished to inspire, nor solicited the avowal of. I shall always detest them both. He can have no true regard for me, or he would not have listened to her; and *she*, with her little rebellious heart and indelicate feelings, to throw herself into the protection of a young man with whom she has scarcely ever exchanged two words before! I am equally confounded at *her* impudence and *his* credulity. How dared he believe what she told him in my disfavour! Ought he not to have felt assured that I must have unanswerable motives for all that I had done? Where was his reliance on my sense and goodness then? Where the resentment which true love would have dictated against the person defaming me – that person, too, a chit, a child, without talent or education, whom he had been always taught to despise?

I was calm for some time; but the greatest degree of forbearance may be overcome, and I hope I was afterwards sufficiently keen. He endeavoured, long endeavoured, to soften my resentment; but that woman is a fool indeed who, while insulted by accusation, can be worked on by compliments. At length he left me, as deeply provoked as myself; and he showed his anger *more*. I was quite cool, but he gave way to the most violent indignation; I may therefore expect it will the sooner subside, and perhaps his may be vanished for ever, while mine will be found still fresh and implacable.

He is now shut up in his apartment, whither I heard him go on leaving mine. How unpleasant, one would think, must be his reflections! but some people's feelings are incomprehensible. I have not yet tranquillised myself enough to see Frederica. *She* shall not soon forget the occurrences of this day; she shall find that she has poured forth her tender tale of love in vain, and exposed herself for ever to the contempt of the whole world, and the severest resentment of her injured mother.

Your affectionate

S. VERNON

Letter 23

MRS VERNON TO LADY DE COURCY

Churchhill

Let me congratulate you, my dearest mother! The affair which has given us so much anxiety is drawing to a happy conclusion. Our prospect is most delightful, and since matters have now taken so favourable a turn, I am quite sorry that I ever imparted my apprehensions to you; for the pleasure of learning that the danger is over is perhaps dearly purchased by all that you have previously suffered.

I am so much agitated by delight that I can scarcely hold a pen, but am determined to send you a few short lines by James, that you may have some explanation of what must so greatly astonish you – that Reginald should be returning to Parklands.

I was sitting about half an hour ago with Sir James in the breakfast parlour, when my brother called me out of the room. I instantly saw that something was the matter; his complexion was raised, and he spoke with great emotion; you know his eager manner, my dear mother, when his mind is interested.

'Catherine,' said he, 'I am going home today; I am sorry to leave you, but I must go: it is a great while since I have seen my father and mother. I am going to send James forward with my hunters immediately; if you have any letter, therefore, he can take it. I shall not be at home myself till Wednesday or Thursday, as I shall go through London, where I have business; but before I leave you,' he continued, speaking in a lower tone, and with still greater energy, 'I must warn you of one thing – do not let Frederica Vernon be made unhappy by that Martin. He wants to marry her; her mother promotes the match, but *she* cannot endure the idea of it. Be assured that I speak from the fullest conviction of the truth of what I say; I *know* that Frederica is made wretched by Sir James's continuing here. She is a sweet girl, and deserves a better fate. Send him away immediately; *he* is only a fool, but what her mother can mean, Heaven only knows! Goodbye,' he added, shaking my hand with earnestness; 'I do not know when you will see me again; but remember what I tell you of Frederica; you *must* make it your business to see justice done her. She is an amiable girl, and has a very superior mind to what we have ever given her credit for.'

He then left me, and ran upstairs. I would not try to stop him, for I know what his feelings must be. The nature of mine, as I listened to him, I need not attempt to describe; for a minute or two I remained in the same spot, overpowered by wonder of a most agreeable sort indeed; yet it required some consideration to be tranquilly happy.

In about ten minutes after my return to the parlour Lady Susan entered the room. I concluded, of course, that she and Reginald had been quarrelling, and looked with anxious curiosity for a confirmation of my belief in her face. Mistress of deceit, however, she appeared perfectly unconcerned, and after chatting on indifferent subjects for a short time, said to me, 'I find from Wilson that we are going to lose Mr De Courcy – is it true that he leaves Churchhill this morning?' I replied that it was. 'He told us nothing of all this last night,' said she, laughing, 'or even this morning at breakfast; but perhaps he did not know it himself. Young men are often hasty in their resolutions, and not more sudden in forming than unsteady in keeping them. I should not be surprised if he were to change his mind at last, and not go.'

She soon afterwards left the room. I trust, however, my dear mother, that we have no reason to fear an alteration of his present plan; things have gone too far. They must have quarrelled, and about Frederica, too. Her calmness astonishes me. What delight will be yours in seeing him again; in seeing him still worthy your esteem, still capable of forming your happiness!

When next I write, I shall be able to tell you that Sir James is gone, Lady Susan vanquished, and Frederica at peace. We have much to do, but it shall be done. I am all impatience to hear how this astonishing change was effected. I finish as I began, with the warmest congratulations.

Yours ever, &c.,

CATH. VERNON

Letter 24

FROM THE SAME TO THE SAME

Churchhill

Little did I imagine, my dear mother, when I sent off my last letter, that the delightful perturbation of spirits I was then in would undergo so speedy, so melancholy a reverse. I never can sufficiently regret that I wrote to you at all. Yet who could have foreseen what has happened. My dear mother, every hope which made me so happy only two hours ago has vanished. The quarrel between Lady Susan and Reginald is made up, and we are all as we were before. One point only is gained. Sir James Martin is dismissed. What are we now to look forward to? I am indeed disappointed; Reginald was all but gone, his horse was ordered and all but brought to the door; who would not have felt safe?

For half an hour I was in momentary expectation of his departure. After I had sent off my letter to you, I went to Mr Vernon, and sat with him in his room talking over the whole matter, and then determined to look for Frederica, whom I had not seen since breakfast. I met her on the stairs, and saw that she was crying.

'My dear aunt,' said she, 'he is going – Mr De Courcy is going, and it is all my fault. I am afraid you will be very angry with me, but indeed I had no idea it would end so.'

'My love,' I replied, 'do not think it necessary to apologise to me on that account. I shall feel myself under an obligation to anyone who is the means of sending my brother home, because,' recollecting myself, 'I know my father wants very much to see him. But what is it you have done to occasion all this?'

She blushed deeply as she answered: 'I was so unhappy about Sir James that I could not help – I have done something very wrong, I know; but you have not an idea of the misery I have been in, and mamma had ordered me never to speak to you or my uncle about it, and – ' 'You therefore spoke to my brother to engage his interference,' said I, to save her the explanation. 'No, but I wrote to him – I did indeed, I got up this morning before it was light, and was two hours about it; and when my letter was done, I thought I never should have courage to give it. After breakfast, however, as I was going to my room, I met him in the passage, and then, as I knew that everything must depend on that moment, I forced myself to give it. He was so good as to take it immediately. I dared not look at him, and ran away directly. I was in such a fright I could hardly breathe. My dear aunt, you do not know how miserable I have been.'

'Frederica,' said I, 'you ought to have told *me* all your distresses. You would have found in me a friend always ready to assist you. Do you think that your uncle or I should not have espoused your cause as warmly as my brother?'

'Indeed, I did not doubt your kindness,' said she, colouring again, 'but I thought Mr De Courcy could do anything with my mother; but I was mistaken: they have had a dreadful quarrel about it, and he is going away. Mamma will never forgive me, and I shall be worse off than ever.' 'No, you shall not,' I replied; 'in such a point as this your mother's prohibition ought not to have prevented your speaking to me on the subject. She has no right to make you unhappy, and she shall *not* do it. Your applying, however, to Reginald can be productive only of good to all parties. I believe it is best as it is. Depend upon it that you shall not be made unhappy any longer.'

At that moment how great was my astonishment at seeing Reginald come out of Lady Susan's dressing-room. My heart misgave me instantly. His confusion at seeing me was very evident.

Frederica immediately disappeared. 'Are you going?' I said; 'you will find Mr Vernon in his own room.' 'No, Catherine,' he replied, 'I am *not* going. Will you let me speak to you a moment?'

We went into my room. 'I find,' he continued, his confusion increasing as he spoke, 'that I have been acting with my usual foolish impetuosity. I have entirely misunderstood Lady Susan, and was on the point of leaving the house under a false impression of her conduct. There has been some very great mistake; we have been all mistaken, I fancy. Frederica does not know her mother. Lady Susan means nothing but her good, but she will not make a friend of her. Lady Susan does not always know, therefore, what will make her daughter happy. Besides, I could have no right to interfere. Miss Vernon was mistaken in applying to me. In short, Catherine, everything has gone wrong, but it is now all happily settled. Lady Susan, I believe, wishes to speak to you about it, if you are at leisure.'

'Certainly,' I replied, deeply sighing at the recital of so lame a story. I made no comments, however, for words would have been vain. Reginald was glad to get away, and I went to Lady Susan, curious, indeed, to hear her account of it.

'Did I not tell you,' said she with a smile, 'that your brother would not leave us after all?' 'You did, indeed,' replied I very gravely; 'but I flattered myself you would be mistaken.' 'I should not have hazarded such an opinion,' returned she, 'if it had not at that moment occurred to me that his resolution of going might be occasioned by a conversation in which we had been this morning engaged, and which had ended very much to his dissatisfaction, from our not rightly understanding each other's meaning. This idea struck me at the moment, and I instantly determined that an accidental dispute, in which I might probably be as much to blame as himself, should not deprive you of your brother. If you remember, I left the room almost immediately. I was resolved to lose no time in clearing up those mistakes as far as I could. The case was this – Frederica had set herself violently against marrying Sir James.' 'And can your ladyship wonder that she should?' cried I with some warmth; 'Frederica has an excellent understanding, and Sir James has none.' 'I am at least very far from regretting it, my dear sister,' said she; 'on the contrary, I am grateful for so favourable a sign of my daughter's sense. Sir James is certainly below par (his boyish manners make him appear worse); and had Frederica possessed the penetration and the abilities which I could have wished in my daughter, or had I even known her to possess as much as she does, I should not have been anxious for the match.' 'It is odd that you should alone be ignorant of your daughter's sense!' 'Frederica never does justice to herself; her manners are shy and childish, and besides she is afraid of me. During her poor father's life she was a spoilt child; the severity which it has since been necessary for me to show has alienated her affection; neither has she any of that brilliancy of intellect, that genius or vigour of mind which will force itself forward.' 'Say rather that she has been unfortunate in her education!' 'Heaven knows, my dearest Mrs Vernon, how fully I am aware of that; but I would wish to forget every circumstance that might throw blame on the memory of one whose name is sacred with me.'

Here she pretended to cry; I was out of patience with her. 'But what,' said I, 'was your ladyship going to tell me about your disagreement with my brother?' 'It originated in an action of my daughter's, which equally marks her want of judgement and the unfortunate dread of me I have been mentioning – she wrote to Mr De Courcy.' 'I know she did; you had forbidden her speaking to Mr Vernon or to me on the cause of her distress; what could she do, therefore, but apply to my brother?' 'Good God!' she exclaimed, 'what an opinion you must have of me! Can you possibly suppose that I was aware of her unhappiness! that it was my object to make my own child miserable, and that I had forbidden her speaking to you on the subject from a fear of your interrupting the diabolical scheme? Do you think me destitute of every honest, every natural feeling? Am I capable of consigning *her* to everlasting misery, whose welfare it is my first earthly duty to promote? The idea is horrible!' 'What, then, was your intention when you insisted on her silence?' 'Of what use, my dear sister, could be any application to you, however the affair might stand? Why should I subject you to entreaties which I refused to attend to myself? Neither for your sake, nor for hers, nor for my own, could such a thing be desirable. When my own resolution was taken, I could not wish for the interference, however friendly, of another person. I was mistaken, it is true, but I believed myself right.' 'But what was this mistake to which your ladyship so often alludes! from whence arose so astonishing a misconception of your daughter's feelings! Did you not know that she disliked Sir James?' 'I knew that he was not absolutely the man she would have chosen, but I was persuaded that her objections to him did not arise from any perception of his deficiency. You must not question me, however, my dear sister, too minutely on this point,' continued she, taking me affectionately by the hand; 'I honestly own that there is something to conceal. Frederica makes me very unhappy! Her applying to Mr De Courcy hurt me particularly.' 'What is it you mean to infer,' said I, 'by this appearance of mystery? If you think your daughter at all attached to Reginald, her objecting to Sir James could not less deserve to be attended to than if the cause of her objecting had been a consciousness of his folly; and why should your ladyship, at any rate, quarrel with my brother for an interference which, you must know, it is not in his nature to refuse when urged in such a manner?'

'His disposition, you know, is warm, and he came to expostulate with me; his compassion all alive for this ill-used girl, this heroine in distress! We misunderstood each other: he believed me more to blame than I really was; I considered his interference less excusable than I now find it. I have a real regard for him, and was beyond expression mortified to find it, as I thought, so ill bestowed We were both warm, and of course both to blame. His resolution of leaving Churchhill is consistent with his general eagerness. When I understood his intention, however, and at the same time began to think that we had been perhaps equally mistaken in each other's meaning, I resolved to have an explanation before it was too late. For any member of your family I must always feel a degree of affection, and I own it would have sensibly hurt me if my acquaintance with Mr De Courcy had ended so gloomily. I have now only to say further, that as I am convinced of Frederica's having a reasonable dislike to Sir James, I shall instantly inform him that he must give up all hope of her. I reproach myself for having even, though innocently, made her unhappy on that score. She shall have all the retribution in my power to make; if she value her own happiness as much as I do, if she judge wisely, and command herself as she ought, she may now be easy. Excuse me, my dearest sister, for thus trespassing on your time, but I owe it to my own character; and after this explanation I trust I am in no danger of sinking in your opinion.'

I could have said, 'Not much, indeed!' but I left her almost in silence. It was the greatest stretch of forbearance I could practise. I could not have stopped myself had I begun. Her assurance! her deceit! – but I will not allow myself to dwell on them; they will strike you sufficiently. My heart sickens within me.

As soon as I was tolerably composed I returned to the parlour. Sir James's carriage was at the door, and he, merry as usual, soon afterwards took his leave. How easily does her ladyship encourage or dismiss a lover!

In spite of this release, Frederica still looks unhappy: still fearful, perhaps, of her mother's anger; and though dreading my brother's departure, jealous, it may be, of his staying. I see how closely she observes him and Lady Susan, poor girl! I have now no hope for her. There is not a chance of her affection being returned. He thinks very differently of her from what he used to do; he does her some justice, but his reconciliation with her mother precludes every dearer hope.

Prepare, my dear mother, for the worst! The probability of their marrying is surely heightened! He is more securely hers than ever. When that wretched event takes place, Frederica must belong wholly to us. I am thankful that my last letter will precede this by so little, as every moment that you can be saved from feeling a joy which leads only to disappointment is of consequence.

Yours ever, &c.,

CATHERINE VERNON

Letter 25

LADY SUSAN TO MRS JOHNSON

Churchhill

I call on you, dear Alicia, for congratulations: I am my own self, gay and triumphant! When I wrote you the other day I was, in truth, in high irritation, and with ample cause. Nay, I know not whether I ought to be quite tranquil now, for I have had more trouble in restoring peace than I ever intended to submit to. This Reginald has a proud spirit of his own! – a spirit, too, resulting from a fancied sense of superior integrity, which is peculiarly insolent! I shall not easily forgive him, I assure you. He was actually on the point of leaving Churchhill! I had scarcely concluded my last, when Wilson brought me word of it. I found, therefore, that something must be done; for I did not choose to leave my character at the mercy of a man whose passions are so violent and so revengeful. It would have been trifling with my reputation to allow of his departing with such an impression in my disfavour; in this light, condescension was necessary.

I sent Wilson to say that I desired to speak with him before he went; he came immediately. The angry emotions which had marked every feature when we last parted were partially subdued. He seemed astonished at the summons, and looked as if half wishing and half fearing to be softened by what I might say.

If my countenance expressed what I aimed at, it was composed and dignified – and yet, with a degree of pensiveness which might convince him that I was not quite happy. 'I beg your pardon, sir, for the liberty I have taken in sending for you,' said I; 'but as I have just learnt your intention of leaving this place today, I feel it my duty to entreat that you will not on my account shorten your visit here even an hour. I am perfectly aware that after what has passed between us it would ill suit the feelings of either to remain longer in the same house: so very great, so total a change from the intimacy of friendship must render any future intercourse the severest punishment; and your resolution of quitting Churchhill is undoubtedly in unison with our situation, and with those lively feelings which I know you to possess. But, at the same time, it is not for me to suffer such a sacrifice as it must be to leave relations to whom you are so much attached, and are so dear. My remaining here cannot give that pleasure to Mr and Mrs Vernon which your society must; and my visit has already perhaps been too long. My removal, therefore, which must, at any rate, take place soon, may, with perfect convenience, be hastened; and I make it my particular request that I may not in any way be instrumental in separating a family so affectionately attached to each other. Where I go is of no consequence to anyone; of very little to myself; but you are of importance to all your connections.' Here I concluded, and I hope you will be satisfied with my speech. Its effect on Reginald justifies some portion of vanity, for it was no less favourable than instantaneous. Oh, how delightful it was to watch the variations of his countenance while I spoke! to see the struggle between returning tenderness and the remains of displeasure. There is something agreeable in feelings so easily worked on; not that I envy him their possession, nor would, for the world, have such myself; but they are very convenient when one wishes to influence the passions of another. And yet this Reginald, whom a very few words from me softened at once into the utmost submission, and rendered more tractable, more attached, more devoted than ever, would have left me in the first angry swelling of his proud heart without deigning to seek an explanation.

Humbled as he now is, I cannot forgive him such an instance of pride, and am doubtful whether I ought not to punish him by dismissing him at once after this reconciliation, or by marrying and teasing him for ever. But these measures are each too violent to be adopted without some deliberation; at present my thoughts are fluctuating between various schemes. I have many things to compass: I must punish Frederica, and pretty severely too, for her application to Reginald; I must punish him for receiving it so favourably, and for the rest of his conduct. I must torment my sister-in-law for the insolent triumph of her look and manner since Sir James has been dismissed; for, in reconciling Reginald to me, I was not able to save that ill-fated young man; and I must make myself amends for the humiliation to which I have stooped within these few days. To effect all this I have various plans. I have also an idea of being soon in town; and whatever may be my determination as to the rest, I shall probably put *that* project in execution; for London will be always the fairest field of action, however my views may be directed; and at any rate I shall there be rewarded by your society, and a little dissipation, for a ten weeks' penance at Churchhill.

I believe I owe it to my character to complete the match between my daughter and Sir James after having so long intended it. Let me know your opinion on this point. Flexibility of mind, a disposition easily biased by others, is an attribute which you know I am not very desirous of obtaining; nor has Frederica any claim to the indulgence of her notions at the expense of her mother's inclinations. Her idle love for Reginald, too! It is surely my duty to discourage such romantic nonsense. All things considered, therefore, it seems incumbent on me to take her to town and marry her immediately to Sir James.

When my own will is effected contrary to his, I shall have some credit in being on good terms with Reginald, which at present, in fact, I have not; for though he is still in my power, I have given up the very article by which our quarrel was produced, and at best the honour of victory is doubtful.

Send me your opinion on all these matters, my dear Alicia, and let me know whether you can get lodgings to suit me within a short distance of you.

Your most attached

S. VERNON

Letter 26

MRS JOHNSON TO LADY SUSAN

Edward Street

I am gratified by your reference, and this is my advice: that you come to town yourself, without loss of time, but that you leave Frederica behind. It would surely be much more to the purpose to get yourself well established by marrying Mr De Courcy, than to irritate him and the rest of his family by making her marry Sir James. You should think more of yourself and less of your daughter. She is not of a disposition to do you credit in the world, and seems precisely in her proper place at Churchhill, with the Vernons. But *you* are fitted for society, and it is shameful to have you exiled from it. Leave Frederica, therefore, to punish herself for the plague she has given you by indulging that romantic tenderheartedness which will always ensure her misery enough, and come to London as soon as you can.

I have another reason for urging this.

Mainwaring came to town last week, and has contrived, in spite of Mr Johnson, to make opportunities of seeing me. He is absolutely miserable about you, and jealous to such a degree of De Courcy that it would be highly unadvisable for them to meet at present. And yet, if you do not allow him to see you here, I cannot answer for his not committing some great imprudence – such as going to Churchhill, for instance, which would be dreadful! Besides, if you take my advice, and resolve to marry De Courcy, it will be indispensably necessary for you to get Mainwaring out of the way, and you only can have influence enough to send him back to his wife.

I have still another motive for your coming: Mr Johnson leaves London next Tuesday; he is going for his health to Bath, where, if the waters are favourable to his constitution and my wishes, he will be laid up with the gout many weeks. During his absence we shall be able to choose our own society, and to have true enjoyment. I would ask you to Edward Street, but that once he forced from me a kind of promise never to invite you to my house; nothing but my being in the utmost distress for money should have extorted it from me. I can get you, however, a nice drawing-room apartment in Upper Seymour Street, and we may be always together there or here; for I consider my promise to Mr Johnson as comprehending only (at least in his absence) your not sleeping in the house.

Poor Mainwaring gives me such histories of his wife's jealousy. Silly woman to expect constancy from so charming a man! but she always was silly – intolerably so in marrying him at all, she the heiress of a large fortune and he without a shilling! *One* title I know she might have had, besides Baronet's. Her folly in forming the connection was so great that, though Mr Johnson was her guardian and I do not in general share his feelings, I never can forgive her.

Adieu. Yours ever,

ALICIA

Letter 27

MRS VERNON TO LADY DE COURCY

Churchhill

This letter, my dear mother, will be brought you by Reginald. His long visit is about to be concluded at last, but I fear the separation takes place too late to do us any good. She is going to London to see her particular friend, Mrs Johnson. It was at first her intention that Frederica should accompany her, for the benefit of masters, but we overruled her there. Frederica was wretched in the idea of going, and I could not bear to have her at the mercy of her mother; not all the masters in London could compensate for the ruin of her comfort. I should have feared, too, for her health, and for everything but her principles – *there* I believe she is not to be injured, even by her mother, or her mother's friends; but with those friends she must have mixed (a very bad set, I doubt not), or have been left in total solitude, and I can hardly tell which would have been worse for her. If she is with her mother, moreover, she must, alas! in all probability be with Reginald, and that would be the greatest evil of all.

Here we shall in time be in peace, and our regular employments, our books and conversations, with exercise, the children, and every domestic pleasure in my power to procure her, will, I trust, gradually overcome this youthful attachment. I should not have a doubt of it were she slighted for any other woman in the world than her own mother.

How long Lady Susan will be in town, or whether she returns here again, I know not. I could not be cordial in my invitation, but if she chooses to come no want of cordiality on my part will keep her away.

I could not help asking Reginald if he intended being in London this winter, as soon as I found her ladyship's steps would be bent thither; and though he professed himself quite undetermined, there was something in his look and voice as he spoke which contradicted his words. I have done with lamentation; I look upon the event as so far decided that I resign myself to it in despair. If he leaves you soon for London everything will be concluded.

Your affectionate, &c.,

C. VERNON

Letter 28

MRS JOHNSON TO LADY SUSAN

Edward Street

MY DEAREST FRIEND – I write in the greatest distress; the most unfortunate event has just taken place. Mr Johnson has hit on the most effectual manner of plaguing us all. He had heard, I imagine, by some means or other, that you were soon to be in London, and immediately contrived to have such an attack of the gout as must at least delay his journey to Bath, if not wholly prevent it. I am persuaded the gout is brought on or kept off at pleasure; it was the same when I wanted to join the Hamiltons to the Lakes; and three years ago, when I had a fancy for Bath, nothing could induce him to have a gouty symptom.

I have received yours and have engaged the lodgings in consequence. I am pleased to find that my letter had so much effect on you, and that De Courcy is certainly your own. Let me hear from you as soon as you arrive, and in particular tell me what you mean to do with Mainwaring. It is impossible to say when I shall be able to come to you; my confinement must be great. It is such an abominable trick to be ill here instead of at Bath that I can scarcely command myself at all. At Bath his old aunts would have nursed him, but here it all falls upon me; and he bears pain with such patience that I have not the common excuse for losing my temper.

Yours ever,

ALICIA

Letter 29

LADY SUSAN VERNON TO MRS JOHNSON

Upper Seymour Street

MY DEAR ALICIA – There needed not this last fit of the gout to make me detest Mr Johnson, but now the extent of my aversion is not to be estimated. To have you confined as nurse in his apartment! My dear Alicia, of what a mistake were you guilty in marrying a man of his age! just old enough to be formal, ungovernable, and to have the gout; too old to be agreeable, too young to die.

I arrived last night about five, and had scarcely swallowed my dinner when Mainwaring made his appearance. I will not dissemble what real pleasure his sight afforded me, nor how strongly I felt the contrast between his person and manners and those of Reginald, to the infinite disadvantage of the latter. For an hour or two I was even staggered in my resolution of marrying him, and though this was too idle and nonsensical an idea to remain long on my mind, I do not feel very eager for the conclusion of my marriage, nor look forward with much impatience to the time when Reginald, according to our agreement, is to be in town. I shall probably put off his arrival under some pretence or other. He must not come till Mainwaring is gone.

I am still doubtful at times as to marrying; if the old man would die I might not hesitate, but a state of dependence on the caprice of Sir Reginald will not suit the freedom of my spirit; and if I resolve to wait for that event, I shall have excuse enough at present in having been scarcely ten months a widow.

I have not given Mainwaring any hint of my intention, or allowed him to consider my acquaintance with Reginald as more than the commonest flirtation, and he is tolerably appeased. Adieu, till we meet; I am enchanted with my lodgings.

Yours ever,

S. Vernon

Letter 30

Lady Susan Vernon to Mr De Courcy

Upper Seymour Street

I have received your letter, and though I do not attempt to conceal that I am gratified by your impatience for the hour of meeting, I yet feel myself under the necessity of delaying that hour beyond the time originally fixed. Do not think me unkind for such an exercise of my power, nor accuse me of instability without first hearing my reasons. In the course of my journey from Churchhill, I had ample leisure for reflection on the present state of our affairs, and every review has served to convince me that they require a delicacy and cautiousness of conduct to which we have hitherto been too little attentive. We have been hurried on by our feelings to a degree of precipitation which ill accords with the claims of our friends or the opinion of the world. We have been unguarded in forming this hasty engagement, but we must not complete the imprudence by ratifying it while there is so much reason to fear the connection would be opposed by those friends on whom you depend.

It is not for us to blame any expectations on your father's side of your marrying to advantage; where possessions are so extensive as those of your family, the wish of increasing them, if not strictly reasonable, is too common to excite surprise or resentment. He has a right to require a woman of fortune in his daughter-in-law, and I am sometimes quarrelling with myself for suffering you to form a connection so imprudent; but the influence of reason is often acknowledged too late by those who feel like me.

I have now been but a few months a widow, and, however little indebted to my husband's memory for any happiness derived from him during a union of some years, I cannot forget that the indelicacy of so early a second marriage must subject me to the censure of the world, and incur, what would be still more insupportable, the displeasure of Mr Vernon. I might perhaps harden myself in time against the injustice of general reproach, but the loss of *his* valued esteem I am, as you well know, ill-fitted to endure; and when to this may be added the consciousness of having injured you with your family, how am I to support myself? With feelings so poignant as mine, the conviction of having divided the son from his parents would make me, even with you, the most miserable of beings.

It will surely, therefore, be advisable to delay our union – to delay it till appearances are more promising – till affairs have taken a more favourable turn. To assist us in such a resolution I feel that absence will be necessary. We must not meet. Cruel as this sentence may appear, the necessity of pronouncing it, which can alone reconcile it to myself, will be evident to you when you have considered our situation in the light in which I have found myself imperiously obliged to place it. You may be – you must be – well assured that nothing but the strongest conviction of duty could induce me to wound my own feelings by urging a lengthened separation, and of insensibility to yours you will hardly suspect me. Again, therefore, I say that we ought not, we must not, yet meet. By a removal for some months from each other we shall tranquillise the sisterly fears of Mrs Vernon, who, accustomed herself to the enjoyment of riches, considers fortune as necessary everywhere, and whose sensibilities are not of a nature to comprehend ours.

Let me hear from you soon – very soon. Tell me that you submit to my arguments, and do not reproach me for using such. I cannot bear reproaches: my spirits are not so high as to need being repressed. I must endeavour to seek amusement, and fortunately many of my friends are in town, amongst them the Mainwarings; you know how sincerely I regard both husband and wife.

I am, very faithfully, yours,

S. VERNON

Letter 31

Upper Seymour Street

MY DEAR FRIEND – That tormenting creature, Reginald, is here. My letter, which was intended to keep him longer in the country, has hastened him to town. Much as I wish him away, however, I cannot help being pleased with such a proof of attachment. He is devoted to me, heart and soul. He will carry this note himself, which is to serve as an introduction to you, with whom he longs to be acquainted. Allow him to spend the evening with you, that I may be in no danger of his returning here. I have told him that I am not quite well, and must be alone; and should he call again there might be confusion, for it is impossible to be sure of servants. Keep him, therefore, I entreat you, in Edward Street. You will not find him a heavy companion, and I allow you to flirt with him as much as you like. At the same time, do not forget my real interest; say all that you can to convince him that I shall be quite wretched if he remains here; you know my reasons – propriety, and so forth. I would urge them more myself, but that I am impatient to be rid of him, as Mainwaring comes within half an hour.

Adieu!

S. VERNON

Letter 32

MRS JOHNSON TO LADY SUSAN

Edward Street

MY DEAR CREATURE – I am in agonies, and know not what to do. Mr De Courcy arrived just when he should not. Mrs Mainwaring had that instant entered the house, and forced herself into her guardian's presence, though I did not know a syllable of it till afterwards, for I was out when both she and Reginald came, or I should have sent him away at all events; but *she* was shut up with Mr Johnson, while *he* waited in the drawing-room for me. She arrived yesterday in pursuit of her husband, but perhaps you know this already from himself. She came to this house to entreat my husband's interference, and before I could be aware of it, everything that you could wish to be concealed was known to him; and unluckily she had wormed out of Mainwaring's servant that he had visited you every day since your being in town, and had just watched him to your door herself! What could I do! Facts are such horrid things! All is by this time known to De Courcy, who is now alone with Mr Johnson. Do not accuse me; indeed, it was impossible to prevent it. Mr Johnson has for some time suspected De Courcy of intending to marry you, and would speak with him alone as soon as he knew him to be in the house.

That detestable Mrs Mainwaring, who, for your comfort, has fretted herself thinner and uglier than ever, is still here, and they have been all closeted together. What can be done? If Mainwaring is now with you, he had better be gone. At any rate, I hope he will plague his wife more than ever.

With anxious wishes,

Yours faithfully,

ALICIA

Letter 33

LADY SUSAN TO MRS JOHNSON

Upper Seymour Street

This *éclaircissement* is rather provoking. How unlucky that you should have been from home! I thought myself sure of you at seven! I am undismayed however. Do not torment yourself with fears on my account; depend on it, I can make my own story good with Reginald. Mainwaring is just gone; he brought me the news of his wife's arrival. Silly woman, what does she expect by such manoeuvres? Yet I wish she had stayed quietly at Langford.

Reginald will be a little enraged at first, but by tomorrow's dinner, everything will be well again.

Adieu!

S. V.

Letter 34

— Hotel

I write only to bid you farewell, the spell is removed; I see you as you are. Since we parted yesterday, I have received from indisputable authority such a history of you as must bring the most mortifying conviction of the imposition I have been under, and the absolute necessity of an immediate and eternal separation from you. You cannot doubt to what I allude. Langford! Langford! that word will be sufficient. I received my information in Mr Johnson's house, from Mrs Mainwaring herself.

You know how I have loved you; you can intimately judge of my present feelings; but I am not so weak as to find indulgence in describing them to a woman who will glory in having excited their anguish, but whose affection they have never been able to gain.

R. DE COURCY

Letter 35

LADY SUSAN TO MR DE COURCY

Upper Seymour Street

I will not attempt to describe my astonishment in reading the note this moment received from you. I am bewildered in my endeavours to form some rational conjecture of what Mrs Mainwaring can have told you to occasion so extraordinary a change in your sentiments. Have I not explained everything to you with respect to myself which could bear a doubtful meaning, and which the ill-nature of the world had interpreted to my discredit? What can you now have heard to stagger your esteem for me? Have I ever had a concealment from you? Reginald, you agitate me beyond expression. I cannot suppose that the old story of Mrs Mainwaring's jealousy can be revived again, or at least be *listened* to again. Come to me immediately, and explain what is at present absolutely incomprehensible. Believe me, the single word *Langford* is not of such potent intelligence as to supersede the necessity of more. If we *are* to part, it will at least be handsome to take your personal leave – but I have little heart to jest; in truth, I am serious enough; for to be sunk, though but for an hour, in your esteem, is a humiliation to which I know not how to submit. I shall count every minute till your arrival.

S. V.

Letter 36

Mr De Courcy to Lady Susan

— Hotel

Why would you write to me? Why do you require particulars? But, since it must be so, I am obliged to declare that all the accounts of your misconduct, during the life and since the death of Mr Vernon, which had reached me, in common with the world in general, and gained my entire belief before I saw you, but which you, by the exertion of your perverted abilities, had made me resolved to disallow, have been unanswerably proved to me; nay more, I am assured that a connection, of which I had never before entertained a thought, has for some time existed, and still continues to exist, between you and the man whose family you robbed of its peace in return for the hospitality with which you were received into it; that you have corresponded with him ever since your leaving Langford – not with his wife, but with him – and that he now visits you every day. Can you, dare you deny it? and all this at the time when I was an encouraged, an accepted lover! From what have I not escaped! I have only to be grateful. Far from me be all complaint, every sigh of regret. My own folly had endangered me, my preservation I owe to the kindness, the integrity of another; but the unfortunate Mrs Mainwaring, whose agonies while she related the past seemed to threaten her reason, how is *she* to be consoled?

After such a discovery as this, you will scarcely affect further wonder at my meaning in bidding you adieu. My understanding is at length restored, and teaches me no less to abhor the artifices which had subdued me than to despise myself for the weakness on which their strength was founded.

R. De Courcy

Letter 37

Upper Seymour Street

I am satisfied, and will trouble you no more when these few lines are dismissed. The engagement which you were eager to form a fortnight ago is no longer compatible with your views, and I rejoice to find that the prudent advice of your parents has not been given in vain. Your restoration to peace will, I doubt not, speedily follow this act of filial obedience, and I flatter myself with the hope of surviving my share in this disappointment.

S. V.

Letter 38

MRS JOHNSON TO LADY SUSAN VERNON

Edward Street

I am grieved, though I cannot be astonished at your rupture with Mr De Courcy; he has just informed Mr Johnson of it by letter. He leaves London, he says, today. Be assured that I partake in all your feelings, and do not be angry if I say that our intercourse, even by letter, must soon be given up. It makes me miserable, but Mr Johnson vows that if I persist in the connection, he will settle in the country for the rest of his life – and you know it is impossible to submit to such an extremity while any other alternative remains.

You have heard of course that the Mainwarings are to part, and I am afraid Mrs M. will come home to us again; but she is still so fond of her husband and frets so much about him that perhaps she may not live long.

Miss Mainwaring is just come to town to be with her aunt, and they say that she declares she will have Sir James Martin before she leaves London again. If I were you, I would certainly get him myself. I had almost forgot to give you my opinion of Mr De Courcy; I am really delighted with him; he is full as handsome, I think, as Mainwaring, and with such an open, good-humoured countenance, that one cannot help loving him at first sight. Mr Johnson and he are the greatest friends in the world. Adieu, my dearest Susan, I wish matters did not go so perversely. That unlucky visit to Langford! but I dare say you did all for the best, and there is no defying destiny.

Your sincerely attached

ALICIA

Letter 39

LADY SUSAN TO MRS JOHNSON

Upper Seymour Street

MY DEAR ALICIA – I yield to the necessity which parts us. Under such circumstances you could not act otherwise. Our friendship cannot be impaired by it, and in happier times, when your situation is as independent as mine, it will unite us again in the same intimacy as ever. For this I shall impatiently wait, and meanwhile can safely assure you that I never was more at ease, or better satisfied with myself and everything about me, than at the present hour. Your husband I abhor, Reginald I despise, and I am secure of never seeing either again. Have I not reason to rejoice? Mainwaring is more devoted to me than ever; and were we at liberty, I doubt if I could resist even matrimony offered by *him*. This event, if his wife live with you, it may be in your power to hasten. The violence of her feelings, which must wear her out, may be easily kept in irritation. I rely on your friendship for this. I am now satisfied that I never could have brought myself to marry Reginald, and am equally determined that Frederica never shall. Tomorrow, I shall fetch her from Churchhill, and let Maria Mainwaring tremble for the consequence. Frederica shall be Sir James's wife before she quits my house, and she may whimper, and the Vernons may storm, I regard them not. I am tired of submitting my will to the caprices of others; of resigning my own judgement in deference to those to whom I owe no duty, and for whom I feel no respect. I have given up too much, have been too easily worked on, but Frederica shall now feel the difference.

Adieu, dearest of friends; may the next gouty attack be more favourable! and may you always regard me as unalterably yours,

S. VERNON

Letter 40

Parklands

MY DEAR CATHERINE – I have charming news for you, and if I had not sent off my letter this morning you might have been spared the vexation of knowing of Reginald's being gone to London, for he is returned. Reginald is returned, not to ask our consent to his marrying Lady Susan, but to tell us they are parted for ever. He has been only an hour in the house, and I have not been able to learn particulars, for he is so very low that I have not the heart to ask questions, but I hope we shall soon know all. This is the most joyful hour he has ever given us since the day of his birth. Nothing is wanting but to have you here, and it is our particular wish and entreaty that you will come to us as soon as you can. You have owed us a visit many long weeks; I hope nothing will make it inconvenient to Mr Vernon; and pray bring all my grandchildren; and your dear niece is included, of course; I long to see her. It has been a sad, heavy winter hitherto, without Reginald, and seeing nobody from Churchhill. I never found the season so dreary before; but this happy meeting will make us young again. Frederica runs much in my thoughts, and when Reginald has recovered his usual good spirits (as I trust he soon will), we will try to rob him of his heart once more, and I am full of hopes of seeing their hands joined at no great distance.

Your affectionate mother,

C. DE COURCY

Letter 41

Churchhill

MY DEAR MOTHER – Your letter has surprised me beyond measure! Can it be true that they are really separated – and for ever? I should be overjoyed if I dared depend on it, but after all that I have seen, how can one be secure? And Reginald really with you! My surprise is the greater because on Wednesday, the very day of his coming to Parklands, we had a most unexpected and unwelcome visit from Lady Susan, looking all cheerfulness and good-humour, and seeming more as if she were to marry him when she got back to town than as if parted from him for ever. She stayed nearly two hours, was as affectionate and agreeable as ever, and not a syllable, not a hint was dropped of any disagreement or coolness between them. I asked her whether she had seen my brother since his arrival in town; not, as you may suppose, with any doubt of the fact, but merely to see how she looked. She immediately answered, without any embarrassment, that he had been kind enough to call on her on Monday; but she believed he had already returned home, which I was very far from crediting.

Your kind invitation is accepted by us with pleasure, and on Thursday next, we and our little ones will be with you. Pray heaven, Reginald may not be in town again by that time!

I wish we could bring dear Frederica too, but I am sorry to say that her mother's errand hither was to fetch her away; and, miserable as it made the poor girl, it was impossible to detain her. I was thoroughly unwilling to let her go, and so was her uncle; and all that could be urged, we *did* urge; but Lady Susan declared that as she was now about to fix herself in London for several months, she could not be easy if her daughter were not with her, for masters, &c. Her manner, to be sure, was very kind and proper, and Mr Vernon believes that Frederica will now be treated with affection. I wish I could think so too.

The poor girl's heart was almost broke at taking leave of us. I charged her to write to me very often, and to remember that if she were in any distress we should be always her friends. I took care to see her alone, that I might say all this, and I hope made her a little more comfortable; but I shall not be easy till I can go to town and judge of her situation myself.

I wish there were a better prospect than now appears of the match which the conclusion of your letter declares your expectations of. At present, it is not very likely.

Yours ever, &c.,

C. VERNON

Conclusion

This correspondence, by a meeting between some of the parties, and a separation between the others, could not, to the great detriment of the Post Office revenue, be continued any longer. Very little assistance to the State could be derived from the epistolary intercourse of Mrs Vernon and her niece; for the former soon perceived, by the style of Frederica's letters, that they were written under her mother's inspection, and therefore, deferring all particular enquiry till she could make it personally in London, ceased writing minutely or often.

Having learnt enough, in the meanwhile, from her open-hearted brother, of what had passed between him and Lady Susan to sink the latter lower than ever in her opinion, she was proportionably more anxious to get Frederica removed from such a mother, and placed under her own care; and, though with little hope of success, was resolved to leave nothing unattempted that might offer a chance of obtaining her sister-in-law's consent to it. Her anxiety on the subject made her press for an early visit to London; and Mr Vernon, who, as it must already have appeared, lived only to do whatever he was desired, soon found some accommodating business to call him thither. With a heart full of the matter, Mrs Vernon waited on Lady Susan shortly after her arrival in town, and was met with such an easy and cheerful affection as made her almost turn from her with horror. No remembrance of Reginald, no consciousness of guilt, gave one look of embarrassment; she was in excellent spirits, and seemed eager to show at once by every possible attention to her brother and sister her sense of their kindness, and her pleasure in their society.

Frederica was no more altered than Lady Susan; the same restrained manners, the same timid look in the presence of her mother as heretofore, assured her aunt of her situation being uncomfortable, and confirmed her in the plan of altering it. No unkindness, however, on the part of Lady Susan appeared. Persecution on the subject of Sir James was entirely at an end; his name merely mentioned to say that he was not in London; and indeed, in all her conversation, she was solicitous only for the welfare and improvement of her daughter, acknowledging, in terms of grateful delight, that Frederica was now growing every day more and more what a parent could desire.

Mrs Vernon, surprised and incredulous, knew not what to suspect, and, without any change in her own views, only feared greater difficulty in accomplishing them. The first hope of anything better was derived from Lady Susan's asking her whether she thought Frederica looked quite as well as she had done at Churchhill, as she must confess herself to have sometimes an anxious doubt of London's perfectly agreeing with her.

Mrs Vernon, encouraging the doubt, directly proposed her niece's returning with them into the country. Lady Susan was unable to express her sense of such kindness, yet knew not, from a variety of reasons, how to part with her daughter; and as, though her own plans were not yet wholly fixed, she trusted it would ere long be in her power to take Frederica into the country herself, concluded by declining entirely to profit by such unexampled attention. Mrs Vernon persevered, however, in the offer of it, and though Lady Susan continued to resist, her resistance in the course of a few days seemed somewhat less formidable.

The lucky alarm of an influenza decided what might not have been decided quite so soon. Lady Susan's maternal fears were then too much awakened for her to think of anything but Frederica's removal from the risk of infection; above all disorders in the world she most dreaded the influenza for her daughter's constitution! Frederica returned to Churchhill with her uncle and aunt; and three weeks afterwards, Lady Susan announced her being married to Sir James Martin.

Mrs Vernon was then convinced of what she had only suspected before, that she might have spared herself all the trouble of urging a removal which Lady Susan had doubtless resolved on from the first. Frederica's visit was nominally for six weeks, but her mother, though inviting her to return in one or two affectionate letters, was very ready to oblige the whole party by consenting to a prolongation of her stay, and in the course of two months ceased to write of her absence, and in the course of two more, to write to her at all.

Frederica was therefore fixed in the family of her uncle and aunt, till such time as Reginald De Courcy could be talked, flattered and finessed into an affection for her – which, allowing leisure for the conquest of his attachment to her mother, for his abjuring all future attachments, and detesting the sex, might be reasonably looked for in the course of a twelvemonth. Three months might have done it in general, but Reginald's feelings were no less lasting than lively.

Whether Lady Susan was or was not happy in her second choice, I do not see how it can ever be ascertained; for who would take her assurance of it on either side of the question? The world must judge from probabilities; she had nothing against her, but her husband, and her conscience.

Sir James may seem to have drawn a harder lot than mere folly merited; I leave him, therefore, to all the pity that anybody can give him. For myself, I confess that *I* can pity only Miss Mainwaring, who, coming to town and putting herself to an expense in clothes, which impoverished her for two years, on purpose to secure him, was defrauded of her due by a woman ten years older than herself.